And the Skipper Bats Cleanup

And the Skipper Bats Cleanup

A History of the
Baseball Player-Manager,
with 42 Biographies of Men
Who Filled the Dual Role

by FRED STEIN

McFarland & Company, Inc., Publishers
Jefferson, North Carolina, and London

Library of Congress Cataloguing-in-Publication Data

Stein, Fred.
    And the skipper bats cleanup : a history of the baseball player-manager,
  with 42 biographies of men who filled the dual role / by Fred Stein.
       p.   cm.
    Includes bibliographical references and index.

    ISBN 0-7864-1228-3 (softcover : 50# alkaline paper) ∞

    1. Baseball player-managers— United States— Biography.   I. Title.
  GV865.A1 S75   2002
  796.357'092'273 — dc21   2001007789

British Library cataloguing data are available

On the cover: Three baseball cards issued by the American Tobacco
Company in 1911 of Frank Chance, player-manager for the Chicago Cubs
(Benjamin K. Edwards collection, Library of Congress)

Manufactured in the United States of America

*McFarland & Company, Inc., Publishers
  Box 611, Jefferson, North Carolina 28640
    www.mcfarlandpub.com*

For my late wife, Phyllis P. Stein,
who helped launch this effort,

and

Doris S. Ahnberg, my close friend,
who helped complete it.

Contents

Introduction

In early baseball days the idea of an individual playing the dual role of player and coach/manager was as natural as any activity in which the strongest, brightest, or best player — often the person who owned the playing equipment — also directed fellow players. But as baseball became commercialized, it became feasible to pay one man to manage the team from the bench. This is the story of the men who remained players while they managed.

This book describes the role of the player-manager from its inception. Forty-two men are described in these pages. The approach has been to cover in sufficient detail the years before and after they were player-managers, but to concentrate on their most important years and accomplishments as player-managers.

This book does not include all player-managers. For example, Frank Robinson, the first African-American to play and manage, is not included because he filled that role almost exclusively as a designated hitter.

Chapter 1 discusses what being a player-manager was like, the player-managers' playing skills, and how they dealt with their fellow players. Chapter 2 describes the early evolution of the player-manager. Chapters 3 through 19 recount the careers of the most important men who played while managing. And Chapter 20 puts the player-manager role in historical perspective, with the help of comments from former player-managers and their players.

There is little chance that there will be any more player-managers. But examining the important role they played should be of interest to both the baseball historian and the more casual fan.

1

Playing and Managing

Baseball at the major league level is a tremendously demanding game to play. Hitting a 95-mile-an-hour fastball or a sharply-moving curveball is a remarkable triumph over the physics involved and, less often recognized, the batter's instinctive fear of being hit by the pitch. The very authoritative Ted Williams has described hitting a round baseball solidly with a round bat as the most difficult act in sports. Fielding a sharply-hit baseball cleanly and consistently, and throwing it accurately to the proper place, requires coordination, dexterity, and experience. Effective base stealing, of course, requires natural speed but also involves correctly reading the pitcher's pickoff moves. These playing activities require raw physical talent, natural baseball instincts, and controlled aggressiveness.

Pitching requires a special set of skills, some inherent and some learned. An adequate, if not an overpowering, fast ball and mastery of at least one other pitch are usually necessary. Good control is the ability not only to throw strikes at will but to deliver them in a plate location where it is difficult for them to be hit solidly. Also extremely important are the abilities to retain concentration regardless of the situation, to hold runners close to the bases, and to field competently. Regardless of the position played, of equal importance as these skills are the temperament and the stamina to maintain a high performance level in the face of continuous pressure over a long, grueling season. These are the necessary attributes of a successful major league player.

Managing skills are similar to those required of a player only as they involve a natural feel for the game and the ability to retain composure as the fortunes of the game ebb and flow. But the manager needs to have other qualities not necessary in a player. He must direct the activities of players, many of them paid much more than he, to maximize their effectiveness. A player can ignore the pressures imposed by the media much more easily than the manager, for whom dealing effectively with the media is most important. Then there is the question of working harmoniously with team management, an infrequent player problem after he has signed his contract. Essentially, the player's basic concern is his performance on the playing field. The manager's functions involve a variety of activities on and off the playing field.

If playing and managing simultaneously require such different functions, it might seem almost incomprehensible to today's fans that years ago major league baseball was awash with player-managers. But employment of player-managers made sense in the past. Simple economics was the fundamental reason for the employment of the player-manager. Major league clubs did not become large corporate entities, truly "big businesses," until after World War II. Before that time, most clubs had a pressing need to reduce or eliminate salary costs wherever possible, otherwise the club owner would personally feel the financial effect. As a result, it was to the owner's direct benefit to pay one salary to have an individual both direct the team and play a position rather than to employ two men. Today, in an era in which it is economically feasible to gamble millions of dollars on the chance that a player might become a bona fide star, it makes no financial sense to economize by paying a player to perform double duty as a player and a manager. It would be foolish to pay a multi-million-dollar-a-year performer a relatively small additional amount and burden him with the added responsibility of managing.

As an example of earlier practice, the Giants paid star rightfielder Mel Ott $18,000 in 1941. Then they hired Ott as their player-manager for the 1942 season, paying him $25,000. In effect, the Giants hired a new manager for a mere $7000 at a time when non-playing managers were being paid two to five times that amount. Similarly, penny-conscious Washington Senators owner Clark Griffith chose Senators second baseman Bucky Harris to serve as his player-manager in 1924 at an equally modest salary increase. Such economy-driven player-manager selections were more the rule than the exception in the game's earlier history.

Relatively young players have become player-managers after demonstrating strong field leadership qualities. Cleveland shortstop Lou Boudreau took over the Indians when he was a tender 24. Shortstop Joe Cronin became the Senators' manager at 26. First baseman Adrian "Cap" Anson and outfielder Fred Clarke became player-managers at 27. And Detroit hired 31-year-old catcher Mickey Cochrane to manage the Tigers.

Popular players also have been promoted as managers in an effort to bolster attendance. Well-liked Joe Cronin was purchased by the Red Sox from the Senators in 1935 to enliven the moribund Boston club, which needed help on the field and at the gate. Sox owner Tom Yawkey anticipated correctly that Cronin's smiling Irish face would be a popular draw with the large number of Fenway Park customers with Hibernian roots. Here, too, the Giants promoted the well-loved Ott in an attempt to revive slipping attendance as the lackluster Polo Grounders fell out of favor with their longtime fans.

There was one promotion of a crowd favorite which proved a complete flop. Vest-pocket-sized shortstop Walter "Rabbit" Maranville, renowned for his crowd-pleasing "basket catch," his ebullient personality, and his drinking exploits, was appointed manager of the last place Cubs in mid-season of 1925. The well-oiled Rabbit celebrated his appointment by waking up his sleeping players in their Pullman berths, pouring ice water on them, and shouting at the top of his lungs, "There will be no sleeping on this train under Maranville management." Not surprisingly, the Rabbit's happy-go-lucky regime lasted only 53 games, with the Cubs still languishing in last place. Hall of Famer Maranville's reign as one of the National League's best-fielding shortstops lasted for another ten years, but, not surprisingly, he never managed again.

Pete Rose provided a special case with his appointment as player-manager of the Cincinnati Reds in mid-season of 1984. Facing an uncertain playing future, Rose began that season as a player with the Phillies and by the time he moved back to the Reds as their player-manager he had accumulated 4,062 hits, 128 fewer than Ty Cobb's record total at the time. Reds owner Marge Schott, whose business acumen exceeded her personality shortcomings, knew a drawing card when she saw one. She brought Rose back to his hometown to virtually ensure that he would eclipse Cobb's record. Manager Rose was able to choose the games in which he would play, and the Reds' attendance figures climbed until he surpassed Cobb's record in 1985.

Player-managers naturally have been closer in age to their players than have bench managers, and this has presented a potential personal relationship problem, particularly when player-managers were promoted from within the ranks. A case in point involved outfielder Billy Southworth, who was elevated to managing the Cardinals in 1929. The 36-year-old Southworth attempted to establish his authority by treating his teammates tyrannically, and, as a result, he lasted only half of the season before being deposed. Southworth went back to the minors, learned how to handle his players with fairness and understanding, and returned years later to become a successful major league manager.

Second baseman Billy Herman took over the managership of the

Pirates in 1947 when he was still a part-time player. He told writer Donald Honig in *The Man in the Dugout* of his experiences during his first year as manager. Herman said:

> When it was announced I was taking over the Pirates, a few
> guys said to me, "Well, you've got to change now. It's going to
> be different." They were right, but I didn't think so at the time.
> Any person who's managing for the first time has to change.
> It's an altogether different situation for you on a ball club. For
> years you were friendly with everybody and were one of the
> boys. Suddenly that's changed. You're not one of the boys any-
> more—you're the boss. But I was determined not to change,
> and that's where I was wrong. I had some great friends on that
> team and we buddied together a lot. I found out later that some
> of the other players resented it. I was naïve about the psychol-
> ogy of a ball club. I shouldn't have been, but I was.

Another problem faced by the player-manager was the relative loneliness of his life in comparison with his earlier role as a player only. After a game or workout, the coaches usually go off by themselves and socialize. But the manager has to stay behind and meet with the media group until they have from him what they need. After that, the writers go off and finish their work and the manager, or years ago the player-manager, would be left alone. The manager might enjoy being with his players but he couldn't socialize with them for fear of appearing to show favoritism. And, of course, when a player was promoted from the ranks, usually he felt he no longer could continue to room with a fellow player no matter how close the two might be.

There was a good example of how boosting a player to a managerial role changed his relationships with his teammates. Giants first baseman Bill Terry held a press conference immediately after taking over the club in mid-season in 1932. Just before the conference ended, Terry asked the writers, "By the way, have any of you fellows seen my roommate, [pitcher] Hal Schumacher? As soon as he heard about my being the new manager, he took off out of our room as though he was scared to death of me and I haven't seen him since." (Actually, Schumacher said years later that he had made himself scarce because he was afraid of dealing with the writers who wanted to learn all they could about the new manager.) On the other hand, Giant third baseman Freddie Lindstrom received the news of Terry's promotion with bitter disappointment because he felt that he had been promised the job by outgoing manager John McGraw before McGraw left the post. As a result, Terry had little alternative but to trade his old friend Lindstrom after the season ended, to the eventual regret of both men—Terry at losing a player of Lindstrom's ability and Lindstrom at losing out on two Giants pennant wins after he left the club.

A fundamental problem faced by playing managers was to maintain their performance on the field despite the pressures of managing. To followers of the Giants in the 1940s, it was obvious that Mel Ott found his playing manager role extremely stressful. The little outfielder always had a nervous habit of tapping the grass in right field with his toe as he stood in the outfield. But by mid-season of his first year as manager, the harassed Ott had reduced a large patch of Polo Grounds right field sod to dirt with his nervous foot tamping.

One day a writer asked Ott, "Mel, has being the manager made any difference in your hitting?"

"No, I hit the same way."

The reporter continued, "I mean psychologically. For instance, when you go up there now do you think about the effect on the team if you, the manager, strike out in the clutch or hit into a double play?"

"Oh, no," Mel answered. "Say, if I went up there thinking about things like that I would never get a base hit."

In his first season as a player-manager, Ott talked to a reporter about the problems of maintaining his concentration on playing while managing. He admitted, "I'm really getting an education even after all my years in the game. Sometimes the decision as to when to pull a pitcher can be murder. My instinct tells me to take him out, but my desire to give him another chance and build up his confidence tells me to leave him in." Mel continued, "Another problem a manager faces is to anticipate plays and circumstances and make the right move in time. Every manager has these problems, but they are more difficult when you also have to concentrate on the game as a player. The other day Pete Reiser hit a fly ball out to me when I was thinking about something else and it actually startled me until my normal reflexes took over and I moved over to make the catch."

Playing managers often were given special consideration when challenging an umpire's decision. An experience of first baseman–manager Bill Terry provides a case in point. His Giants met the Cardinals in an important game in 1933 at the Polo Grounds. With the Giants leading in a late inning, Cardinal second baseman–manager Frankie Frisch sent a high "Baltimore Chop" bouncer to Terry at first. Bill grabbed the ball and dashed to the bag, arriving there just as Frisch dove in. Umpire Ted McGrew called Frisch safe, and the usually calm Terry blew his top.

Terry charged McGrew and uttered some unacceptable words. McGrew emphatically waved Terry out of the game, and the normally undemonstrative Terry responded by flinging his cap and glove to the

ground and kicking them several feet. The fans contributed to the frenzied protest by throwing pop bottles onto the field. Mel Ott raced in from
right field and, along with Giants coach Tom Clarke, tried to calm down
the raging Terry. When order finally was restored, McGrew astonished the
onlookers by ordering peacemakers Ott and Clarke off the field but permitting Terry to remain in the game.

After the game, *New York Journal-American* writer Garry Schumacher
said to Ott, "Mel, what in the world went on out there?" Ott drawled,
"Garry, you're not going to believe this. McGrew told Terry, 'I can't take
that, you're out of here.' Bill shouted back, 'You can't throw me out. I'm
the only first baseman we've got, and besides that I'm the manager.' So,
I'll be darned if McGrew didn't turn on me and Clarke, and shout, 'O.K.,
Terry stays but you guys have to go.'"

Theoretically, the catching position would appear to be the most log-
ical position for a player-manager. From his position behind the plate the
catcher has the best visual perspective of his eight teammates as they face
him from their defensive positions. He appears best able to station his
players because he has the clearest view of the spaces between them as they
defend against the hitter. Another theoretical advantage is that the catcher
is in the best position to monitor the speed and movement of the pitcher's
deliveries. One of the manager's most important functions is to decide if
and when to remove the pitcher, and he often solicits his catcher's opinion as to whether a pitcher is losing his effectiveness. This brings to mind
the story of the manager who ventured out to the mound to determine if
a pitcher who had given up a succession of first pitch, line drive hits had
lost his stuff. As the story has it, the manager asked the catcher, "What's
going on? Is he losing it?" The catcher shook his head and answered,
"Damned if I know; I haven't caught a pitch yet."

Other than the catcher, the infielders appeared to be the most logi-
cal men to play and manage simultaneously. Infielders are relatively close
to the action, most of which occurs within the infield. They also are close
to the bases, where most plays take place. Also, infielders are well situated
to exert field leadership, both in assisting and exhorting their teammates,
and in carrying complaints to umpires.

Managing from the outfield would appear to be difficult because
outfielders are far removed from the infield action. It is far less physically
demanding for a shortstop, for example, to confer with the pitcher than
for an outfielder to travel to and from his position. And it is much easier
for an umpire involved in a disputed play to use the argument to an
outfielder-manager, "How can you dispute my call when you were so far
from the play?" Moreover, many outfielders, often in the lineup for their

offensive skills, admit that their distance from the action reduces their exposure to field situations that catchers and infielders face routinely.

Pitchers were least likely to be player-managers and, given the intense concentration required of a pitcher when he is pitching a game, it is highly unlikely that he could focus adequately on other aspects of the game at the same time. Pitchers tend to be most involved with the special problems they face in one-on-one confrontations with hitters and less involved with offensive or defensive techniques of position players. Although there were exceptions, pitchers were considered to be specialists who were not as likely to possess the attributes of managers, who need general experience in all phases of the game.

There were wide differences in the number of games participated in by player-managers. Some player-managers, particularly the younger ones, were regular players who played in almost every scheduled game for a number of seasons. Other player-managers were regulars for only one or two seasons. Still others were part-time players.

Appendix Table 1 ranks 47 major player-managers by the number of games they played as player-managers. Only seven of these 47 men played and managed in more than 1000 games. First baseman Cap Anson heads the list with 2155 games. He is followed by outfielder Fred Clarke (1848 games), first baseman Charles Comiskey (1312), shortstops Joe Cronin (1291) and Lou Boudreau (1285), first baseman/third baseman Patsy Tebeau (1011), and outfielder Patsy Donovan (1002). Outfielders Ty Cobb, Tris Speaker, and Fielder Jones played regularly while managing in more than 700 games.

The aforementioned theories about suitable positions for player-managers were not borne out in actual practice, either in the case of catchers or outfielders. None of the top 30 player-managers in games played include a catcher. Red Dooin caught the most games as a catcher-manager (354), and Roger Bresnahan was a playing manager in 324 games, 309 as a catcher and 15 games in other positions. Also, contrary to what might have been expected, outfielders comprised as many as four of the top 10 player-managers in games played. Of the 47 player-managers listed in Appendix Table 1, there were 26 infielders, eight outfielders, seven catchers, and six who frequently played more than one position. Appendix Table 2 lists three Hall of Fame pitchers and John Montgomery Ward, who was a pitcher as well as an infielder, all of whom managed while they played.

As a group, playing-managers were excellent players, no matter where they played. Of the top 10 non-pitching player-managers, in terms of games played while managing, eight were elected to the Hall of Fame. And of the top 47 position player-managers, more than two-thirds have been enshrined at Cooperstown. All of the four top pitcher-managers—Ward, Al Spalding, Kid Nichols, and Clark Griffith—have been elected to the Hall.

Seven player-managers, almost half of the 16 men who managed existing major league teams for all or part of the 1934 season, were eventually elected to the Hall of Fame as players. In that year five of the eight National League clubs had player-skippers. The Cardinals were managed by second baseman Frankie Frisch, and the Giants by first baseman Bill Terry. First baseman Charlie Grimm managed the Cubs; the Pirates were led by third baseman Pie Traynor, and the Phillies by catcher Jimmie Wilson. When Carl Hubbell struck out five future Hall of Famers in a row in his legendary 1934 All-Star game performance, he was heavily supported by infielder-managers Frisch, Terry, and Traynor.

This leads to the question of how important playing excellence has been considered to managing. Baseball writer-maven Bill James, in his book *Baseball Managers,* has determined that from 1901 through 1945 there was an increase in the employment of managers, many still active players, who could be considered good or outstanding players, an increase from 56 percent to 82 percent. But since 1945 that trend has turned around, and by 1990 only 39 percent were considered to have been good or outstanding players.

Major League Managers

	1901	1916	1930	1945	1960	1975	1990
Outstanding Players	7	7	6	8	6	5	3
Good Players	2	5	3	6	6	7	10
Fringe Players	5	14	7	2	8	13	12
Didn't Play	2	2	1	1	1	5	8
Percentage Rated Good or Outstanding	56%	43%	53%	82%	57%	40%	39%

Source: Adapted from *The Bill James Guide to Baseball Managers from 1870 to Today,* Bill James, 1997, Scribner

In analyzing his numbers, James pointed out:

> The three managers [in 1990] who were listed as outstanding players were Frank Robinson, Joe Torre, and Red Schoendienst, although arguments can be made that Davey Johnson and Lou Piniella would also deserve to be called outstanding. It may be that the percentage of managers who have been outstanding players was pushed downward from 1950 to 1990 because many of the best players were blacks and Latins, who were almost never hired to manage. In recent years Felipe Alou, Cito Gas-

ton, Don Baylor, and Dusty Baker have all gotten a chance to manage, and have all had some success. Thus, it may be that the number of managers who were outstanding players is now headed *upward,* not downward.

2

Wright, Spalding, and Ferguson

The concept of the player-manager (originally more of a player–field leader–"boy scout" leader) goes back at least as far as 1842 with the first organized baseball team, the Knickerbockers Base Ball Club of New York. This was essentially a social club with an upper crust membership dominated by local professional men. A rather snobbish Board of Directors ran the organization. As recounted in Harold Seymour's classic *Baseball— The Early Years*, the Board determined what clubs to play, chose team captains, and controlled the conduct of all games, or "matches," as they were called. The team captain ran the club on the field and, since many captains also were players, these men could be considered the forerunners of the player-manager as the role would evolve. Members of the Knickerbockers were not permitted to leave a game without the permission of the captain. Players refusing to obey the captain were fined 50 cents, and the fine for disputing an umpire's decision was 25 cents. And if a captain left the field before the end of a game, or neglected his duties in any other way, he was fined one dollar. When the Knickerbockers gathered on the field, the club president, acting on behalf of the Board, picked the captain to direct the team, and, theoretically at least, every club member was entitled to a fair chance to be selected as captain. The team captains, in a game between two of the club's teams, chose up sides from the club members on hand and assigned them to their positions. A coin toss would follow to determine which side batted first, the captains would select an umpire, and the game would begin.

The game rules changed continually. There were variations in the size and weight of the balls and bats used, in the distances between the bases and between the pitcher and catcher, and in most of the other rules governing play. Then, after the game, emphasis would shift to social activities, such as club entertainment and lavish dinners. The Knickerbockers were only one of a number of other such clubs in New York, Boston, Philadelphia, and other northeastern areas. After a game between these clubs, it was customary for the captain of the losing team to present a game ball to the victors. The winning team's captain would respond graciously and the ball would be placed in an honored place in the winning club's trophy room. The subsequent festivities were usually long and liquor-enhanced.

These "gentlemen's sports" activities continued through the 1860s. By that time the game had become a more sophisticated pastime as players began to specialize in playing and mastering specific field positions. Captains, who took on a more established position as permanent team leaders, emphasized more and more the need for team discipline and serious training and practice. Working class members, usually artisans and clerks, formed their own teams, and spirited rivalries sprang up between labor and other groups in neighboring cities and regions.

HARRY WRIGHT

In 1869 the legendary Cincinnati Red Stockings became the first fully professional team, as all of its players were paid salaries. This new approach was led by Red Stockings player-manager Harry Wright and Aaron B. Champion, a local lawyer. Albert G. Spalding, in his book *America's National Game*, expressed his admiration for the moral courage displayed by Wright, Champion, and their associates in paying all of their players. Spalding cited major concerns with which Wright's group had to deal. One concern was the feeling of much of the general public that baseball was simply an ordinary form of an outdoor leisure sport played by "gentlemen" for exercise and only incidentally for public entertainment. This view held that professionalism would hurt the game by bringing into it rowdies, drunkards, and deadbeats. Another major concern was that professionalism would stimulate gambling on games. This presumed an increase in the bribing of players and, as a result, a public loss of confidence in the game's integrity and the honesty of players' efforts.

Harry Wright had been an excellent player for many years. The Red Stockings, or Reds as they were called even then, came out of nowhere, as baseball of any organized fashion did not exist in Cincinnati before 1867. Wright, who also served as the Reds' trainer, was considered the most effective team leader of the day. *The New York Clipper*, a leading sports journal, wrote that Wright was "unapproachable in his good generalship and management." Henry Chadwick, the most important baseball writer of the pre–1900 period, wrote that Wright's players were "better trained and more practiced" than players on any other team, and that the most prominent New York teams should adopt Wright's methods.

Wright worked his players hard as he stressed the importance of fundamentals and the need for close teamwork. His efforts were rewarded as his team won 57 of its 58 games. The high-scoring Reds' streak began in Buffalo. Spectators at that game were impressed by the Red Stockings' field discipline, as none of the Cincinnati players uttered a word on the field except for player-manager Wright. The club swept through western New York, then traveled through Massachusetts and on into New York City. In New York the Reds beat the highly rated Mutuals in a low-scoring 4-2 game in what amounted to a pitchers' duel for that era. The Reds continued on through Philadelphia, Baltimore, and wound up their eastern tour in Washington. This was the first tour of a professional baseball team, and Wright's club defeated all of the best-known teams of the time.

The Red Stockings toured the West Coast and returned home still undefeated. Harry Wright kept a

Harry Wright, the first player-manager, served as his team's trainer, ticket seller, outfielder-pitcher, field leader, and gentle disciplinarian. His all-winning Cincinnati Red Stockings club was the first team comprised of paid professional players.

comprehensive record of the triumphant tour. In these 57 games the Red Stockings scored a total of 2395 runs to their opponents' 574 runs. The

Reds hit 169 home runs, averaging nearly three home runs per game. The club traveled by rail and boat for almost 12,000 miles. Their leading hitter was shortstop George Wright, Harry's younger brother, who played in 52 of the 59 games, hitting for a .518 batting average with 59 home runs. Harry Wright's record of the trip did not discuss its financial aspects, but it was widely understood that the club had ended up turning a profit. Harry Wright played in most of the games.

Although the tour was a great team victory, it also was considered an impressive personal triumph for Harry Wright. Off the field he had been the team's business manager, responsible for arranging games likely to be profitable and negotiating contracts with his players. But most of the praise directed at him had to do with his skillful handling of his players on and off the field. Warren Goldstein wrote in his *Playing for Keeps—A History of Early Baseball*:

> Harry Wright was more involved in the lives of his players than any previous captain had ever been. He directed and supervised their practices, decided who played where or when, maintained morale, and kept an eye on their eating, drinking, and sleeping habits. He was in effect the first modern baseball manager.... The key to Wright's importance as baseball's first real manager was the way he firmly established his control over the players in every aspect of the game. His control over the players' lives off the field was never as complete as he would have liked, but he did establish the *principle* of that authority.

The paternalistic, elder statesman Wright was 34 during his club's magnificent year, older by seven years than the next oldest player, pitcher Asa Brainard, and almost 12 years the senior of the average player on the team. Although his players were well trained and generally well disciplined, a few of them gave him problems—missing trains, avoiding practice, or drinking too much. Brainard, a world-class hypochondriac and night owl, missed games with imagined ailments and off-the-field carousing, and Harry Wright had to leave his center field position and take over the pitching burden when Brainard was not available. The gifted George Wright was a high-spirited player who occasionally angered his brother by missing practice. And alcohol consumption was enough of a problem that a local newspaper suggested sarcastically that 1870 player contracts contain a clause forbidding whiskey use "unless prescribed by a physician in good standing."

The total payroll of the 1869 club was $9300, distributed among the 13 players who had other jobs during the off season. The breakdown of occupations and salaries for 10 of the 13 players (on whom information is available) was as follows:

Harry Wright (jeweler)	center field	$1200
George Wright (engraver)	shortstop	1400
Asa Brainard (insurance)	pitcher	1100
Fred Waterman (insurance)	third base	1000
Cal Sweasy (hatter)	second base	800
Charles Gould (bookkeeper)	first base	800
Doug Allison (marble cutter)	catcher	800
Andy Leonard (hatter)	left field	800
Cal McVey (piano maker)	right field	800
Dick Hurley (trade not known)	substitute	600

It is surprising to note that Harry Wright, who took on every possible job with the team, is listed as being paid less than his brother George. Years later George Wright questioned the accuracy of these salary figures, saying that Harry was paid $2000, and he, George, was paid $1800.

Cincinnati's enthusiasm for the team slacked off and financial losses forced a decision to have the Reds revert back to an amateur club in 1871. As a result, the enterprising Wright moved the Red Stockings to Boston for the 1871 season. There were hard feelings when he made the move, as he took his best players with him. And Wright added insult to injury when he took with him to Boston the treasured name "Red Stockings."

Wright's first Boston team was staffed by several of his Cincinnati players—first baseman Charles Gould, shortstop George Wright, leftfielder Andy Leonard, catcher-outfielder Cal McVey, and, of course, playing manager Harry Wright. The most important new player was a 20-year-old righthander, Al Spalding, who would become one of the game's most important figures.

In that first season Wright's club finished third, barely missing a second place berth in the new eight-club league. The Red Stockings were highly competitive, losing out to the first place Philadelphia Athletics by only 1½ games. Harry Wright played his usual consistent game with a .267 average on 43 hits in the 42 games in which he played. He had protested the Athletics' pennant win as unfair, complaining that his Red Stockings had played three more games. The resulting spirited rivalry between the two clubs made the quiet but extremely competitive Wright especially determined to win the 1872 pennant, and Wright got his revenge. The two clubs fought on even terms through the first half of the 1872 season until a key game in which Boston crushed the visiting Athletics 13–4, a game highlighted by a superb catch by player-manager Wright. Harry reportedly responded to the cheering crowd "by politely" doffing his cap. After that win the Red Stockings were unstoppable. They went on to win the pennant with a 39–8 record, 7½ games ahead of the second place Athletics. Harry Wright played decently enough, but the real star was young Al Spalding with a splendid 37–8 record. The offense was led by George Wright and second baseman Ross Barnes, who hit .404. This was still the era in which base hits were credited on ground balls that landed in fair territory but went foul before reaching first or third base. The small (5 foot 8, 145 pound) Barnes specialized in guiding such ground balls, and he wound up with a .379 career batting average. During the season Harry Wright wore his usual number of hats—player, field manager, trainer, and handler of all of the team's financial, scheduling, and other off-field functions.

Wright's club captured another pennant win over the Athletics in 1873, this time by only four games as the Red Stockings rebounded from a ten game deficit behind the Athletics in August. Spalding again led the league with 41 wins, and the offense was led by Barnes, George Wright, and two rookies, outfielder Jim O'Rourke and catcher Jim "Deacon" White. The 1874 season included a trip to England, arranged by the enterprising Spalding at Wright's request, during which the Red Stockings played eight of 14 regular season games with the Athletics. The trip was a financial failure because the baseball games were poorly attended, and the players were forced to take pay cuts to compensate the Boston club for the lost revenue. Wright's club won the pennant again, defeating the second place New York Mutuals by 7½ games, as Spalding had an overpowering 57-win year and Cal McVey, Spalding, Andy Leonard, and Jim O'Rourke led the hitters. Harry Wright had a respectable .307 batting average in his last season as a regular player.

The 1875 season was the last year of the National Association's operation. During the league's five years, a number of teams were forced to quit playing during the season because of on-field inadequacies, which led to heavy financial losses. It was clear that the imbalance between teams was destroying interest in the game, and before the 1875 season ended, efforts were undertaken to eliminate the Association and, with it, Boston's dominance. It became common knowledge before the season ended that William A. Hulbert, president of the Chicago club of the soon-to-be-formed National League, had lured Spalding, McVey, Barnes, and White from the Red Stockings, with their transfer to take effect after the season. This was the effective end of Harry Wright's powerhouse.

Baseball historian David Q. Voigt wrote in the first edition of *Total Baseball:*

> "... the pioneering National Association was by no means a failure. For all its weaknesses the Association had popularized professional baseball. Supporters like Henry Chadwick, the

innovative sportswriter, ... publicized the league by his coverage of games.... The Association's most solid innovator was
Harry Wright, who set high standards for professional promotion. Wright's Boston payroll was baseball's highest until
the early 1880s. As Boston's manager, Wright presided over a
$35,000 annual budget and dealt creatively with such problems
as proper groundskeeping, equipment design and procurement,
advertising, and the recruiting and training of players. Wright's
mastery paid off in his team's astonishing success. He was honored in these years as the "Father of Professional Base Ball," and
his envious colleagues also referred to the National Association as "Harry Wright's League."

Wright continued to manage the Red Stockings, now in the newly-
established National League, for the next six seasons. Even without the
four stars who had moved to Chicago, his clubs won pennants in 1877 and
1878, and finished in second place the following year (behind the Providence club). But the Red Stockings collapsed in 1880 and, after a sixth place
finish in 1881, Harry Wright left the Red Stockings and managed Providence for two years with only fair success. He took over the Philadelphia
Phillies in 1884 and managed them for the next 10 years, but with only
one first place finish and one second place season. Phillies owner John
Rogers fired him after the 1893 season, creating a considerable stir because
of the popularity of the 58-year-old Wright. As a result, the National
League created the position of chief of umpires for him, and he remained
in it until his death two years later. Over his 23 years as a major league
manager, Wright had a 1225–885 (.581) record and a .274 career batting
average. His long-overdue election into the Hall of Fame came in 1953.

Wright's accomplishments as a player-manager and team executive
were not surprising considering his extensive background in sports. He
was born in Sheffield, England, in 1835 and was heavily involved in sports
from the start. Harry began his athletic career with the St. George cricket
team before joining the Knickerbocker baseball club in 1858. He was an
excellent outfielder but possessed a barely adequate throwing arm. He was
a run-of-the-mill hitter, not nearly as good as his brother George, but
Wright was considered a decent hitter when it counted. He is thought to
be the first pitcher to throw a change-of-pace, which is especially intriguing since he was not a fast ball pitcher. Wright's involvement in sports
extended off the field to a sporting goods business he operated with his
brother George.

Wright was a handsome man and a neat dresser, in keeping with his
strong sense of propriety. The graceful 5 foot 9, 157-pounder presented a
striking presence, with his luxuriant sideburns, long mustache, and neatly

trimmed beard. He was a gentle but firm manager who expected his players to behave like professionals. Wright related well to his players and was especially helpful to young hopefuls. He wrote to a youngster who asked for advice on how to become a professional player: "In regard to diet, eat hearty, Roast Beef [sic] rare will aid, live regularly, keep good hours, and abstain from intoxicating drinks and tobacco." As for developing the requisite skills, he continued, "learn to be a good catch, a good thrower—strong and accurate—a reliable batter, and a good runner, all to be brought out—if in you—by steady and persevering practice."

Baseball historian Lee Allen described Wright as a decent, quiet man who did not believe in playing baseball on Sunday, and who, in an uncouth age, had the respect of even the rowdiest of players and was, in many ways, much like Connie Mack. Bill James wrote that Wright's strongest point as a manager was his almost phenomenal ability to persuade people to go along with his plans. In his *Baseball Managers*, James answered the question as to what Harry Wright would have done with his life had there been no professional baseball by observing "There wasn't any professional baseball. He invented it."

AL SPALDING

Albert Goodwill Spalding was born into a wealthy family in Byron, Illinois on September 2, 1850. When he was eight he and his widowed mother moved to the larger town of Rockford, Illinois. A natural athlete, by the time he was 15 he was pitching for Rockford's semi-professional Forest City club. The high point of the righthander's years in Rockford came in 1870 when he pitched in a 12–5 victory over Harry Wright's Red Stockings. After that season, when Wright prepared to move his Red Stockings from Cincinnati to Boston in the new National Association, Wright raided the Forest City team, signing Spalding for an impressive $1500 salary, along with second baseman Ross Barnes, and leftfielder Fred Cone.

Twenty-year-old Al Spalding was a sensation in his first year in Boston. The 6 foot 1, 170-pound youngster was the top pitcher in the league as Boston won the pennant in each of the next four seasons. Spalding was a commanding presence on the mound, with excellent control, a blazing fastball, and an effective change of pace. He had mastered the art of keeping hitters off balance either by quick-pitching or by stalling on the mound and upsetting the batter's concentration. He also specialized in feinting throws to first base before this practice was ruled a balk, and

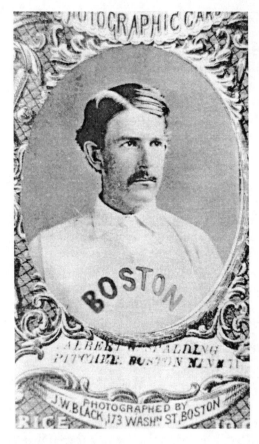

Albert Spalding was a great righthanded pitcher and competent outfielder with a career 252–65 pitching record and a .313 batting average. After a monster season as the pitcher-manager of the pennant-winning 1876 Chicago club, he later became the National League's foremost off-field leader and a prominent sporting goods industry executive.

he intimidated hitters by pitching high and inside. A good fielder, Spalding was credited with perfecting the technique of intentionally dropping pop ups to start double plays. He was not a powerful batter but he was a good contact hitter and was especially adept at hitting to the opposite field, always an asset to a righthand hitter. Over his five years with Boston, Spalding won 204 games out of the 225 games won by the Red Stockings. Playing in the outfield when he was not pitching, he hit for an average of .323 during the five years.

Despite his great success in Boston, Spalding was deeply concerned about the long-term outlook for the game. He saw the negative impact on the game of Boston's dominance, and he realized that the lack of competition would hurt the game's stability and, most important to Spalding, its profitability. His concern was borne out as six of the 13 teams starting the 1875 season ceased operations before the season ended. Spalding also was troubled by other problem areas. He worked hard at maintaining his public image and did not smoke or drink, in public at least, and he was contemptuous of other players who did not approach that standard. And he was upset by the corrupting influence of gamblers at ball parks.

Spalding felt that the solution lay in changing the system under which baseball was operating. As he saw it, club owners should relieve the players "… of all care and responsibility for the legitimate functions of management, require of them the very best performance of which they were capable … for which service they were to receive commensurate pay." In other words, businessmen should handle the business end of the game and the players should concentrate on playing the game. Spalding, a very mature 25-year-old, joined with other baseball figures in pushing this idea.

In March 1875 Spalding met William A. Hulbert, a wealthy Chicago businessman and a generally powerful mover and shaker in the Windy City. He was Spalding's kind of man and, moreover, he was taking over as president of the Chicago club in the up-and-coming National League. The two men actually drafted the constitution for the National League in Hulbert's home. The constitution provided that alcohol would not be sold on the teams' grounds and gambling would not be tolerated. All teams were obligated to play complete schedules, with each franchise representing a city of at least 75,000. Most important, it would be a National League of *clubs*, not players. Owners would have complete control and the League would be run as a business.

Spalding agreed to jump his contract and move to Chicago as the White Stockings' player-manager. He convinced catcher Deacon White, first baseman Cal McVey, and second baseman Ross Barnes to go with him. He also recruited two Philadelphia stars, first baseman Adrian "Cap" Anson and third baseman Ezra Sutton. The players wanted the signings to be kept secret, but well before the season ended the story came out. Spalding fought his way through the resulting public condemnation. He went all out to prove that the Chicago deal would not affect his ability to perform well for the rest of the season in Boston. In characteristic style, Spalding won 54 games and lost five, with a 1.59 ERA with Boston.

Spalding negotiated a generous contract for himself—an impressive $2500 base salary plus 25% of the gate receipts. In addition, he received an ownership interest in the team and was given the position of club secretary. For these considerations, pitcher-manager Spalding produced a monster year in 1876, the National League's first season. His club won the pennant by six games—in a 66-game season. On April 24 he pitched the first National League shutout, earning a 4-0 victory at Louisville, and he won Chicago's first home game, with a 6-0 win over Cincinnati. Spalding led the league with 47 wins, as his club won 52 games, and he also hit .312. He was rivaled on the mound only by righthander George Bradley of the St. Louis Cardinals. Spalding's club had a .337 season batting average, .66 higher than any other team, and four of the top five hitters in batting average played for Chicago.

To begin his great year, player-manager Spalding moved from his home in Rockford to Chicago with his brother J. Walter to open a sporting goods store. Spalding became acquainted with that industry while working with the Wright brothers, and he found that he enjoyed it. Making good use of his baseball contacts in an era in which a conflict of interest was of little concern, in 1878 the enterprising Spalding obtained a contract to supply the official baseballs used in all National League games. The A.G. Spalding Company also began publishing the official National League baseball guide and later published guides and instruction manuals for all sports, all designed to promote the company's ever-expanding product lines. Before the end of the century, Spalding's aggressive company became the country's largest sporting goods business, far outstripping Harry Wright's company, Wright & Ditson, and putting the Spalding brothers well into the millionaire class.

Spalding's baseball fortunes tumbled in 1877. His overworked pitching arm gave out and he pitched in only four games. He made his last start as a pitcher on June 5 and he failed to retire any of the five hitters he faced before literally being knocked out of the game when a vicious line drive through the box struck him in the chest. Spalding returned to the lineup a few days later, playing first base for the remainder of the season. The White Stockings also fell apart, finishing the season in fifth place in a six-team league. That was the end of Spalding's player-manager tenure and his playing career. He retired at 27 with an outstanding pitching record of 252 wins and only 65 losses (.795), a career 2.04 ERA, and a .313 career batting average. As a player-manager, his teams had a 78-47 (.624) record.

After Spalding retired from field activities he became the secretary of the Chicago White Stockings (while running his thriving company) and eventually replaced William Hulbert in 1882. The 32-year-old Spalding became the club's president and principal stockholder. He took the lead in attempting to suppress the Players' Brotherhood before the Players League came into operation in 1890, and some baseball historians have credited him with saving the National League by helping to crush the new league after its one year of operation.

Spalding relinquished the Chicago club's presidency in 1891, but he remained a heavily involved, behind-the-scenes owner until he sold his controlling interest in the club in 1902. By that time he had attained status as the "Father of Baseball' and of the National League. He moved to California and, in 1910, attempted to enter politics as a progressive Republican, but he was less successful in convincing party insiders to accept him than he had been with his baseball colleagues, and he was refused the nomination. He died of a stroke at age 65 in 1915. Spalding was inducted into the Hall of Fame in 1939, an honor he deserved both as a player and as one of the most important figures the game has ever known.

BOB FERGUSON

Infielder Bob "Death to Flying Things" Ferguson, who replaced Spalding, was another important player-manager throughout the 1870s. His off-the-wall nickname derived from his defensive skills as a second and third baseman, as he was only a fair hitter as a player-manager for five different teams from 1871 through 1884. He had a mediocre managerial record (417–616), never finishing higher than third place. Yet he must have been highly respected as a player-manager because only 10 men in major league history served as player-managers for longer than the 714 games in which he filled that role.

The Brooklyn-born Ferguson's primary contribution to the game was his forthright, unflinchingly honest presence in a period when many players were men of low moral character with a high susceptibility to the bribery efforts of gamblers. This was reflected in Ferguson's election to the presidency of the National Association of Professional Baseball Players, which led to the establishment of the National League in 1876. Ferguson's integrity compensated for his blunt, tactless manner in handling players when he managed, as well as when he later became an umpire.

Ferguson's explosiveness was displayed on July 24, 1873, when he got into an argument with catcher Nat Hicks of the New York Mutuals over a play Ferguson called that went against Hicks. Ferguson became so enraged at a remark Hicks made that he grabbed Hicks' bat and broke the catcher's arm. Surprisingly, the two men reconciled after the game, but Hicks was unable to play for two months.

Warren Goldstein discussed the changing relationship between managers and their players in the late 1800s:

> By the latter 1870s and 1880s the playing captain was on the way out. [According to Bill James, this was not completely the case.] Players remained roughly the same age, then, as their managers grew older.... The popularity of the nickname "Pops" for baseball managers and coaches suggests the quasi-filial attitude held by thousands of players toward their managers over the years. But "Pops," of course, could be used ironically or sarcastically as well, and when players rebelled against managerial authority, they did so frequently as errand boys staying out late, running off without telling the manager, sulking over real or imagined poor treatment, objecting to being treated as children.

3

Anson and Donovan

CAP ANSON

Adrian Constantine "Cap" Anson is generally considered the greatest non-pitching player and the foremost player-manager of the pre–1900 period. He was born on April 11, 1852, in Marshalltown, Iowa, in the central part of the state, some 300 miles from the Illinois border. His father, Henry, was the first white settler of Marshalltown, which he laid out and began to develop the year before his son Adrian was born. The younger Anson grew to be a huge man for his time, over 6 feet tall and almost 230 pounds, no surprise considering that his mother, Jeannette, was a tall, heavy woman and his father was a hulking man. Anson learned to play ball on the local sandlots, and at 14 he played on the Marshalltown Stars team, along with his father and his brother, which won the Iowa state championship several times. Anson attended both Iowa State and Notre Dame, but he was not a good student and left college after a year.

When he was 19 the burly young man joined the Forest City team of Rockford, which needed new players to replace Al Spalding and Ross Barnes who had left to join Harry Wright's Boston club. Anson, then called "Baby" Anson because he was only 19, signed with Forest City for $66 a month. The husky, righthand-hitting young man played third base and caught, and had a commendable .325 average. When Rockford dropped out of the National Association after the 1870 season, Anson signed with the Philadelphia Athletics for $1250. With the Athletics he developed into a powerful hitter and more versatile fielder. The high points of his stay with the Athletics came in 1872 when he hit .417, and in 1874 when the Athletics joined Harry Wright's club on its tour through England and Ireland.

24

While he played for Philadelphia, Anson did not live a monk-like life. One night he got into a bar fight with a policeman and was dragged, badly bruised, to the police station. He was extremely fortunate though because the police commissioner also was the president of the Athletics. Anson repaired to another bar to celebrate his release and had several more drinks. While there he met a very young woman and apparently it was love at first sight. It was love on his part, at least, because the first reaction of the young girl, Virginia Fiegal, was to express her disgust with men who drank too much and who were arrested after being involved in barroom fights. (It was not clear as to what sort of men she expected to meet in a bar.) If Anson's reaction, as expressed in his 1900 autobiography, *A Ballplayer's Career*, is to be fully believed, he stopped going to bars, cut back his drinking, and engaged in no more street fights.

Anson almost upset his wedding plans when he received a $2000 offer from the newly-organized Chicago National League club that had picked up four of Harry Wright's star players, including player-manager designate Al Spalding. When Anson told Virginia that he had committed to play in Chicago, she insisted that she would not leave her native Philadelphia. The lovesick Anson sought to buy his release from the White Stockings, but Chicago club president William Hulbert refused Anson's offer of $1000 for his release. The young lady reluctantly agreed to relocate with her fiancé, and they were married before the 1876 season. The union produced seven children, three of whom died when they were infants.

Al Spalding saw to it that Anson became the White Stockings' player-manager in 1879. In his autobiography Anson recalled that he and Spalding had developed a strong mutual respect 10 years before when Spalding was a young pitcher for Forest City against the Marshalltown Stars. The professional club's players were disappointed at "only" winning by 18–3, and Spalding and his teammates stayed in Marshalltown overnight and won a hastily scheduled second game by a more satisfactory 35–3 score. Anson wrote that Forest City had unfairly substituted a livelier ball to run up the second game score. During the second game the 18-year-old Anson got into a spirited argument with Spalding, and the impressed Al Spalding brought Anson to Chicago.

Anson, who threw righthanded, had a fine offensive year as Chicago's regular third baseman in 1876, hitting .356 average, but he had a butcher-like .883 fielding average. Anson, still playing third base, had another good offensive year in 1887, although the White Stockings slipped down to fifth place and Spalding was replaced as manager by shortstop Bob Ferguson. The club showed only slight improvement in 1878, and Chicago catcher Frank "Old Silver" Flint replaced Ferguson. Flint's first step was to move

Anson to first base from left field. But the club started poorly and Al Spalding appointed 27-year-old Anson to replace Flint after only 19 games. The White Stockings responded smartly to their new player-manager's tough leadership and won two-thirds of their remaining games.

In 1880 player-manager Anson had his best year up to that point, earning a .337 average and leading his team in winning the pennant by an impressive 15 games. The big Iowan had become a patient, scientific hitter, and, despite his large size, he was more of a skillful place hitter than a pure power hitter. He stood erectly at the plate with his feet close together, and he was strong enough to use an unusually heavy bat. His hitting strategy was to take the first pitch and often wait to offer at a pitch until he had two strikes on him. Despite this habit, he struck out infrequently, less than once in every 31 at-bats over his long career.

The White Stockings had a number of outstanding players in addition to Anson. Third baseman Ned Williamson was a good hitter and one of the best third basemen in the game. Outfielder George Gore was a solid, dependable player. And catcher-outfielder Mike "King" Kelly, although semi-literate, was one of the most prominent players of the day. He was a talented hitter, a rifle-armed fielder who played several positions well, a skilled baserunner, and one of the most colorful players of the day, whether drunk or sober. Anson's other two stars were two new pitchers, lefthander Larry Corcoran and righthander Fred Goldsmith. Both pitchers did so well early in 1880 that Anson decided to rotate their starts. Before that, teams usually had one player who pitched most of the games. Anson's idea of alternating his starters was revolutionary and, as it turned out, extremely successful. Supported by a strong club, the fastballer Corcoran and slow-ball pitching Goldsmith pitched the White Stockings to a 35–3 start and a 67–17 season record, for a .798 winning percentage, the best in National League history. The same group of players carried the White Stockings to two more pennant wins, in 1881 and 1882, a second place finish in 1883, and, with the replacement of Corcoran and Goldsmith by righthanders John Clarkson and Jim McCormick, two more pennants in 1885 and '86. Anson considered Clarkson the best pitcher the White Stockings had up to that point.

Through it all, Cap (for Captain) Anson was the league's dominant figure, as a player, manager, innovator, and personality. Over the 1880–86 period he led the National League in hitting twice. He led the league in RBI in six of those years, missing only in 1883 when he tied for fourth. He could hit with power even in that dead ball era, as he showed on August 5 and 6, 1884, when he hit five home runs in two consecutive games, a record that stood for 41 years. And despite a reputation as a mediocre fielding first baseman, he twice led the league in fielding average during that period.

Anson was one of the game's more imaginative managers and important innovators. He was the first manager to take the rudimentary step of rotating his pitchers. He started the practice of coaching base runners from third base. When his team was at bat, and he was not at the plate or on the bases, Anson stood along the third base line, and as a runner approached third base Anson would shout instructions to him. He also used this proximity to the pitcher to harass him with more force than could be exerted from the bench. Other practices that Anson either initiated or expanded were the use of offensive and defensive signals, having his fielders back each other up on all fielding plays, using the hit-and-run play, and increasing the use of base stealing.

Anson is credited with developing spring training in an early version of the pre-season phase it would become. Actually, he was not the first manager to bring his team south for conditioning and early practice. But he made spring training a more organized team activity, especially in bringing his players down to Sulphur Dell, Tennessee, to melt off excess weight accumulated during the off-season.

Anson never stopped trying to get an edge. Before 1881 there was no rule requiring that each team's batting order be provided to the umpire before the game. But such a rule took effect that year and Anson was the reason for it. Before the rule change Anson used to take advantage of developments as the first inning progressed. The heavy-hitting White Stockings manager waited to see if the first two men got on base, in which case he would bat next. If no men were on base, Anson would send up another hitter, saving himself for a later chance to hit.

Writer Robert Smith, in his *The Hall of Fame*, described Anson:

> Anson was six feet two, an erect, square-shouldered, lop-eared man, tightly muscled, of a slightly dour countenance. His eyes were deep and his gaze level and clear. His mouth was firm, his nose curved and badly proportioned, like something a child might draw. There was a fierceness in his nature which took the form of a stubborn honesty and independence, a grim clinging to prejudice, a tendency to express his mind loudly and directly, and a desire to go his own way—and have his own way.

After being named manager Anson lost no time in establishing his toughness. He scheduled daily long, hard workouts for his players. He was especially rough on his players during their pre-season training drills, and woe to the player who tried a short cut. Christy Mathewson wrote in his *Pitching in a Pinch*:

After hours of practice, [Anson] would lead the men in long
runs, and the better he felt, the longer the runs. One hot day....
Anson was toiling around the park ... at the head of a string of
steaming, sweating players, ... when a player discovered a loose
board in the fence on the back stretch, pulled it off, and dived
through the hole.... [Almost all of the other players followed
suit] ... [Anson] kept grimly on, alone, until he had finished,
and then he pushed his red face through the hole in the fence
and saw his men. "Your turn now, boys," he said, and while he
sat in the grandstand as the sole spectator, he made that crowd
of unfortunate athletes run around the track twice as many
times as he himself had done.

   Early in Anson's first season as player-manager, Al Spalding came on
the field to protest an umpire's call. Furious at Spalding's intervention,
Anson lit into his boss with a
string of expletives and Spalding almost meekly moved back
to his seat. Then Anson took
up the battle with the umpire,
either because he thought the
umpire was wrong or because
he felt the umpire could be
intimidated. And Anson had
an intimidating voice, remarkably like a foghorn.

   Anson was loved by Chicago fans for his gruff, tough,
plain-speaking style and his
bravado as he led his team
onto the field. The baseball
writers liked him, not neces-
sarily as a person, but because
he was a highly opinionated
talker on such diverse topics
as baseball, politics, and bil-
liards. He was respected but
not loved by his players, and
some of them detested him.
He was described by Chicago
writer Harry Palmer as "mat-
ter-of-fact, calculating, and
practical" in handling his

Adrian "Cap" Anson is generally considered
the greatest non-pitching player and most successful, domineering, and innovative playing
manager of the pre-1900 period. First baseman Anson was a player-manager in 2155
games, winning five pennants over a 20-year
period, with a lifetime .329 batting average.

charges. The burly player-manager appeared to be indestructible, rarely missing a game because of illness or injury. He expected his players to display the same fortitude, and he forced them to play with bruised fingers or with various ailments.

Anson was enthusiastically supported by the teetotaling Spalding. Late one night while checking player curfews, Anson found a locked room and he diagnosed the situation correctly. A player was covering for a teammate who was out on the town. The big player-manager climbed up a chair to peek through the transom and lit a match. With that a pillow thrown from inside the room snuffed out the match and knocked Anson down. He retaliated by fining both roommates.

Anson was the largest man on his club and he was not above enforcing his edicts with his fists. He did have at least one weakness as a manager, though. He played cards with his players for big stakes. There was the time that Anson and his third baseman, Ned Williamson, almost got into a violent brawl over a poker game. It seems that Anson, with a hand of four jacks, lost a sizable pot to Williamson, who held four kings. Convinced the game was not on the up-and-up, Anson refused to pay. The enraged Williamson responded by grabbing a metal water pitcher and preparing to split Anson's skull. Fortunately, the would-be combatants were pulled apart before any real violence took place. Later Williamson gave a vintage, if ungrammatical, critique of player-manager Anson, grumbling, "Cap's all right as a player but he don't count for cornstalks as a man."

In 1886 the White Stockings, now known as the "Colts," were a weaker club than in previous years, beating out second place Detroit by only 2½ games. They were led on offense as usual by player-manager Anson who hit .371 and led the league with 147 RBI. Chris Von der Ahe, the colorful owner of the pennant-winning St. Louis Browns of the rival American Association, challenged the Colts to play the Browns for the championship. The two clubs had played an "exhibition" post-season series in 1885 that ended in a controversial tie, although there was a general feeling that Anson's players had not taken the Browns seriously and had been outplayed. Anson, who looked down his nose at the American Association, took Von der Ahe's challenge in the 1886 post-season series, but only under the condition that the winning team would "take every penny of the gate." Al Spalding, who had been bitter about the Colts' poor performance in the 1885 exhibition series, promised his players suits of clothes and half of the gate receipts if the club won. This time Anson's team had real incentive to win, and the gamblers felt that the Browns would not win a game.

The teams opened their best of seven series on October 18 as the Colts' John Clarkson shut out first baseman-manager Charles Comiskey's team. But the Browns rebounded to take three of the next four games. Clarkson started the sixth game. Going into the bottom of the eighth, the Colts led 3–0. But the Browns pulled to within 3–1, with the tying runs on base. With more than 10,000 fans crowded around the field and screaming wildly, Browns third baseman Arlie Latham rifled a triple to tie the game. In the bottom of the tenth, Browns centerfielder Chris Welch sprinted home on a pitch that catcher King Kelly could not handle, sliding in with the Series-winning run, a play that became known as the famous "$15,000 slide." Some time later Latham told a writer a dirty little secret—the players on both teams had agreed among themselves to split the game receipts (which actually amounted to $13,920, not $15,000). This statement was never proved or disproved.

In his *Baseball Managers*, Bill James wrote:

> Cap Anson would remain a proud and imposing figure until the day he died thirty-five years later, but in a very real sense Anson's life passed its peak at that moment, and was lived forever after on a downward spiral. King Kelly, beloved by the fans but never a favorite of Anson's (or Spalding's for that matter) due to his heavy drinking, was sold to Boston. George Gore, the star center fielder, had fought with the Colts constantly for more money; Anson sold him, too, to the New York Giants. "I'll go," said Gore, "but if I do, you'll never win another pennant."

And he was right. Gore and Kelly would play for championship teams again. But Anson never would.

Spalding was a temperance fanatic and, before the 1886 season, he actually had coerced his players, notably heavy drinking King Kelly, Ned Williamson, and John Clarkson, into pledging not to partake of wine, beer, or liquor. Fellow prohibitionist Cap Anson administered the oath to the players in Spalding's sporting goods store. After it became clear that his players were violating their oaths, Spalding went so far as to hire Pinkerton Agency detectives to follow the players. After receiving reports of player misdeeds, Spalding called in a number of the identified players; all of them expressed their regrets except Kelly, who deeply resented the intrusion on his privacy. At that point, Spalding and Anson, and probably Kelly himself, knew that Kelly's days with the club were numbered.

The Colts missed Kelly, Gore, pitcher Jim McCormick, and leftfielder Al Dalrymple in 1887, as they finished in third place, 6½ games off the pace. It was a big disappointment to Spalding and Anson, since their club was tied with Detroit for first place at the end of August but by mid–September the Colts had fallen out of the race. Anson had another great season personally, hitting a league-leading .347, and Clarkson led all the pitchers in the league, with 38 wins. The season was notable because of a display of Anson's racial bigotry. His prejudice had surfaced as early as 1882 when he objected violently to having his team play an exhibition game against Toledo of the American Association because Toledo catcher Moses "Fleet" Walker was black. Anson finally relented when he was given the alternative of playing the game or pulling his team off the field and losing his team's share of the gate receipts.

On June 19, 1887, the Colts were scheduled to play an exhibition game against the Newark club of the International League. Newark had a black pitcher, George Stovey, who appeared to have major league potential. On the day of the game Anson refused to let his team take the field against Stovey, saying, "Get him off the field, or I get off." With that, Stovey agreed to leave the field in order to avoid an embarrassing confrontation. Shortly after, the International League banned the employment of black players in 1888, and there would not be a black player on a major league team until Jackie Robinson's debut with the Brooklyn Dodgers in 1947.

The 1888 season was a carbon copy of the previous year—another outstanding season for Anson (who led the league in hitting and in RBI) but not for his team, which finished in second place, nine games behind the New York Giants. The year started out well for Anson when he signed a ten-year contract to continue managing the Colts and received 130 shares of stock in the club. But his team suffered a big loss when the talented but temperamental Clarkson threatened to quit the game unless he was traded to Boston, near his hometown, leaving Spalding with no choice but to make the deal. As a result, Clarkson won 33 games for Boston instead of winning a comparable number for Chicago, and that was the story of the season. Anson was one of Spalding's partners on a world tour during the off-season after the 1888 season. In his autobiography, Anson himself told of the disgraceful, bigoted way in which he had treated Clarence Duval, a black man whom Anson had made the team mascot a few years before the trip.

After a third place finish in 1889, Anson had to deal with the problems brought on by the establishment of the Players League in 1890. Most of the National League's stars had elected to move to the new league, and Anson, a minority owner of the Colts, condemned the jumpers as disloyal and greedy. Anson put together a team of young, inexperienced replacements who were nicknamed the "Cubs," the first use of one of the most famous baseball team names. The veteran Anson now was widely called

"Pop" Anson. His young "Cubs" gave a respectable performance, finishing in second place, largely due to their redoubtable player-manager. In his nineteenth major league campaign, Pop Anson hit a commendable .312, with 107 RBI.

After the Players League folded, Anson integrated a number of returning defectors into his lineup with some success. His club finished in second place, 3½ games behind the Boston Beaneaters. The Cubs had their best day of the season on September 4, when they beat the Beaneaters 5–3 to move into what appeared to be a commanding seven game lead over Boston. But Anson's mood changed over the next few weeks as his club slumped badly and the Boston club spurted to victory. Anson accused veteran players with New York of throwing games to Boston, and he appeared to have a point because the Giants had not played three of their stars—first baseman Roger Connor, catcher Buck Ewing, and pitching ace Amos Rusie—in the last three games of the season against Boston. After the season the National League officially dismissed Anson's charges of collusion, although for the rest of his life he stoutly maintained that he had been cheated out of the 1891 pennant.

Tiring of the criticism of the fans he had received for selling his star players, Spalding had stepped down as club president before the 1891 season and appointed James A. Hart, one of his disciples, to replace him. Spalding assured Anson that his job was not in jeopardy but, nevertheless, Hart and Anson did not hit it off from the start. The Cubs finished fifth in a 12-team race in 1892 and, by that Fall, Anson was openly feuding with Hart. The two men constantly bickered as the Cubs' fortunes declined over the next five years. Anson continued as player-manager, and he played respectably as he approached his mid–40s. But the feuding between Anson and Hart came to a head in 1897 when Anson's ten-year contract ended. After a tough loss, the irascible Anson goaded Chicago writer Hugh Fullerton into writing the following story: "Captain A.C. Anson desires me [Fullerton] to announce, in black type at the head of this column, that the Chicago baseball club is composed of a bunch of drunkards and loafers who are throwing him down."

That, of course, was the effective end of Anson's career with Chicago. Spalding refused to support his old friend and Anson's contract was not renewed. Spalding tried to ease the pain of Anson's firing by beginning a campaign to raise $50,000 for a testimonial dinner for Anson. But the proud veteran, who had become bitterly angry with Spalding for a number of reasons, spurned the effort with the statement, "The public owes me nothing. I am neither old nor a pauper. I can earn my own living."

Anson signed to manage the New York Giants in June 1898, but he quit after 31 games because Giants owner Andrew Freedman would not give him a free hand to manage as he saw fit. After that he was involved in an unsuccessful attempt to bring back the American Association. He also bought a billiard parlor and was elected city clerk of Chicago. He also played on his semipro ball club until he was nearly 60, and even campaigned unsuccessfully for the job of baseball's first commissioner after the Black Sox scandal in 1919. But he was ruined financially by bad investments and was too proud to accept charity.

Anson had a lifetime batting average of .329, leading the National League in hitting four times and in RBI eight times. Anson had 2995 hits as a National Leaguer, but his 423 hits in the National Association brings his major league total to 3418 hits. During Anson's career, teams did not play the 154 or 162 game schedules that came later. If Anson had played these longer seasons, he almost surely would have had more than 4000 hits.

Anson was arguably the best player-manager ever. He played in more games while managing (2155) than any other player-manager in baseball's history. He was a player-manager in Chicago for an incredible 20 years, winning five pennants during that period. Overall, clubs Anson managed won 1296 of 2288, for a commendable .578 winning percentage. He was a highly successful manager when he had talented players, and his clubs finished in the first division in each of his first 14 years as a player-manager. Anson, who died penniless at age 70, was inducted into the Hall of Fame in 1939.

Patsy Donovan

Patrick Joseph "Patsy" Donovan was born in County Cork, Ireland, on March 16, 1865. He came to the United States when he was three and his family settled in Lawrence, Massachusetts, where his younger brother, former Yankees manager" Wild Bill" Donovan, was born. After four years in the minors, the handsome, dark-haired Patsy began a 17-season career in the majors, playing with National League clubs in Boston, Washington, Pittsburgh, St. Louis, and Brooklyn, as well as one season with the Washington Senators.

Donovan had his best years with Pittsburgh from 1893 through 1899, batting over .300 in six of seven years, and with the Cardinals over the next four years. He gained recognition as one of the best right fielders in the game, with a strong, accurate throwing arm and speed in the outfield and on the bases. He stole 518 bases, averaging more than 30 stolen bases a season. Not a power hitter, he hit for an average of .301 over his 17-season career.

Donovan was a player-manager for Pittsburgh in 1897 and 1899, with his clubs finishing eighth and tenth. He played and managed for the Cardinals from 1901 through 1904, and with Washington in 1905, with no more success. After retiring as a player, he managed the Dodgers and the Red Sox. Donovan's teams consistently lacked the horses to compete successfully. None of his teams finished higher than fourth, and he had the misfortune of leaving the Red Sox helm in 1911, the year before the club acquired players with the skills to help it dominate the American League for the next several years.

His career managerial winning percentage was a poor .438 (684–879), next to the lowest for anyone who managed for more than 10 years in the major leagues. His winning percentage as a player-manager was an even lower .428. Yet the respect that baseball people had for his knowledge of the game is best reflected in the fact that only six men were player-managers in more games than Donovan's 1002. Donovan died on December 25, 1953, in Lawrence, Massachusetts.

4

Ward, Ewing, and Mack

JOHN MONTGOMERY WARD

John Montgomery "Monte" Ward, one of the most important player-managers of the late 1800s, would gain far greater influence and fame as a key figure in the development of the game. He was born on March 3, 1860, in Bellefonte, Pennsylvania, the son of tobacconist James and Ruth Ward. The bright, aggressive youngster pitched for semipro teams before he entered nearby Penn State. But his stay there ended abruptly during his freshman year when he objected so strenuously to being hazed that he knocked an upperclassman down a flight of stairs. Writer Byron Di Salvatore, in his biography of Ward, *A Clever Base-Ballist, The Life and Times of John Montgomery Ward*, reported that Ward also was cited for stealing chickens. He was summarily kicked out of school.

The 5 foot 8, 165 pounder started his professional career in 1878, pitching in the Iowa League before joining the Providence Grays of the National League. Even at 18 the stocky, sandy-haired righthander baffled hitters with a sharp curve and good control, winning 22 and losing 13 for Providence. He had a great year the following season under shortstop-manager George Wright, with a remarkable 47 and 19 record as the Grays won the pennant. Apparently the strong-willed Ward had to overcome differences with his manager, as Wright later said that Ward was "obstinate."

On June 12, 1880, Ward pitched only the second perfect game in National League history, in Providence against Buffalo. Later that season 20-year-old Ward became the Grays' interim pitcher-manager for the last 32 games of the season. Monte pitched for Providence for the next two seasons until he was traded to the New York Giants, beginning their first year in the National League.

In 1884 Ward injured his throwing arm running the bases, a serious injury that ended his pitching career. He taught himself to throw left-handed with enough accuracy and power to become a proficient outfielder. Within a few years his righthand throwing had recovered sufficiently for him to play shortstop. Near the end of the 1884 season, Ward replaced Giants manager Jim Price for the last 16 games of an uneventful Giants season. Ward was known for his aggressiveness, but he outdid himself in one of those late-season games. He disputed a call by umpire John Gaffney and punched Gaffney in the face, cutting his eye. Ward escaped with a fine and a brief suspension because he apologized immediately.

Ward became the Giants' team captain before the 1885 season. He had full authority on the field, which made him, for all practical purposes, the Giants' player-manager. By that time the improved Giants had developed into a genuine pennant contender. Catcher Buck Ewing, first baseman "Dear Old Roger" Connor, and centerfielder "Orator Jim" O'Rourke had become stars. Ward had established himself at shortstop, although he was not yet as good a hitter as he would later become. "Smiling Mickey" Welch was a canny little righthander with a good fastball, and a deadly curve ball and change-of-pace. Fellow righthander "Sir Timothy" Keefe was a superb power pitcher, transferred from Giants president John B. Day's Mets (Day owned both clubs) to the Giants before the 1885 season. The Giants finished only two games behind Cap Anson's Chicago club.

After the 1885 season Ward took the lead in forming the Brotherhood of Professional Base Ball Players, a group of players seeking to unionize professional athletes and fight salary restrictions and the abuses of the reserve clause. Ward and several teammates set about organizing similar groups on other National League clubs. Within a year the Brotherhood had enrolled 107 players.

The Giants were not yet able to challenge Cap Anson's Colts seriously in 1886. But the resourceful Ward characteristically turned a misfortune to his advantage. He was beaned early in the season batting righthanded and realized he had become gun-shy—he could no longer hang in at the plate without stepping in the bucket. So he turned around at the plate and learned to bat lefthanded. He felt that he had less power from the new side, but his batting average rose after he became a switch hitter.

Ward had his best offensive year in 1887, hitting .338 and leading the League with 111 stolen bases. He also led all shortstops in fielding percentage. But the Giants finished in fourth place despite fine years by other players as well. The popular Connor ranked high in home runs and triples, and Keefe and Welch had good years.

In addition to running the Giants on the field, much of Ward's attention was directed to off-the-field activities. The public became aware of the existence of the Brotherhood by late 1886. Ward gave the complete story to *Sporting Life* and, in doing so, gained the support of its influential editor, Francis C. Richter, and other well-respected baseball journalists. Ward, by then a full-fledged attorney, wrote a series of articles attacking the reserve rule, the blacklisting of players, and the inequitable contracts offered players. He wrote one particularly brilliant essay, *Is the Base Ball Player a Chattel?*, which was helpful in explaining the Brotherhood's positions on various issues. That essay stimulated the establishment of a three-man player committee to present their grievances to the owners, who were led by Al Spalding.

Other than his on-field and Brotherhood activities, Ward kept well occupied off the field. Always an excellent student, he studied law and political science at Columbia University and graduated from law school in 1885 with honors. Unlike most of his teammates who lived near the Polo Grounds, Ward lived at the fashionable Grand Central Hotel in mid-town. He was also very much the eligible young man about town, well-spoken, handsome, and unmarried.

Ward fell deeply in love with Helen Dauvray, a prominent Broadway actress and classic buxom beauty. Without night games to keep him away, as Noel Hynd described it in his *The Giants of the Polo Grounds*, Ward would be seen "... waiting in the gaslit wings of the legitimate theatres waiting for Helen to finish her performance. Then the couple would go out on the town, sometimes till 5 A.M." But impassioned young love demands continual contact, and it particularly abhors road trips. Since the couple did not live together, when Ward was in New York he often felt the need to communicate with his beloved before games. He accomplished this by sending steamy love notes to Dauvray via a young messenger. The good news is that Ward and Dauvray were married in 1887 at a fashionable Presbyterian church. The unhappy news is that the marriage ended in divorce three years later, the victim of Ward's relentless philandering.

Jim Mutrie, more of a promoter and businessman than a baseball man, had managed the Giants since their entrance into the League in 1883. But it was well recognized that Ward was the Giants' de facto field leader, a position he held through the 1887 season when he resigned as captain over a salary dispute. Buck Ewing took over the captaincy for the next two seasons. The Giants started off uncertainly in 1888, but in July the team came on strong, winning 18 of 23 games, and the Giants were on their way to their first pennant win. Their pitching staff was by far the best in the league, with a remarkable staff ERA of 1.96. Tim Keefe and Mickey Welch accounted for 71 of the team's 84 wins. The Giants went on to defeat the St. Louis Browns six games to four as Connor and Ewing did the power hitting, Ward hit .379, and Keefe sparkled with four of the Giants' six wins.

One reporter wrote some time later, "He [Ward] was considered ... the model ballplayer of the country." Another wrote, glowingly, "He was the most dashing, daring and winning player the Giants ever had. The fans swore by him." Ward was recognized widely for his leadership qualities and his intelligence, both on and off the field. As another writer put it, "He is quick to see and take advantage of any opportunity. His keen perception helps him to win many games." To illustrate the point, Ward convinced Ewing to employ a new stratagem—the intentional walk.

In November 1888, while Ward was touring overseas as player-manager of an all-star team, wealthy clothing manufacturer John T. Brush bought the Indianapolis club of the National League. Brush succeeded in obtaining league approval of a scheme called the Classification Plan. Under the Plan, players would be placed in five categories, A to E, according to "habits, earnestness, and special qualifications" exhibited in the previous season. The owners and managers would do the grading, and players would be paid as follows:

Class	Yearly Salary	Class	Yearly Salary
A	$2500	D	1750
B	2250	E	1500
C	2000		

After returning from the tour, a furious Ward was refused an immediate hearing of a Brotherhood committee by the League. The players talked of striking, but Ward feared they would lose public support if they walked out on a legal agreement. That left the players in the impossible position of trying to negotiate a settlement with the season under way.

Meanwhile, the National League season proceeded under a cloud. The Giants had largely the same pennant-winning cast. Roger Connor, rightfielder "Silent Mike" Tiernan, and Buck Ewing led the offense; Welsh and Keefe combined for 55 wins; and Ward hit .299 while directing the club's defense. The Giants won the pennant when Tim Keefe defeated Cleveland 5–3 while the fifth place Pittsburgh Pirates beat the second place Boston Beaneaters. So the victorious Giants returned home and prepared to take on the Brooklyn Bridegrooms in a post-season "World Series."

Just a week before the Series started, Ward met with Giants owner John Day to inform him that he and most of Day's players would be starting their own New York club in a new Players League in 1890. In the first game the Giants led 10–8 after seven innings, but the umpires refused to call the game because of darkness, perhaps fearing the wrath of the Brooklyn home crowd. The Bridegrooms came back to score four runs in the deepening darkness and pull out the win. The Giants evened the series the next day before a Series record-breaking crowd of 16,172 as Giants righthander Ed "Cannonball" Crane held off the Bridegrooms for a 6–2 win.

Brooklyn won the next two games for a three-to-one Series lead. In the third game, ahead 8–7 in the sixth inning, the Bridegrooms began to stall, waiting for darkness to fall. The score was still 8-7 when the game was called in the top of the ninth—when the Giants had the bases loaded and only one out. For a second time a game was called because of darkness to help the Brooklyn cause. The Giants had overcome a 7-2 Bridegroom lead to tie the game in the top of the sixth inning, but in the bottom of that inning, rightfielder Tom "Oyster" Burns homered in the dark for a 10–7 Brooklyn lead. With that, the umpires called the game.

Ed Crane won the fifth game 11–3. Moving to the Polo Grounds for the remaining games of the Series, Giants righthander Hank O'Day won a 2–1 pitchers' battle against Brooklyn's Bill "Adonis" Terry. Ward starred for the Giants, stealing second and third bases in the ninth to score the tying run, and then driving in the winning run in the 11th inning. The Giants battered the Bridegrooms heavily in the next two games to take a five to three lead in games.

The last game of the Series was played before 3,067 chilled, wet fans at the Polo Grounds. It was a repeat match between Adonis Terry and Hank O'Day. With their backs to the wall, the overmatched Bridegrooms held a 2–1 lead after five innings. But the Giants tied the game in the sixth; then in the seventh Roger Connor scored the deciding run on a passed ball, and O'Day blanked Brooklyn after the first inning. The Giants had overcome bad breaks to win the Series.

The Giant fans raced onto the field and mobbed their heroes, not realizing that the Giants' consecutive Series wins would be ended by the advent of the new Players League. They saluted the feats of all of the Giants and shouted especially loud and long for Ward, who had sparked the club all season and topped off the year by leading the Giants in the Series with 10 stolen bases, 15 hits, and a .417 batting average.

A week later Ward officially announced that the Brotherhood would begin operating the Players League in 1890. He also revealed he would be the player-manager of the new Brooklyn team. Ward spent much of the off-season traveling the country in leading the effort to stock the new league's teams. The National League responded with a number of lawsuits.

The Giants sought an injunction to prevent Ward from playing in the Players League. But, with Ward representing himself in court, Judge O'Brien of the State Supreme Court ruled that Ward's 1889 contract had not fixed the time and place contemplated by the reserve clause. The Judge ruled that Ward's contract was lacking in fairness and in equity, as it bound him to the Giants for life, while the Giants could terminate the club's obligation to Ward after 10 days' notice.

The Giants lost heavily in terms of personnel. In response, the National League took the unusual step of completing a deal whereby John T. Brush (he of the odious Classification Plan) sold his entire Indianapolis club roster to the Giants. The Giants of 1890 comprised players from the defunct Indianapolis club, plus Mickey Welch and Mike Tiernan, who elected to remain with the Giants. Typical of many National League players who had moved to the Players League team in their city, all of the other 1889 Giants players had moved to the New York club of the new league. Buck Ewing became the club's player-manager.

Ward took over the Brooklyn entrant in the Players League. With the Brooklyn Bridegrooms moved into the National League to replace Indianapolis, both the National League and the Players League opened their seasons on April 19, 1890. Ward's club was a pleasant surprise to the writers and fans. The team started well, ran into a slump, but recovered to finish second, 6½ games behind the Bridegrooms. Ward's playing and managing were highly praised. The 30-year-old player-manager took advantage of the hopped-up baseball used in the new league, hitting .335 and scoring 134 runs, the highest total of his career. Some observers felt that Ward, despite his pending divorce from Helen Dauvray, was an even more effective field general than he had been in 1888–89. Certainly he had maneuvered his club into a much better season than Jim Mutrie's badly depleted Giants had experienced.

Despite its fine performance, Brooklyn's Brotherhood team lost money, competing with four other teams in New York City and Brooklyn. Losses faced by Players League club owners forced them to consider merging some Players League clubs with National League clubs. Brotherhood League players became disenchanted when they learned that Players League financial backers were seeking deals without consulting them. Ward made an impassioned plea for player participation in National, American Association, and Players Leagues affairs. But he was opposed successfully by the National League. Al Spalding had succeeded in splitting the Players League players from the league's owners. The Players League club owners could see the handwriting on the wall, and the owners made individual deals. The Players League was dead.

Mark Alvarez wrote in SABR's 1996 publication, *Baseball's First Stars*:

> Although it put a better product on the field and outdrew the
> NL (National League), the PL (Players League) failed. For more
> than three quarters of a century, the baseball establishment
> pointed to its collapse as proof that players couldn't run the
> business of baseball, that the owners could, and that the reserve
> clause was necessary to maintain order in the game.... But it
> was a poor analysis of what really happened. The PL under
> Ward's guidance out-organized, out-hustled and out-fought
> the NL right down the line.... The difference, in the crunch,
> was the inability of any of the PL's financial backers to match
> the foresight and acumen of Al Spalding, who led the fight for
> the NL.... Ward was a great organizer and an inspirational
> leader, but he didn't have the financial clout to stiffen the
> resolve of his backers by example, as Spalding had been doing
> for NL owners all year. When push finally came to shove, the
> PL had no businessman with the guts, the will, and the simple
> business acumen to match Spalding, who ran the most spec-
> tacular bluff in the history of the game.... No one on the scene
> in the late 1880s could have organized and led the Brotherhood
> War but Ward. No one on the scene in 1890 could have won it
> for the NL but Spalding.

In retrospect, baseball historian David Q. Voigt examined why the high-powered Ward had wanted to lead the Brotherhood revolt of lesser men than himself. Ward was well paid, although he might have worried about the Classification Plan's restrictions on salaries. But it also was true that Ward was a good lawyer, a personal friend of Al Spalding's, and the recipient of repeated offers of an important job with the Giants. So Voigt concluded that the high-principled Ward had a deep, altruistic sense of mission for his fellow players, who in turn respected and trusted him, and that was what drove Ward.

Ward remained in Brooklyn for the 1891 season as player-manager of the Bridegrooms. He had a reputation as an innovator and was credited for instituting the practice of holding morning workouts for young prospects. The Bridegrooms played their games in Eastern Park, the 12,000-seat former Players League park. The field was located near a complex of street cars and suburban railroad lines, which forced the fans to dodge trolleys on their way into the park. This led in time to the nickname "Trolley Dodgers," which was shortened to the name "Dodgers." Ward's club included most of the players who had played on the Brooklyn club which had won the National League pennant. But the reconstituted 1891 National League teams were much stronger, and the Bridegrooms finished sixth in the eight-club race.

In 1892 the National League expanded to 12 teams with a 154-game schedule, with the winner of the first half playing the winner of the second for the pennant. The Dodgers were an improved club, finishing with the third best season-long winning percentage, but Ward's men did not come close to winning either half of the season. Ward, who had moved to second base, led the National League with 88 stolen bases. In *The Hall of Fame Giants* yearbook, published in 1986 by Woodford Publishing, it was reported: "Ward was ... a renowned gambler, especially known for betting on his own teams. In 1892 he won twenty percent of the Giants stock from a director of the club, putting himself in an unusual conflict of interest. The league conveniently ignored the problem until it went away when Ward eventually sold his stock."

Ward resigned after the season and returned to the Giants as their playing manager for 1893. It also was reported in Woodford Publishing's 1986 yearbook that Ward's return to the Giants came only after Brooklyn managed one of baseball's oddest trades by accepting the cash-poor Giants' offer of a percentage of New York's gate in exchange for Ward's contract. Ward's club finished a disappointing fifth in the 12-team league. The Giants received solid years from third baseman George Davis, fastballing righthander Amos Rusie (33–21), Roger Connor, and second baseman–manager Ward, who hit .328. The Giants "borrowed" King Kelly from Boston, but he and Ward clashed and Kelly was released after playing in only 20 games.

Ward's last year as a player or manager in 1894 was a success, his club finishing in second place behind the John McGraw–led Orioles. Ward's club started slowly, but by mid-season he figured out what to do—pitch alternately his two Indiana-born righthanders, Amos Rusie and Jouett Meekin. Between them they won 69 of the Giants' 88 victories. This was the year of the Temple Cup. William Chase Temple, a wealthy former president of the Pittsburgh Pirates conceived the idea of having the teams finishing first and second play each other in a seven-game post-season series, with the winning players to receive two-thirds of the gate receipts. But he had not envisioned an idea dreamed up by Ward after the Oriole's John McGraw protested that it was unfair for his first place team to have to take a one-third share of the gate receipts in the event that it lost the Series.

Ward suggested to McGraw that the players of both teams split their shares of the Series receipts evenly, regardless of which team won. A furious Temple threatened to withdraw the ceremonial Temple Cup if this scheme were to be carried out by the players. The players decided to play under Temple's original scheme. But, behind the scenes, several of the players made private deals to split their checks with their opposite numbers on the opposing team.

The Giants won the first game in Baltimore 4–1 behind Rusie's overpowering pitching. Some 200 policemen were on hand the next day to protect the umpires and the players from the crowd and the abusive Orioles. The Giants took the second game 9–6. After that, with the games moving to New York, the Giants polished off the Orioles behind Rusie and Meekin. The Polo Grounders had swept the rugged Orioles in four straight. Second baseman–manager Ward hit .294 in his last appearance in a major league game.

Much-disliked Andrew Freedman purchased controlling interest in the Giants after the season. One of his first acts was to fire Ward, apparently because Ward was too powerful a baseball personality to be controlled. Only 34, Ward was in demand by other major league clubs, but he had no interest in further involvement in baseball politics. But he did take one last parting shot at the reserve clause as it related to him a year and a half after he left the Giants. He filed an objection to being retained on the Giants' reserve list, and the National League upheld his appeal, making him a free agent.

Ward established a full-time, prosperous law practice, but he stayed in close touch with the game. He represented many players with considerable effectiveness in their grievances against baseball management. Ward returned to baseball twice after leaving the Giants. He barely missed election to the presidency of the National League in 1909. Then he served as president of the Boston Braves in 1911–12. And in 1914, still fighting the battle against the powerful, established major league teams, Ward became business manager of the Brooklyn Tip Tops of the Federal League.

In addition to his monumental efforts off the field, Ward was a major player-manager. He served in this dual capacity, both as a pitcher and then as a non-pitcher, in 854 games, a number exceeded only by seven player-managers. These numbers do not include the 1885–1887 period when he was the Giants' de facto playing manager. His managerial record of 412–320 (.563) included no pennants, but it did include three second place finishes in the seven years in which he managed. Ward had a 164–102 pitching record, with a 2.10 career ERA, and he accumulated 2104 hits for a lifetime batting average of .275. He was elected to the Hall of Fame, but his plaque makes no mention of his powerful efforts to better conditions for his fellow players. Ward died at age 65 in Augusta, Georgia.

BUCK EWING

William Buckingham "Buck" Ewing, one of the great catchers, also was a player-manager in the 1890s. Ewing was born in Hoaglands, Ohio, on October 17, 1859. When he was two, his family moved to Cincinnati. The first organized team he played with was the local East End Pendletons. The solidly-built youngster gravitated to catching, with his strong throwing arm, quick reflexes, steadiness, and his natural feel for the game. Then, at 19, he joined the Mohawk Browns, a strong local semipro team, where he was primarily a catcher. Meanwhile, he worked as a wagon driver for a local distillery, driving a team of horses ten hours a day, every day except Sunday.

In 1880, when Ewing was 21, he signed his first professional contract with Rochester of the National Association, and he finished the season with Troy of the National League. By 1881 he was Troy's regular catcher, receiving the deliveries of Mickey Welch and Tim Keefe. In his third year at Troy the versatile young man played more games at third base than he did behind the plate. The newly-formed Giants called him up in 1883, and the righthand-hitting Ewing broke in with a bang, hitting .303 with a league-leading 10 home runs. At the time that was the most home runs a player had hit in any major league season. Ewing continued to establish himself as the best National League catcher over the 1883–1889 period. He hit over .300 in six of those seven years.

He was so highly regarded that when Monte Ward resigned as team captain just prior to the 1888 season, 29-year-old Buck Ewing was chosen to succeed him. Ewing was the Giants' playing manager in the Giants' first pennant-winning season. He was a heavy contributor to the Giants' success that year, hitting .306, filling in competently for Ward at shortstop when Monte was sidelined, and stealing a career-high 53 bases. Although Ewing had just average speed, he was an excellent base stealer. The stocky (5 foot 10, 188 pound) catcher was so adept at taking extra bases that he was the Giants' leadoff man during the 1888 season. Ewing joined Ward in leading the Giants to a repeat pennant win the following season.

Ewing was the player-manager for the New York entry in the 1890 Players League season. His club led the Players League in hitting, with a solid offense led by Roger Connor and player-manager Ewing, who hit .338. But the pitching was only fair and the club finished in third place, 2½ games behind Monte Ward's Brooklyn team. During the season the National League owners continued their attempts to win back the players who had jumped to the Players League. One effort apparently centered on Ewing. A National League official was rumored to have drafted a statement for Ewing's signature which would declare that Ewing planned to rejoin the Giants in 1891 because he did not think the Players League would survive. As baseball historian Harold Seymour described the matter in his *Baseball— The Early Years*:

> Ewing was the player chosen not only because he was a star but because he had expressed sympathy for his employer, John B. Day, on the eve of the players' revolt.... The scheme fell through because Ewing reneged when other players refused to join him. Ewing denied everything when confronted, claiming that he was merely spying for the Brotherhood.... However, the players were unconvinced and for some time they refused to have anything to do with him.

Ewing rejoined the Giants in 1891, playing only a few games, but he came back in 1892 to hit .310 while playing most of the season at first base and catching only on a part-time basis. The Giants traded Ewing to Cleveland where he had an excellent 1893 season as a full-time outfielder, hitting .344 with 122 RBI. After a poor 1894 season he moved to Cincinnati as the Reds' player-manager.

Ewing, who at 35 had slowed up, moved from the outfield to first base. He hit a respectable .318, but he was unable to pull his mediocre team above eighth place in the 12-club league. Ewing ended his playing career as his club produced a better season in 1986, finishing in third place without the benefit of an outstanding year from any of his players, and with a pitching staff that yielded more runs than any other in the league. Ewing managed the Reds from the bench to three straight first division finishes before returning to manage the Giants in 1900. But his second stay with the Giants was short and not particularly sweet. Andrew Freedman did not get along with any of his managers, and he fired Ewing in mid-season, with the team languishing in last place and racked by internal dissension.

Long before Ernie Lombardi, Johnny Bench, or Ivan "Pudge" Rodriguez mastered the art of throwing to bases while remaining in a crouch behind the plate, Ewing was intimidating would-be base runners with his quick snap throws from that position. He also was one of the pioneers in the development of catching equipment and the first catcher to use a large "pillow" glove, despite being called a sissy by other catchers of the time, to whom gnarled, misshapen fingers were a mark of honor. These accusations ended with the realization that the innovation had made Ewing the surest receiver in baseball.

Ewing, a pleasant, congenial man, did much to include strategic thinking and psychology in going about his catching and managing duties. Playing in an era when players routinely snarled at umpires and generally treated them with disrespect, Ewing was one of the first catchers to treat home plate umpires respectfully, no matter how off the mark their calls appeared to be. Ewing explained to his critics that he wasn't being soft or charitable, but only predisposing umpires to make future close calls in his favor.

Ewing hit over .300 in 11 of his 18 seasons, making for a career .303 average. He was basically a catcher, although he played every other field position when necessary. The sturdy Ohio native was considered the best catcher to play the game through the 1920s, before talented receivers like Gabby Hartnett, Mickey Cochrane, and Bill Dickey came along. The 50th anniversary yearbook of the Hall of Fame museum described Ewing as "perhaps the finest player of the 19th century and a great field leader."

Ewing had a winning percentage of .553 as a manager, surprisingly good considering that his teams finished no higher than third place in any of his seven managerial seasons. He was well liked by his players. One of them told a writer that when Ewing wanted to rebuke a player, he "voiced his remarks good-naturedly and never left a sting behind." Most refreshing for a manager in the 1890s, he was unlike Charles Comiskey, Bob Ferguson, or Patsy Tebeau in that he was not an umpire-baiter or a team leader who thrived on controversy. Ewing retired from the game after leaving the Giants. He died of diabetes and paralysis at 47 and was elected to the Hall of Fame in 1939.

CONNIE MACK

Any discussion of baseball managers and player-managers must of necessity mention Connie Mack. Actually, Mack's career as a playing manager is barely worth mentioning. He was a catcher-manager with Pittsburgh from 1894 through 1896, although he was the regular catcher only in 1894 when he was appointed manager for the last 23 games of the season. Mack has always been thought of as a dignified, calm manager, waving his players into position with his scoreboard without ever losing his cool. But in his brief stint as Pittsburgh's catcher-manager the younger Mack showed a different side. SABR's 1996 publication, *Baseball's First Stars*, described a situation involving player-manager Mack:

> As a playing manager in 1895, Mack had his team in first place as late as August 9.... But then the Pirates slid to seventh in the

12-team league. On September 6, in New York, a few close calls
in the fifth inning that went against his team teed Mack off,
and he blew up at his former Washington batterymate, umpire
Hank O'Day. After a lengthy harangue by Mack, O'Day fined
him $100 and ordered him off the field for "using insulting and
abusive language." Mack refused to leave. When one policeman
came out to get him, Mack shook him off and stood his ground
until several bluecoats arrived to usher him out.

5

Comiskey, Tebeau, and Davis

CHARLES COMISKEY

Charles Albert Comiskey was born in Chicago on August 15, 1859, the son of an Irish immigrant. The elder Comiskey, a local alderman, wanted his son to become a plumber, but the ambitious 17-year-old youngster rebelled and instead chose to play semipro baseball in the Chicago suburbs. In 1878 he signed on with the Dubuque Rabbits of the Northwest League and played there for four seasons, starting as a pitcher and trying other positions before settling in at first base.

"Commy," as Comiskey was called, impressed the fans and players in Dubuque with his deft fielding, daring base running, and his generally aggressive, heads-up play. When the Dubuque franchise folded after the 1881 season, the St. Louis Browns of the American Association picked him up, and by mid-season he had become their regular first baseman. Comiskey established himself immediately as a dependable fielder, playing his first 11 games with the Browns without an error, impressive in an era before players used gloves. Commy, who hit a mere .243 that year, although he was a decent clutch hitter, was even more impressive as a base runner, shaking up the opposition with his aggressive, almost reckless, style. He was one of the first players to use the headfirst slide.

The Browns were owned by Chris Von der Ahe, a heavy-set, boastful, German-born saloon owner who made up in bombast and showmanship what he lacked in baseball knowledge. Although his heavy accent and heavy-handed style made him the butt of many jokes, he was one of the founders of the American Association. But his ignorance of the game was appalling, as was his craving for recognition. Both characteristics were illustrated when he told a group of ballpark visitors that he had "the

48

'piggest baseball diamond in da' world." Comiskey, by that time the club's player-manager, hastily pulled him aside and whispered, "Chris, all baseball diamonds are the same size." Never one to admit a mistake, Von der Ahe amended his story with the assured boast, "Vell, ve haf da' 'piggest infield."

Von der Ahe's boorish manner made him a difficult employer. Ted Sullivan, the man who brought 18-year-old Charlie Comiskey to Dubuque, was the Browns' manager in 1883. He appointed Comiskey captain in Commy's second season with the Browns. Sullivan, exasperated with Von der Ahe's constant interference, quit the second place club after 79 games, and first baseman Comiskey took over as manager for the rest of the season. Under his managership, the club finished the season in second place as he hit a respectable .294. The scenario was much the same in 1884, as Von der Ahe hired an unknown, Jimmy Williams, to manage the Browns. Williams lasted six more games into the season than had Sullivan, then threw in the towel, refusing to stand for any more of Von der Ahe's meddling. So again first baseman Comiskey took over the club's field direction for the rest of the season, as the Browns finished the season eight games out of the running.

Von der Ahe grandly proclaimed that in 1885 he himself would manage the Browns and that Commy would remain the team captain. In fact, given the owner's lack of baseball knowledge, this was tantamount to naming the 25-year-old Comiskey field manager. Comiskey's first move was to rid the team of several heavy drinkers and troublemakers. After that he built a team that would play his kind of baseball, with heavy emphasis on an improved defense and more aggressive base running. Holdover regulars from the 1884 club were Comiskey himself, shortstop Billy Gleason, and third baseman Arlie Latham. Others were rightfielder Hugh Nichol, leftfielder Yank Robinson, and righthanders Dave Foutz and Bob Caruthers. The important new players were centerfielder Curt Welch and catcher Albert "Doc" Bushong.

Comiskey was one of the game's early defensive strategists. Many baseball historians credit Comiskey with being the initial first baseman to play off the bag. However, the evidence is that Comiskey was not the first to play off the bag but the first to insist that the first baseman play deeper than usual to permit the second baseman to play deeper and closer to second base. He also insisted that his pitchers cover first base when the first baseman ranged far to his right to field a ground ball. On balls hit to the outfield, Comiskey taught his pitchers to back up the appropriate base. The great second baseman and baseball student Johnny Evers commented years later, "Comiskey won pennants in St. Louis by his inventiveness and

Charles Comiskey was a player-manager in 1312 games, a total exceeded only by Cap Anson and Fred Clarke. An aggressive first baseman and sometimes abusive field leader, he hit .264 but had a .608 winning percentage as a manager. He became owner of the Chicago American League club in the new American League in 1901.

it is a remarkable thing that every team he ever handled had great fielding pitchers."

The 1885 team played in a league that had reduced the number of franchises from 12 in 1884 to eight. Commy's team was a revelation, winning the pennant by 16 games in a 112-game season. The keys to the Browns' runaway triumph were excellent defense, aggressive base running required by the player-manager, and superb pitching. The fiery Comiskey was limited to playing in only 83 games, as he suffered a broken collarbone on August 8. But he recovered in time to hit .292 in the World Series against Cap Anson's Chicago club.

The Series, which included games in Pittsburgh and Cincinnati, as well as Chicago and St. Louis, ended in a controversial three-all tie because of a wild scene in the second game. A Chicago bouncer down the first base line, which appeared to be foul until it suddenly twisted into fair territory, was muffed by first baseman Comiskey. This allowed the go-ahead Chicago run to score. Comiskey almost convinced the umpire that the ball should be ruled foul, but he lost the argument when Cap Anson insisted on seeing the rule book. With his bluff called, Commy pulled his team off the field and the game was forfeited to Chicago. The Series ended with each team having won three games, plus a first game tie, although the bitter Comiskey insisted that his team had rightfully won the Series.

Comiskey's 1885 team and those that followed reflected their player-manager's rough-tough style. He pioneered the questionable strategy of inciting the home team fans as a regular practice. St. Louis fans, egged on by Comiskey and his players, were so abusive that they actually successfully intimidated opposing teams. Umpire Ben Young called Comiskey "a most aggravating player," especially when he pretended to converse with a player within an umpire's earshot. His "private conversations" actually were a cover for a torrent of insults intended for a nearby umpire's ears.

The Browns overpowered the American Association again in 1886, winning the pennant by 12 games. In a game in May against Cincinnati, the 180-pound Comiskey prevented a double play by running full speed into the Reds' second baseman covering the base, leading the Browns to a 2–1 win. The Cincinnati fans were furious when the umpire allowed the play to stand. The Browns, led by their aggressive player-manager, were making "breaking up the double play" an accepted part of the game. The league also introduced the first lined coaches' boxes specifically designed to prevent third base coach Comiskey from chasing umpires around the field. The boxes did limit Comiskey's movements, but they did little to prevent his constant stream of abuse directed at the umpires. Comiskey was fined continually for this abuse, but he responded with simple direct-ness—he simply refused to pay them. He was threatened with expulsion from the league in July 1886, but Von der Ahe paid the fines himself.

Browns third baseman Arlie Latham was Comiskey's accomplice in crime. Nicknamed "The Freshest Man on Earth," Latham, a handsome man with a luxuriant mustache, took over the third base coaches' box when Comiskey was otherwise occupied. An excellent fielder and leadoff man, he was a crowd favorite with his comedic actions. But he was a merciless heckler who infuriated opposing players with his cutting remarks. His presence was a mixed blessing to Comiskey because he often created unrest by antagonizing fellow team members. His personal conduct off the field in that Victorian age also gave Comiskey some heartburn— Latham almost drove his first wife to the point of killing herself, and his second wife filed for divorce, citing "perversion, assault, desertion, and infidelity."

The Browns won the 1886 Series from Anson's White Stockings four games to two. Player-manager Comiskey contributed, with a respectable .292 average and seven hits. Under the winner-take-all agreement in effect for the Series, the Browns received $13,000, of which Von der Ahe kept $6900, with each player receiving $580. At the time, Comiskey earned $4000, the highest salary in the American Association.

For the third straight year, the Browns won the pennant easily in 1887 after a sluggish start early in the season. This was essentially the same team that had overpowered the league in the two previous seasons, but with one exception. The canny Comiskey picked up righthander Charles "Silver" King from the Kansas City club, where he had been ineffective, and King won 32 games. It was an explosive offensive year, as hitters were favored by a rule change allowing them four strikes and counting a walk as a hit. As a result, Browns outfielder Tip O'Neill led the league with a lofty .435 batting average. And Comiskey had his best offensive year, hitting .335 with 117 stolen bases.

The Browns lost the marathon 15-game series to the Detroit Wolverines 10 games to five, a series played in eight different cities. The fickle Von der Ahe claimed that his players had not even tried to win and refused to share the Browns' $12,500 gate receipts with them. He had complained about the players' high salary demands even before the season started and, to the complete disgust of Comiskey, his first post-season move was to sell two star pitchers, Bob Caruthers and Dave Foutz, to Brooklyn. Catcher Doc Bushong also was sent to Brooklyn, and outfielder Curt Welch was sold to Philadelphia.

The ever-resourceful Comiskey struggled to find competent replacements. Battling against the potent Brooklyn club, Commy's rejuvenated team fought its way into first place in August. The crucial hit for the Browns was supplied in early August by Comiskey, a three-run homer to tie a game against second-place Brooklyn. The Browns won in extra innings, and went on to win the pennant by 6½ games. The Browns battled the powerful Giants through several games in a 10-game post-season series. But they were unable to solve the pitching of righthander Tim Keefe and the Giants won, six games to four, with Keefe winning four games for the Giants. Comiskey led his team with 11 hits, but his club was clearly outclassed. The final two games meant nothing to the series' outcome, a fact recognized by all fans except for the 711 rooters who attended the ninth game and the 412 diehards who went to the last game.

The Browns' streak ended in 1889 in a season during which Comiskey constantly placated his players, who feuded all year with the irascible Von der Ahe. Over his managerial years, Commy had learned how to finesse some of Von der Ahe's capricious orders. Typically, when Von der Ahe insisted on fining a player, often for trivial offenses, the player-manager avoided potentially serious morale problems by offsetting such fines with bonuses. But in 1889 the players' dislike of the owner could not be papered over by the smooth-talking Comiskey.

The Browns lost the 1889 pennant to the Brooklyn Bridegrooms by two games. The American Association's Board of Directors had to make several important decisions before the winner was determined. On September 7, for example, the most controversial game in the Association's history was played in Brooklyn between the Browns and the Bridegrooms.

The Browns led 4–2 in the ninth inning, and Comiskey and his players protested loudly that it was too dark to continue the game. Finally, they left the field in protest before the game had been completed, and the game was ruled a forfeit. Several Browns players were hit with bottles as they left the field. Fearing for his players' safety, Comiskey did not let his team play the following day, and the game was declared a forfeit. Some time later the league heads met in an emergency meeting and reversed the forfeit of the 4–2 game, awarding it to the Browns.

The Players League came into being in 1890 and Comiskey left the Browns to take over as player-manager of the Chicago team in the new league. His team was in the running through the first half of the season but fell back after Commy was injured, finishing in fourth place. With the Players League's disbandment after the 1890 season, Comiskey returned as playing manager of the Browns. His club finished the season in second place but well behind the Boston club. After the 1891 season, Comiskey left the Browns, exhausted by his endless efforts to act as a buffer between the blustery Von der Ahe and his unhappy players.

Commy moved to the National League with the Cincinnati Reds as their player-manager for the next three seasons. But, in his new surroundings, he had to contend with something even worse than the usual disciplinary problems—inept players. Comiskey's teams finished in the second division in each of the three years. This marked the end of his major league playing and managing career, in which he played and managed in a total of 1312 games, a total exceeded only by Cap Anson and Fred Clarke. He had a mediocre .264 career batting average but a fine managerial record of .608, with 839 wins and 542 losses. This remains the third best record in major league history.

While Commy was in Cincinnati he became friendly with *Cincinnati Commercial-Gazette* sportswriter Ban Johnson. A man of lofty ambition and oversized ego, Johnson had become head of the Western League. As part of his reorganization, he invited Comiskey to purchase the Sioux City, Iowa, club in that league. Commy bought the club, moved it to St. Paul, and installed himself as manager. He remained there until 1900 when Johnson renamed his league the American League and moved its franchises into major cities. Comiskey took his team to the South Side of Chicago and named it "White Stockings."

The American League gained recognition as the "other major league" the following year.

Comiskey, utilizing all of his experience as a team builder, put together a team of major league castoffs and promising youngsters. Then he hired pitcher Clark Griffith to manage his team in 1901, and Griffith pitched and managed the White Sox to the pennant in their first year. Over its first 10 years, Comiskey's club became a box office success and a solid team. Comiskey admitted netting more than $700,000 during that period, and by 1912 his annual profits were around $150,000. (Harold Seymour, in his classic *Baseball—The Golden Age*, wrote that Comiskey also had a "financial interest" in the Cleveland club, an odoriferous, but prevalent, practice involving interlocking ownership of more than one team during the formative years of the American League.) During their first decade, the White Sox won two pennants and a World Championship, and only in 1903 did they finish out of the first division. In 1910 Comiskey opened Comiskey Park, a fire-resistant park built on the site occupied by the Players League team he had managed in 1890.

Comiskey's clubs performed decently over the 1911–1920 period, with two pennant wins, a World Championship in 1917, and five first division finishes. That is, they performed decently if the 1919 "Black Sox" were excepted. In the first four years of the decade Comiskey decided that he had to spend money on real talent if his club was to compete successfully. In 1912 he bought righthander Ed Cicotte from the Red Sox, and he picked up several other quality players—shortstop Buck Weaver, catcher Ray Schalk, lefthander Claude "Lefty" Williams, righthander Red Faber, outfielders "Shoeless Joe" Jackson and Happy Felsch—and, most important, the Philadelphia Athletics' great second baseman, Eddie Collins. The dominating and experienced Comiskey was a difficult owner to work for, as previous White Sox managers had found out. But in 1915 Clarence "Pants" Rowland, an undistinguished baseball man, took over as manager. He gave Captain Eddie Collins considerable latitude in handling the club on the field, and this proved a good move, as the Sox finished third in 1915 and a strong second (only two games out) in 1916. The 1917 club, under Rowland's gentle handling and the fiery Collins' continued needling, won the pennant with relative ease.

The White Sox went on to defeat John McGraw's Giants in the World Series, four games to two. After a poor 1918 season Comiskey's club came back to win the 1919 pennant. They were heavily favored to beat the Reds in the Series. But the Reds won five games to three, and the "Black Sox" story began. The story has been the subject of many books and articles, but two intriguing questions remain—first, what part did Comiskey's salary policies play in triggering the event and, second, what actions did he take after the reality of the fix became known to him?

The White Sox never recovered from the Black Sox scandal during the remaining years of Comiskey's reign. During the 1921–31 period he spent large sums on unproven minor leaguers who did not deliver. He apparently lost his touch, and possibly his desire to win, during that period, as his club finished in the second division every year. Elected to the Hall of Fame in 1939, Comiskey was a bitter, sick man for much of his last five years before he died at age 62 at his country home in Wisconsin.

PATSY TEBEAU

Oliver Wendell "Patsy" Tebeau was born in St. Louis on December 5, 1864. He began his professional career as a second baseman with St. Joseph, Missouri, in the Western League. He played third base in 20 games with the Chicago White Stockings in 1887 before being sent to the minors. He was signed by the Cleveland Spiders of the National League in 1889, and was the player-manager of the Cleveland club in the Players League the following season. Tebeau rejoined the Spiders in 1891 and became the club's infielder-manager through the 1898 season. He moved to the St. Louis Cardinals as their first baseman–manager in 1899.

Although not a great player, Tebeau batted at least .300 in four seasons, with a lifetime .280 average. But he is remembered mostly as one of the most aggressive, "dirty" field leaders of his time. He was an outspoken advocate of the rough-and-ready baseball played in the 1890s. In the best Charles Comiskey tradition, Tebeau continually harassed umpires and opponents, and he admitted to a writer, "My instructions to my players are to win games and I want them to be aggressive. A milk and water, goody-goody player can't wear a Cleveland uniform."

As shown in Appendix Table 1, only five other men player-managed in more games than Tebeau. Over his managing career, his teams had a respectable .555 winning percentage, reflecting his aggressive temperament, as they excelled in the "grind-out-the-runs" style of the 1890s. His teams regularly led the National League in drawing walks, stealing bases, and employing the hit-and-run play.

The Cleveland club owners bought the St. Louis Cardinals franchise in 1899, and Tebeau, in his last season as a player-manager, took over as field leader of the Cardinals. After a successful season he resigned angrily in mid-season of 1900, claiming that the owners planned to replace him with John McGraw. McGraw had left the Orioles that season to become the Cardinals' third baseman. Actually, the Cardinals replaced Tebeau with one Louie Heilbroner, rather than McGraw. Tebeau left baseball after leaving the Cardinals, and eventually opened a saloon in St. Louis. The fiery Tebeau, apparently no easier to live with than to play against, separated from his wife and later shot himself to death in his saloon at age 54.

George Davis

George Stacey Davis was born in Cohoes, New York, on August 23, 1870. He began his career at 19 with an independent team in Albany before joining the Cleveland Spiders under manager Patsy Tebeau in 1890. The youngster, who played both the infield and outfield, entered the major leagues at 20, his early entrance facilitated by the large exodus of players who deserted the National League for the Players League. In that season the speedy young man, who had an unusually strong arm, led all major league outfielders in assists. In 1893 Davis was traded to the New York Giants for Buck Ewing. Giants manager Monte Ward installed Davis at third base, and he remained there until 1897 when he moved to shortstop, the position for which he was best suited, for the rest of his career.

The switch-hitting New York State native batted well over .300 for the next nine seasons, including a sensational season in 1893 when he led the league with 27 triples, still the all-time record for switch-hitters. Interestingly, it was an unusual feat considering that Davis during that season had five fewer doubles than triples, a reflection of his great speed. Over his 20-year playing career Davis hit .295 with 2660 hits, and an impressive 1437 RBI and 616 steals.

Monte Ward left the Giants to make use of his law degree, and the 25-year-old Davis became the Giants' player-manager. Very bright and a good student of the game, Davis appeared to have all the tools to be a successful manager. But after the Giants played under .500 ball over the first quarter of the season, the mercurial Andrew Freedman removed him as manager, replacing him with "Dirty Jack" Doyle. Despite his problems as the Giants' embattled skipper, and hampered by a shoulder injury, Davis hit .340 with 50 extra base hits.

Buck Ewing, who had managed the Cincinnati Reds for four reasonably successful seasons, returned to the Giants as their new manager in 1900. At first he appeared to have a good relationship with Davis and, citing Davis' easy manner in dealing with umpires, he appointed Davis team captain. But the Giants started off the season poorly as the players broke into two feuding factions, a holdover group and players Ewing brought with him from the Reds. Ewing accused Davis of leading the holdover group and attempting to undermine him. He also accused Davis of faking a knee injury so that he could remain in New York while the struggling Giants went on the road. A few days later Ewing resigned under pressure as the Giants staggered badly in mid-season.

Davis replaced Ewing and suspiciously returned to the lineup immediately, and the club's performance improved. The shortstop-manager missed 30 games but still played well, hitting .319 and becoming the most effective shortstop in the league. The Giants finished last in 1900, but the season is remembered best because it was the year of righthander Christy Mathewson's debut with the club. The future pitching great joined the Giants as a nervous 19-year-old during a morning practice, and Davis wasted no time in testing what the Giants had received for the $2,000 they had paid the Norfolk club.

Davis himself stepped up to the plate and told the youngster to throw everything he had. The player-manager nodded approvingly as Matty showed his fast ball. But the manager drove Mathewson's slow sidearm curve ball deep into the outfield, and he shook his head in disapproval. Davis shouted out to the mound, "Do you have a drop?" [the term used at the time for an overhand curve]. Mathewson shook his head affirmatively and threw the pitch. Davis swung and missed.

"Pretty good, kid," Davis called out. "Got anything else?" Still nervous, Mathewson walked towards the plate and answered, "I've got a freak ball, sir, but I'm still working on it." The youngster walked back to the mound and prepared to pitch. He wound up, snapped his pitching wrist in the opposite way as he would a standard curve ball and threw the ball down and inside to the righthand-hitting manager. Davis swung and missed. "Throw that one again," he shouted out. Matty delivered and the lunging Davis missed the reverse curve ball again. He walked out to the mound and asked, "What the hell do you call that one?" The young right hander responded, "I don't have a name for it. It's hard to control but I'm getting better at it."

Davis sent up several of his lefthand hitters but none of them could hit the unusual pitch solidly. Davis told one of his veterans, "It's the craziest pitch I've seen. It kind of fades out of sight, the opposite of a regular curve." And that was the origin of the term "fadeaway," the pitch which was largely instrumental in Mathewson's subsequent success. Years later, lefthanders Carl Hubbell and Fernando Valenzuela were highly successful in throwing the same pitch, which had become known as the "screwball."

Davis returned as the Giants' player-manager in 1901, but he was dismissed after a disappointing 52–85, sixth-place season. Ignoring the reserve clause in his 1901 contract, Davis signed an apparently solid contract to play for the Chicago White Sox in 1902. The Giants did not contest the move, and Davis went on to have a decent season for Charles Comiskey's club.

Under the new management of John McGraw, who took over the Giants in mid-season of 1902, the Giants signed Davis to a contract for the 1903 and 1904 seasons. When Comiskey took legal action against the Giants' move, court injunctions prevented Davis from playing more than a few games for the Giants in 1903. Monte Ward was involved in much of the legal wrangling, as he had drawn up Davis' contract to play for the White Sox and then was in the awkward position of advising Davis that he could break that contract and return to the Giants. Eventually, in order to keep peace within the major league owner fraternity, the Giants relented and Davis returned to the White Sox for five more seasons before finishing his playing career.

William F. Lamb wrote in the 1998 SABR publication, *The National Pastime*:

> Davis's failures as a manager remain perplexing, for he was undeniably an astute baseball man.... There is evidence that Davis was not much of a disciplinarian. He seemed to have had trouble commanding the respect of strong-willed players. Dirty Jack Doyle ... publicly berated skipper Davis throughout the latter part of the 1900 season. Following that season, moreover, Davis was ousted as manager-captain of a Giants-laden squad headed for postseason play in Cuba in what appears to have been a players' revolt. And when Doyle found himself on the trading block that winter, he excoriated Davis as an incompetent, and claimed ... that virtually all the other Giants had little respect for Davis.

After his release by the White Sox in 1909, Davis managed in the minors and later coached college ball and scouted for the Yankees and the St. Louis Browns. He disappeared from public sight after 1918 and remained lost from view for nearly 50 years. In 1968 persistent research by the Hall of Fame determined that Davis had died in October 1940. Investigation of hospital records showed that he had died of paresis, the creeping paralysis and dementia that mark the terminal stage of syphilis. Davis' long overdue election to the Hall of Fame came in 1998.

About half of the teams in the 1890s had player-managers. But there was a rapid turnover in both player-managers and bench managers in the decade. Most of the managers were in their thirties, with some younger but very few over 40. The only managers older than 50 were Harry Wright, who managed until 1893 when he was 58, and a few men who filled in for part of a season. The turnover in managers reflected the fact that baseball in the 1890s retrogressed from the expanding markets and exciting races of the preceding years. As Bill James pointed out, "Baseball on the field became a crude, violent game dominated as much by intimidation as by skillful play, granting that strategies and 'scientific baseball' did continue to evolve through this phase.... The managers of the 1890s were, in the main, *not* professional managers. They were mature players, in their late thirties, who shepherded herds of ruffians from one hotel to the next."

6

Griffith and Nichols

As discussed in Chapter 1, the pitching position does not lend itself to the simultaneous role of managing. So it is no surprise that only four active starting pitchers also were managers at the same time they pitched. Clark Griffith was the most active in this role, pitching in 146 games while he managed. Monte Ward, before injuring his arm and becoming a great infielder, was a pitcher-manager in 117 games. In his relatively short playing career, Al Spalding pitched in 61 games as a manager. And Kid Nichols was a pitcher-manager in 36 games. (See Appendix, Table 2.)

CLARK GRIFFITH

Clark Calvin Griffith was born on November 20, 1869, in Clear Creek, Missouri, near the Kansas border. His father, Isaiah Griffith, was a commercial hunter and trapper. The family lived in a log cabin and struggled to make a living from Isaiah's meager earnings from hunting and trapping, and its struggles intensified after he was killed in a hunting accident. At the time, Clark, who was the youngest of five children, was only three. Before young Clark was ten he had become an accomplished trapper, catching raccoons, possums, and other animals and selling their skins. But he came down with malaria when he was 11, and he was in poor health for some time. By that time, his mother Sarah had moved her brood to Bloomington, Illinois.

Too small to play high school baseball, Griffith played sandlot baseball in nearby Bloomington where he gained recognition as a pitcher. He was fortunate enough to come under the wing of Bloomington resident Charles "Old Hoss" Radbourne, one of the greatest big league pitchers of that era. By the time Griffith was 16 he was playing semipro ball, and within two years he was signed by the local Bloomington club of the Interstate League (later to become better known as the Three-Eye League). His impressive 10 and 4 record earned him a promotion to Milwaukee of the Western Association, and he pitched well enough over the next two years to be picked up by Charlie Comiskey's St. Louis Browns for the 1891 season. He had a decent 14 and 9 season with the Browns and Boston, both teams in the American Association in its last year of operation.

The American Association folded after the 1891 season and Griffith found himself back in the minors with Tacoma of the Northern Pacific League. This league also folded before the season ended and Griffith signed with Oakland in the California League in 1893. He compiled a fine 30 and 17 record before having another team shot out from under him when the league quit operations. After a short stint in vaudeville in San Francisco's Barbary Coast district, the diminutive (5 foot 6, 156 pound) Griffith joined the Chicago Cubs, still managed by Cap Anson.

Griffith was an excellent pitcher for Chicago, winning more than 20 games in each of the next six seasons. By that time he had mastered every trick in the pitching trade. He exploited batters' hitting weaknesses, and he was one of the first pitchers to openly use the scuffed ball. He accomplished this by brazenly banging the ball against his spikes and claiming innocently that he was merely ridding his spikes of mud. Griffith also was accused of throwing an "emery" ball, so called because rubbing sandpaper or another abrasive against the ball caused it to move unpredictably. He also threw a primitive inshoot, later referred to as a screwball, a quick-pitch delivery, and a spitball. To further upset batters, the canny little righthander was one of the slowest-working pitchers of his era. He purposely delayed, stalled, and fooled hitters with pitches they least expected. Before he was 30, Griffith was referred to as "The Old Fox" because he outsmarted rather than overpowered hitters. David Pietrusza described a Griffith antic in SABR's *Baseball's First Stars*:

> One celebrated Griffith confrontation involved [good-hitting Washington outfielder] Kip Selbach, with runners on second and third, and Griffith's Cubs just one run ahead. Goading Selbach with such taunts as "You big stiff, you couldn't hit this one with a board," Griffith tossed balls deliberately outside the strike zone, but nonetheless got the count to three-and-two on the overanxious outfielder. Griffith then yelled, "Here, hit this you big bloke," and lobbed the ball slow as can be to the plate underhand. Selbach was so unnerved, he swung wildly before the ball reached the plate—so wildly he fell to his hands and knees.

In the late 1890s, with the Brotherhood League long gone, there were a series of hostile incidents between the players and the owners. As a result, by 1900 the players took a step towards unionization by forming The Protective Association of Professional Ball Players, and Griffith was elected vice president of the Association. The Association sent the owners a number of demands. Within a short time, the new American League agreed to some of the players' demands, and the National League had no option but to agree to them as well.

The ambitious Griffith looked around for advancement opportunities, and he found them in September 1900 when he joined Ban Johnson and Charles Comiskey in helping to convert the Western League into the second major league, the American League. Griffith, who was highly regarded by his fellow players, set about the task of stocking the new American League teams by convincing some National Leaguers that they would gain higher salaries and other benefits if they signed on with the new league. Griffith was highly successful, snaring 39 National League players to join him. Of the players he approached, only Pittsburgh Pirates star Honus Wagner decided not to join the American League.

Griffith was rewarded for his organizational efforts by being appointed pitcher-manager of Comiskey's new Chicago White Sox club. And pitch and manage he did as he led the White Sox to the pennant by a four-game margin in 1901. Stars of the club were second baseman Sam Mertes, rightfielder Fielder Jones, centerfielder William "Dummy" Hoy, and righthanders Jim "Nixey" Callahan and Roy Patterson. But the biggest Sox star was Griffith himself, who led the new league with a sparkling .774 percentage, based upon a 24–7 record, and tied Cy Young for the league lead with five shutouts.

Pitcher-manager Griffith's club started off well in 1902, leading the league at mid-season. But this was a different year. The club's hitting and pitching fell off, and even Griffith slipped to a 15–9 record. Ban Johnson had become convinced that the infant American League would never be secure until it had a prosperous club in New York City. Johnson anticipated that Giants owner Andrew Freedman, who had powerful connections within New York City's Tammany Hall, would do all that he could to keep the American League out of New York. But, fortunately, Tammany Hall had recently suffered a defeat at the polls by a reform slate. This had reduced Freedman's chances of stopping the movement of another team into the valued New York market. Accordingly, Johnson arranged to put a club in New York.

Johnson installed Griffith as the pitcher-manager for the brand-new Highlanders. For the second time in two years, Griffith concentrated his efforts on stocking a new team. He lured a number of National Leaguers by offering them higher salaries. Griffith skimmed off the cream of the Pittsburgh Pirates' pitching staff, picking up spitballing righthander Jack Chesbro and little lefthander Jesse Tannehill. Chesbro and Tannehill between them had won 48 games for the Pirates as they won the National League pennant in 1902 by 27½ games. Chesbro, in particular, was a spectacular pitcher in 1902, with a 28–6 record, eight shutouts, and a 12-game winning streak. The legendary Willie Keeler, of "Hit 'em Where They Ain't" fame, was obtained from Brooklyn. He was past his peak, but he was a proven winner and was only 31. Norman "Kid" Elberfeld, a scrappy little shortstop, came over from Detroit early in the season. And then there was pitcher-manager Griffith, well past his prime but still able to pitch effectively. Griffith's Highlanders did reasonably well for a team starting from scratch, but they were completely outclassed by the Boston Puritans who won the pennant by 14 ½ games. Chesbro pitched well, winning 21 games, and Tannehill won 15, but they missed the support they had with the Pirates. Griffith won 14 of 25 decisions, and Keeler played up to expectations.

Griffith was not easy on the umpires, even in the American League, which discouraged umpire-baiting much more than the rough-and-ready National League. Griffith

Clark Griffith was a small righthander who was called "The Old Fox" because he won games on guile and mastery of the pitching art. As a pitcher-manager he led the White Sox to a pennant win in the first American League season in 1901 and later gained greater fame as the owner of the Washington Senators.

had one encounter with umpire Tim Hurst that became the talk of the league. Hurst was a colorful and extremely tough man, as is frequently the case with men as small as the stocky 5 foot, 5 inch umpire. He refused to wear spikes, preferring to umpire wearing patent leather dress shoes. In the heat of an argument between Hurst and the Highlander pitcher-manager, Griffith intentionally stepped all over Hurst's shoes, puncturing them with his spikes. An inning later, as Hurst bent over to dust off the plate, he discovered what Griffith had done. Hurst called time and strolled casually over to the water bucket in the New York dugout and began drinking from a cup with his left hand. Griffith sat next to the bucket. Suddenly, Hurst drove his right hand fist squarely into Griffith's chin, knocking the little pitcher-manager out cold. With that done, Hurst walked slowly back to the plate and shouted, "Come on boys, let's play ball." Griffith's men, some of them trying futilely to hide their amusement, did all they could to revive their fallen leader before taking the field.

It was a different story in 1904, even though Griffith's club was unchanged except for Tannehill who moved to the Puritans. The Highlanders remained close to the Boston Pilgrims through midsummer, caught them in August, and gained and lost the lead several times until early October. The Highlanders captured a half-game lead on October 7 when Jack Chesbro won his 41st game, still a record. The Pilgrims came back to win the next two games to take the lead as the teams played a doubleheader on October 10, the final day of the season. With the score tied at two-all in the top of the ninth and a Puritan runner on third base, Chesbro threw a spitball that escaped his catcher, rookie Red Kleinow. The wild pitch permitted the Boston runner to score with what proved to be the pennant-winning run. In a world class example of family pride, more than 80 years later Chesbro's descendants mounted a futile legal attempt to have the fatal pitch retroactively ruled a passed ball.

It was a bitter loss for Griffith and Chesbro. The spitballer had one of the most overpowering years any pitcher had ever had. He had a league-leading 41 and 12 record, and he led all American League pitchers in games pitched, innings pitched, and in complete games (with an eye-opening 48 in 51 starts). Chunky righthander Jack Powell, who had been picked up from the St. Louis Browns, won 23 games, and Willie Keeler hit .343. It was an especially difficult year for Griffith, not only because of the tough loss but because his relations with the team's owners had deteriorated, and winning the pennant would have improved his position within the Highlanders organization.

Griffith could do little with the 1905 Highlanders, who finished in sixth place. Chesbro slipped to a 19 and 15 season, and Griffith, in his last year as an active pitcher-manager, won only nine games. Even more aggravating to Griffith, the New York press became more critical. Griffith further alienated the writers by ignoring them, to the detriment of his team's press coverage. The Highlanders came back in 1906 to finish in second place, three games behind the White Sox, dubbed "the hitless wonders."

Griffith left the Highlanders after a poor 1907 season and moved to the National League, managing the Cincinnati Reds for three undistinguished years. The hard-boiled Griffith, not as vicious a needler from the coaching box as some of his vituperative managing predecessors (like Comiskey and Tebeau), could be rough on young pitchers. In his *Pitching in a Pinch*, Christy Mathewson told of a time when Griffith's needling was counterproductive. Pitching for the first time against Griffith's club in 1911, young Grover Cleveland Alexander was being harassed by the sharp-tongued Griffith. In a tense situation with men on base, Griffith shouted out to the young pitcher from the coaching box, "Now here is where we get a look at the 'yellow.'" According to Mathewson's obviously sanitized version, Griffith shouted to Alexander that he was "going to make that big boob show such a yellow streak that you won't be able to see any white." Alexander dispatched the hitter on a strikeout. An approving Mathewson wrote, "Griffith had tried the wrong tactics."

Griffith was never happy with the lackluster teams he had in Cincinnati and he remained an American Leaguer at heart. So, after the 1911 season Griffith accepted an offer to return to the American League as the manager and part owner of the Washington Senators. Griffith went into heavy debt on the mortgage on his Montana ranch. But he obtained a 10 percent share in the Senators, making him the team's largest individual stockholder. When Griff took over, the Senators were considered the league's weakest franchise. The club had little established talent, except righthander Walter Johnson, whose future greatness was readily apparent, and Clyde Milan, a steady, fleet-footed centerfielder. Griffith put together a young team in his own image—a team with little power but with speed, motivation, and baseball smarts.

The 1912 Nationals started slowly and languished in the second division at the end of May. But, with the benefit of a magnificent 33-game victory season by Walter Johnson, Griffith's youngsters finished in second place. Smoky Joe Wood, the Red Sox' great righthander who matched Johnson win for win, spoke in awe of Johnson's pitching prowess. He told a writer after the season:

> If he'd had the club behind him that I had behind me, he never
> would have lost a game. That's the unfortunate part of Wal-

ter's pitching—he had a bad club behind him all the time....
He was the only pitcher I ever hit against that I didn't know
whether I swung under the ball or over the ball, I just missed
it ... and I don't know how.

Griffith's club finished 14 games behind Boston. But, most importantly, he had gained the all-out support of his players. His meal ticket,
Johnson, said of him: "One thing about Griff as a manager—the Washington ballplayer was always right. No matter what the argument, he stood
behind his players. In a row with the umpire, Griff was the first man in a
Washington uniform to come to his player's support."

In many ways, his first Washington club was the team in which
Griffith took the most pride. Throughout the rest of his long career he
referred to this team affectionately as "My Little Ballclub." The 1913 season was a mirror image of the previous season. Griff's club finished in
second place again, this time beaten out by 6½ games by Connie Mack's
Philadelphia Athletics, featuring his "$100,000 infield" comprised of first
baseman Stuffy McInnis, second baseman Eddie Collins, shortstop Jack
Barry, and third baseman Frank "Home Run" Baker. Johnson had one of
the most dominating pitching seasons ever. He had a 36–7 record and led
both leagues in wins, innings pitched, complete games, ERA, strikeouts,
and shutouts. Clyde Milan provided another bright spot, leading the league
with 75 steals, and rightfielder Danny Moeller was second with 62 steals.
Again Griffith gave Washington fans a hustling, aggressive team, but one
which was outclassed by a much more powerful club.

Griffith continued managing the Senators through the 1920 season,
but the story of each of those years was essentially the same—fabulous
pitching by Johnson, which was largely instrumental in lifting the Senators into third place finishes in 1914 and 1918, but an offense too weak to
be consistently competitive. Griffith's problem was that he simply did not
have the money to purchase outstanding hitters. Then, too, the Senators
played in National Park, later re-named Griffith Stadium, with large
dimensions that did not lend themselves to the hitting game.

Tiring of his fellow Senators owners' unwillingness to spend money,
Griffith worked out a buyout plan before the 1920 season. He and William
Richardson, a Philadelphia grain exporter, bought an 80 percent interest
in the Senators, a $145,000 investment for each of them. Griffith managed
the team to another dreary sixth place finish and then appointed George
McBride as his successor. After a fourth place finish, McBride was replaced
by Clyde Milan, then in his last season as a player. McBride could do no
better than a sixth place finish and he was supplanted by another player-
manager, third baseman Donie Bush, then finishing his playing career.

After another sixth place finish, Griffith selected his third consecutive playing manager just before spring training in 1924. He named 28-year-old second baseman Stanley "Bucky" Harris to run the club.

By this time Griffith had become one of the toughest team owners when it came to bargaining with his players. But he had changed in other ways. In his wonderful biography *Walter Johnson*, Henry W. Thomas wrote of Griffith after he relinquished the manager's role:

> The Old Fox had reached his final destiny as owner and pres-
> ident of the Washington Nationals. Shedding his uniform as
> owner and field boss after the 1920 season, Griffith embarked
> on the longest and most satisfying phase of his monumental
> 70-year career in baseball. A seemingly effortless transition saw
> him transformed from fiery, fighting manager into a soft-spo-
> ken, distinguished, white-haired gentleman and pillar of the
> community. Revered by several generations of ordinary Wash-
> ingtonians, Griffith was at the same time personal friends with
> many of the most powerful men in the country, including a
> long succession of U.S. presidents. The donning of a new outfit
> —three-piece suits and his ever-present cigar—seemed to bring
> about a change even in Griffith's countenance, the furrowed
> brow and piercing eyes replaced now by a gracious, grandfa-
> therly smile. Indeed, he ran his ballclub like a big family.

The appointment marked the beginning of Griffith's most success-ful years in baseball, with nine first division finishes and three pennants over the next 10 years. Bucky Harris' clubs won two pennants, a World Championship, and had first division finishes in each of his five years as the club's player-manager (see Chapter 12). Walter Johnson, who com-pleted his playing career in 1927, took over for Harris in 1929, and he managed the club through 1932, finishing in the first division in three of those years.

Johnson's 1930 club challenged the Athletics, pulling to within 5½ games of the A's by Labor Day before finishing in second place, eight games out. The key to the Senators' improvement was an advantageous trade in mid–June in which Griffith swapped outfielder Leon "Goose" Goslin to the Browns for outfielder Heinie Manush and righthander Alvin "General" Crowder. Manush hit .362 and Crowder won 15 after the trade. Shortstop Joe Cronin attained full stardom during that season.

The Senators played .600 ball in both of the following seasons but could not pass the two powerhouses, the Athletics and the Yankees, who each won a pennant. 1932 was the make-or-break year for Johnson, who had signed a one year extension to manage the Senators, and Griffith approached him about making a managerial change. The two men were so close personally that, as Henry Thomas put it, Griffith called Johnson into his office and, "in effect, asked permission to fire him." Griffith said, "We need a change, Walter. How are you fixed? If you don't need the job, let me get a new manager." Johnson agreed with Griff, and 26-year-old shortstop Joe Cronin became the new player-manager.

As described in Chapter 18, Cronin led the Senators to the pennant in 1933. But after that the financially strapped Senators were not competitive. Griffith, always a tight man with a dollar, had it particularly hard during the Depression. Still, Luke Sewell, the Senators' catcher for the 1933 pennant-winners, said that The Old Fox supported four or five families during those difficult years. But money was in such short supply that in the clubhouse after the Senators clinched the pennant the team celebrated their triumph with orange pop from their concession stand.

In Walter Langford's *Legends of Baseball*, Sewell told a story that illustrated the Senators' weak financial situation:

> That was about the time that air conditioning was coming in on the trains. They had a kind of locker under each end of the car and they'd put six 300-pound blocks of ice in them and blow a fan over them to bring cool air into the car.... So we were after Griff to get us some air conditioned cars. But he said, 'No, it's bad for the pitchers' arms.' We had a trip in the middle of the summer, with the temperature over 100, from Washington to St. Louis, about 22 hours. And we went to Griff and said 'If you'll let us have air conditioned cars, we'll pay for the ice.' And right away Griff said, 'Why don't we try it?'"

During the last 20 years of Griffith's presidency his club continued to deteriorate, finishing in the second division in 16 of those years. Bucky Harris, in his second managerial stint with the Senators, managed only one fourth place finish from 1935 through 1942. Ossie Bluege handled the club over the next five years with more success, finishing in second place twice during the World War II years. His success was the result of a weakened league in which the Senators did not suffer the personnel losses sustained by other teams, and by Griffith's importing Latin-American players who were not subject to the military draft. Joe Kuhel managed two poor teams without success. And the long-suffering Bucky Harris came back to manage five more second division teams as the Griffith era ended.

Griffith's marriage to Addie Ann Robertson did not produce any children. However, the couple did not lack for a family. After Mrs. Griffith's brother died, the Griffiths raised seven nieces and nephews in their home and adopted several of them. The children included Calvin Griffith, who took over as the Senators' president after The Old Fox died in October

1955. Calvin's sister Thelma married Joe Cronin, and Calvin's brother, Sherry Robertson, was a utility player for the Senators for 10 years. Two other brothers were executives in the Senators organization.

Griffith was an innovator. He and John McGraw were among the first managers to utilize relief pitchers routinely. As an example, Griffith himself started 30 of 35 games in which he pitched in 1901, but four years later, still a pitcher-manager, he started in only seven games of the 25 in which he appeared. Griffith also took advantage of his location in Washington, D.C. to originate the custom of inviting Presidents to throw out the first ball on Opening Day. He became the game's most important contact with Presidents, notably President Roosevelt before and during World War II when the game needed government acquiescence in playing through the war. And Griffith was the first major league executive to scout and sign Latin-American players.

Griffith merited his selection to the Hall of Fame in 1946, either as a pitcher or as a manager/executive. He won more than 20 games in seven of the 13 seasons in which he was a regular starting pitcher, with a career record of 237–146 (.619), and a 3.31 ERA. His best performance as a pitcher-manager came in 1901 when he won his only pennant as a manager and pitched to a 24–7 record. He pitched in 146 games during the 1901–1906 period when he managed the Chicago and New York American League clubs.

Griffith had a 1491–1367 (.522) career as a manager. Over his 20-year managerial career his teams finished in the first division 11 times, with one first place finish and four second place finishes. It was not until years after Griffith left the bench that the familiar wisecrack took hold: "Washington, first in peace, first in war, and last in the American League." Clark Griffith died in Washington, D.C. on October 27, 1955.

KID NICHOLS

Righthander Charles August "Kid" Nichols was born in Madison, Wisconsin, on September 14, 1869. He signed his first professional contract in 1886 at a youthful 17 (the source of his nickname) with Kansas City in the Western League. Nichols joined Boston's National League club in 1890, and broke in with a bang with a 27–19 season for a fifth place team. He won a remarkable 297 games in the 1890s, 30 more than the great Cy Young. Nichols won at least 30 games in seven of his 12 seasons with Boston, but he left after the 1901 season because of a salary dispute.

Nichols was involved in an amusing—and future rule-making—encounter with Cap Anson in the pitcher's first year in the majors. As Bill James described it in his *Baseball Managers*:

> Just as Nichols would get set to pitch, Anson would jump to the other side of the plate, batting left-handed, then right-handed, etc. Nichols looked at him as if he were half-crazy, which wasn't necessarily false, and waited for him to stand in and hit.... At last the Boston coach asked the umpire to tell Anson to cut it out.... Anson continued to jump around, and the umpire ... refused to order him to stop. At last the umpire sent Anson to first base, ruling that he was entitled to first base since Nichols had refused to pitch to him. So they [eventually] made a rule about that, that if a hitter switched positions in the batter's box after the pitcher is set he is called out.

In 1902 Nichols became part owner and pitcher-manager for the Kansas City Blue Stockings of the Western League. He had a fine 26–7 record and led his team to the Western League pennant, then won 21 games in 1903 while his club finished in third place. The St. Louis Cardinals brought him back to the majors as their pitcher-manager in 1904, and he had his last successful major league season with a 21–13 performance. But the Cardinals finished a disappointing fifth, and Kid managed only 14 games into the 1905 season before being fired. He pitched for the Philadelphia Phillies for the rest of that season and in 1906 before retiring.

Nichols ranks sixth in major league wins, with a career total of 361 out of 569 decisions, for a .634 winning percentage. He had a career 2.95 ERA, with 48 shutouts. Nichols was a durable overhand pitcher with a smooth delivery who relied on his control and an outstanding fastball. He attributed his lack of arm trouble to his reluctance to throw curves or other arm-wrenching deliveries. Nichols was elected to the Hall of Fame in 1949, four years before his death in Kansas City, Missouri.

There were more player-managers in the major leagues in the decade beginning in 1900 than in any other since 1880. Players managed 57 percent of the teams. Bill James commented on the tremendous change from 1900 to 1915 in the role of all managers. He cited four major factors precipitating the change. First, there was a rapid development of game strategies and tactics, such as the increased use of the bunt, pinch hitters, and relief pitchers, requiring greatly increased game decisions of the manager. Second, the teams began to hire coaches. This changed the relationship of the manager to his players, making the manager more of a chief of staff and less of a hands-on instructor. Another factor was expanded press coverage, forcing the manager to devote much more time to the press. (The subsequent development of radio and television has vastly increased the time managers are involved in dealing with the media.) Finally, the rapid expansion of the minor leagues after 1900 changed the way teams acquired player talent. The manager had the increased responsibility for overseeing the work of scouts and other team personnel who were employed to keep the team re-stocked with fresh players. These four factors had to place an increasing burden upon the playing manager who, while handling these heavier responsibilities, also had to maintain his own performance as a player.

7

Clarke and McGraw

FRED CLARKE

Fred Clifford Clarke was born in Winterset, Iowa, on October 3, 1872. His parents moved to Des Moines, Iowa. While still a teenager, young Clarke played in the Des Moines City League. The compactly-built (5 foot, 10 inches and 165 pounds) youngster played for a semipro team in Carroll, Iowa, before beginning his professional career with the Hastings, Nebraska, minor league team in the Nebraska State League. Clarke went on to play for teams in the Western Association and the Southern League.

In 1894 Clarke joined the Louisville club of the National League and, in his first game, he went five for five before tapering off to hit .268 in 75 games. The intense youngster went on to hit .347 and .325 in 1895–6 as the club's regular leftfielder. Impressed by his drive, skill, and baseball savvy, several National League teams offered the Louisville club cash and players for Clarke, but the team responded by promoting him to manage the team in mid–June of 1897. Unaffected by his new responsibilities, Clarke gave an impressive offensive performance as the club's leadoff hitter, with a career-high .390 average and 57 stolen bases. But his club played poorly, finishing eleventh in a twelve-club league. Clarke's club improved slightly in 1898, finishing ninth as Clarke himself had a relatively poor season. Louisville had another lackluster season the following year, with the only bright spots provided by third baseman–outfielder Honus Wagner, righthanders Deacon Phillippe and Bert Cunningham, and playing manager Clarke. Wagner was an unpretentious, almost shy, young man who needed an aggressive, demanding boss like Clarke during his early days with Louisville. Wagner recalled his first week with Louisville when he attempted to take batting practice and veteran teammates forced him out of the batters box. This was a typical bullying tactic employed by established players to protect their jobs. When Wagner returned to the dugout, Clarke walked over to him and asked:

"Why didn't you take your cuts?"

"They won't let me," the mild-mannered kid said.

"Get back in the box, or get the hell off this ball club!" the manager shouted.

Wagner marched back to the plate, threatened the snarling veterans with his bat, and forced his way back into the batting cage.

A few weeks later Wagner played in his first game against the rowdy Baltimore Orioles. He clubbed a potential triple to deep center but, as he rounded first base, Orioles first baseman Jack Doyle gave him the hip, knocking him off stride. Shortstop Hughie Jennings blocked second base and forced Wagner to lose a second rounding the bag. At third base John McGraw blocked him off the bag, then knocked the wind out of him with a hard tag to the pit of his stomach. Clarke cussed out Wagner and threatened to send him out to the minors if he didn't retaliate. Wagner recalled his response:

> I hit another to deep center for extra bases. I dumped Doyle on his behind at first, left Jennings in the dirt at second, and trampled all over McGraw's feet coming into third. Clarke was so tickled to see McGraw fuming and cussing that he walked over to the coacher's box and said, 'Nice day, ain't it, Muggsy?'

For all of his take-no-prisoners attitude, Clarke had a sense of humor. Wagner told of the first time that Clarke ordered him to "lay one down." The green Wagner hit away and blasted a homer instead of bunting. Still, he had a hard time explaining to Clarke that he had never heard the expression before. The next time that Wagner came up when the situation called for a bunt, Clarke beckoned him over. "Lay one down, Dutch," he rasped, adding with a wink, "like the last time."

Early in his career Wagner insisted, "I'm an outfielder who can play third base and first base, but I really prefer center field." The wily Clarke, who realized Honus' great potential as a shortstop, moved third baseman Tommy Leach to shortstop, with Wagner playing third base. Then Clarke told Leach, "Work on the Dutchman. Tell him that you haven't got near the range of a big fellow like Wagner. Butter him up and belittle yourself. Try to shame him into playing the position." After a week of Leach's nagging, Wagner agreed to move to shortstop.

After the 1899 season the Louisville club was transferred to Pittsburgh and Clarke's career as a player-manager took off. The new owner

Fred Clarke was one of the most effective player-managers in history, with a 1109–674 record, four pennants, and four second place finishes in 12 seasons. He ranks second to Cap Anson in the number of games in which he was both player and manager. Clarke, an outfielder, had a lifetime batting average of .312 over 21 seasons.

of the Pirates, Barney Dreyfuss, brought the best of the Louisville players to Pittsburgh, including Clarke, Wagner, Leach, and righthander Charles "Deacon" Phillippe. Clarke had his first successful year as a player-manager in 1900 as his Pirates finished second in the modified eight-team National League, 4½ games behind the Brooklyn Superbas. The team leaders were the gifted Wagner, still playing right field, and Clarke.

The Pirates dominated the National League over the next three seasons, winning the pennant by 7½ games in 1901, by an overwhelming 27½ game margin the following year, and by 6½ games in 1903. The club's success in 1901 was attributable in part to Clarke's good fortune in losing only his regular third baseman to the newly-established American League while other National League teams were more seriously affected by defections. But still the club won on its merits. The offense was led by Wagner, still alternating between the outfield and shortstop, and by Clarke. Wagner had become the National League's most potent offensive player, and Clarke was rated among the best run producers and fielding leftfielders in the game. Phillippe and righthander Jack Chesbro led an excellent pitching staff.

The Pirates' powerful performance in 1902 was a matter of everything falling into its proper place. Clarke's players led the league in almost every offensive category, and the honors were well distributed throughout the lineup. Wagner led the league in runs, RBI, doubles, slugging percentage, and stolen bases; and Clarke hit .316 and ranked just behind Wagner in runs, doubles, and slugging average. Chesbro had 28 wins to lead all of the pitchers. The 27½ game lead over second place Brooklyn remains the major league record.

The Pirates won their third straight pennant in 1903 despite losing

Chesbro to the New York Highlanders. Wagner barely beat out Clarke for
the batting title, and Clarke led the league in slugging percentage. The
1903 season marked the beginning of the fiery competition between player-
manager Clarke and player-manager John McGraw, whose Giants finished
in second place. On one occasion Clarke and McGraw almost came to
blows during a game when Clarke came to the defense of one of his pitchers who had been taunted by McGraw. Clarke also had problems with at
least one other Giants player. In his *Rowdy Richard*, Dick Bartell wrote:

> When Clarke was managing the Pirates, the Giants had a big
> rawboned catcher, Frank Bowerman [who had played under
> Clarke in 1898–9].... Clarke and Bowerman had words after a
> game. The next day Bowerman invited Clarke into an empty
> room in the clubhouse. They locked the door. Both teams could
> hear them thumping around in there. When Clarke came out,
> the Pirates knew there had been a real battle, and Clarke had
> lost.

Clarke was renowned for his ability to get into the minds of opposing players, to the Pirates' advantage. Christy Mathewson told of the time
that Clarke threw wacky, but talented, lefthander Rube Waddell completely off his game by inviting Waddell out to Clarke's Kansas ranch to
hunt after the season. After Clarke offered to give Waddell a hunting dog,
the childish pitcher lost his concentration, and the Pirates scored five runs
in the next inning.

Pirates' owner Barney Dreyfuss arranged with the fledging American
League's champions, the Boston Pilgrims, to play a best-of-nine series in
the first World Series (although this first modern Series was called the
"Championship of the United States"). Clarke's club was matched against
the Boston Pilgrims, managed by their third baseman, Jimmy Collins.
Acrimonious disputes between leaders of the National League and the
upstart American League had prevented a post-season series in 1901 and
1902, and this was a set of games to answer the question: Was the American League truly qualified to compete against the well-established
National League to decide baseball's best team?

The first game was played at Boston's Huntington Avenue Grounds,
and Deacon Phillippe outpitched legendary righthander Cy Young. The
clubs split the next two games as Phillippe, the only healthy Pittsburgh
starter, won the second of the games, pitching on only one day's rest.
Phillippe also won the next game, played two days later because of a Sunday travel date and a rain postponement. But with Clarke's team ahead
three games to one, Boston came back to win the next three games as Cy

Young returned to defeat Phillippe in the seventh game. After another rainout, the valiant but exhausted Phillippe lost 3–0 to Boston righthander Bill Dineen (later a prominent American League umpire). The Pirates were outclassed in losing the series five games to three. The verdict was in—the American League was indeed qualified to play the best the National League had to offer.

Clarke's teams faltered over the next four seasons, overmatched by John McGraw's Giants and player-manager Frank Chance's Cubs. These seasons were marked by Wagner's continuing brilliance and Clarke's strong leadership and sound outfield play. At the time, prominent players managed three of the eight National League teams, including the Cubs' first baseman, Frank Chance; the Braves' first baseman, Fred Tenney; and Clarke. Player-managers were singled out for their playing accomplishments. As an example, the 1999 edition of *Total Baseball* carried the following item on two games played on April 28, 1906: "It's the only time two player-managers steal home on the same day, though not in the same game. Cubs pilot Frank Chance steals in the ninth to give Chicago a 1–0 win over the Reds, and Fred Clarke matches him in the Pirates' 10–1 win over the St. Louis Cardinals."

The Pirates became competitive again in 1908 on the strength of a magnificent year by Wagner and excellent seasons by lefthander Albert Leifield and righthander Vic Willis. In one of the closest National League races, the Cubs edged out the Pirates on the last day of the season. The clubs started the game dead even, with 98–55 records, and the Cubs won 5–2 before 30,247, the largest turnout at the Cubs' West Side Park. In downtown Pittsburgh, some 50,000 people followed the game on temporary scoreboards. This was the historic season when the Giants were denied a crucial win on Fred Merkle's famous "boner." The Giants and the Pirates finished in a second place tie, a game behind the Cubs.

In 1909 the Pirates had a great year. They moved into the new concrete and steel Forbes Field and won the pennant over the Cubs by 6½ games, with a team record 110 wins. Wagner led the league in hitting for the fourth straight year, and, as usual, he was among the leaders in all of the meaningful offensive categories. Clarke, in his sixteenth season as a player, had one of his better years. The Pirates faced the Detroit Tigers in the World Series, and rookie righthander Charles "Babe" Adams beat righthander George Mullin. Clarke hit a home run for the Pirates' first run in their 4–1 victory. The publicity focus of the first game was on the two superstars, Wagner and the Tigers' Ty Cobb. Writing in his *Super Stars of Baseball*, St. Louis sportswriter Bob Broeg described their first meeting in the Series:

> When Ty Cobb reached first base the first time ... the fiery
> Detroit star cupped his hands and shouted down to the Pirates'
> shortstop, 'Hey, Krauthead, I'm coming down on the next
> pitch.'... 'I'll be waiting,' Wagner answered Ty the Terrible. In
> this first and actually only confrontation between players
> regarded by many as the best each major league has developed,
> Cobb came off a painful second best. When Ty slid into sec-
> ond, spikes high, Wagner was there, not only holding his
> ground to make the putout, but applying the tag so forcefully,
> trying to stuff the ball down the tyrannical Ty's throat, that
> Cobb wound up with a lacerated lip.

The clubs took turns winning the next five games. In the deciding
seventh game, Adams won his third game of the Series. The redoubtable
Wagner had six RBI during the Series, and Clarke more than matched
him with two home runs and seven RBI. Clarke's second homer of the
Series brought in three runs in the pivotal fifth game and broke a 3–3 tie
as the Pirates went on to win 8–4. The Pirates' player-manager was
euphoric in the clubhouse following the game in view of his club's crush-
ing defeat in the first World Series six years before.

By 1909 there was a noticeable increase in the number of women
attending major league games. This presented something of a strain on
the many managers and players known for their use of profanity on the
field, and Clarke was one of the major offenders. Honus Wagner remi-
nisced, "Women were beginning to come to the ball parks. I remember
Clarke's wife bawlin' the devil outa him for the language he was using as
he'd come in from the outfield to squawk about some decision."

The triumvirate of Clarke, Chance, and McGraw were continually at
each others' throats during those years. There was a time during the 1908
season when the Cubs manhandled the Pirates in a series, both artistically
and in a number of spikings and fights. The battered Pirates returned to
Pittsburgh and prepared for another set of games with the Cubs. A very
angry Clarke called his players together before the first game and proclaimed loudly, "I'll give a hundred bucks to the guy who does the most
damage to the Cubs." Righthander Howie Camnitz volunteered, "I'm
gonna win that money, I'll get two strikes on all these guys and then knock
em' down on the next pitch." Clarke warned, "That sounds good, but if
I catch one of you guys talkin' to those birds, except to cuss 'em out, it
will cost you fifty bucks."

Two Cubs were carried off after the first two games, and, before the
third game, Frank Chance walked into the Pirates clubhouse to talk to
Clarke. The men began arguing excitedly, and after ten minutes they suddenly began waving their arms at each other and shaking their fists. Honus

Wagner decided to break up the fight before anyone was hurt. "When I got there," laughed Wagner, "they were going at it hot and heavy, cussin' out John McGraw. They already had agreed to stop playin' dirty against each other and concentrate on cripplin' McGraw and his Giants." That was the year that the Cubs won after the "Merkle boner." That was the end of Clarke's days as a pennant-winning manager. For the remainder of his managerial career, Clarke's teams were never serious challengers. After two successive second division finishes, he retired to his prosperous 1320-acre ranch near Winfield, Kansas, following the 1915 season. In a classic case of the rich getting richer, oil was discovered on his property.

Clarke remained out of baseball until 1925 when he invested in the Pirates. He rejoined the team as a coach that season and subsequently became a club vice president. The Pirates won the World Series that year, and there was a suspicion that Clarke was trying to take credit for the team's success. Some Pirates players thought that Clarke was working to replace manager Bill McKechnie. During the following season, Clarke antagonized several of the players, in particular outstanding outfielder Max Carey, and the team split into factions over problems Clarke had caused. Many baseball men felt this dissension was the reason for the club's third place finish in 1926. The upshot was that, after the season, the very competent McKechnie was fired, Carey was placed on waivers, and Clarke left the club.

A lefthand hitter and righthand thrower, Clarke had a lifetime average of .312 over 21 seasons, with 2672 hits, 1619 runs scored, and 506 stolen bases. As a player-manager he had a marvelous 1109–674 (.622) record with Pittsburgh from 1900 to 1911, with four pennants, four second place finishes, three third places, and one fourth place finish. Some baseball historians consider him the best player-manager in the history of the game. He played and managed in 1848 games, second only to Cap Anson. Even more impressively, he managed in more than 82 percent of the 2242 major league games in which he played. Elected to the Hall of Fame in 1945, he was considered deserving of the honor both as a player and as a manager. Clarke died in Winfield, Kansas, shortly before his 88th birthday.

JOHN MCGRAW

John Joseph McGraw was born on April 7, 1873, in Truxton, New York, a small town in the center of the state. He played local town ball until he was seventeen. That year he signed a contract with the Olean, New York, team in the newly-formed New York–Pennsylvania League.

After failing with Olean he was picked up by Wellsville in the Western New York League, where he hit an eye-catching .365. The following year, 1891, the aggressive little bantam (he was 5' 6½" tall and weighed 121 pounds) played at Cedar Rapids in the Illinois-Iowa League before being purchased by the Baltimore Orioles, then in the American Association. His playing career took off in 1893 when he began seven consecutive years in which he batted at least .321.

McGraw specialized in getting on base and scoring runs. He had little power because of his small size, but also because he choked up on the bat and swung with a short, chopping stroke that tended to produce ground balls which bounced high and permitted the fast-moving youngster to beat out delayed throws to first base. His ability to draw walks was largely attributable to his skill at deliberately fouling off pitches.

Much has been written about McGraw's years with the colorful Orioles. Early in McGraw's playing career with the Orioles he became the club's field leader. With the enthusiastic encouragement of Orioles manager Ned Hanlon, the 21-year-old McGraw began to devise plays calculated to upset opponents. He worked with teammate Willie Keeler to perfect the hit-and-run play. And he led the team in developing its bunting game, and he invented so many trick plays and "dirty" plays that new rules had to be written and old rules revised, in order to deal with them. In his *McGraw of the Giants*, Frank Graham wrote:

> McGraw helped to hasten the advent of the two-umpire system by a simple trick that he worked successfully for a long time. With an opposing runner on third base, poised to dart for the plate when a fly to the outfield had been caught, McGraw would hook his fingers in the runner's belt—unseen, of course, by the umpire, who would be watching the flight of the ball. In the instant the ball had been caught and the umpire whirled to see if the runner had left third ahead of the catch, McGraw would let go but, nine times out of ten, the runner would be thrown out at the plate. Protests went unavailing. The umpire could base a decision only on what he had seen; obviously, he couldn't watch the ball and McGraw at the same time.

McGraw's best year as a player came in 1899, his first year as player-manager. He hit for a career-high .391 and led the league in runs scored and walks, despite missing most of the last month of the season. Even with his sparkling on-field performance, McGraw's Baltimore club could do no better than a fourth place finish in the twelve-club National League. McGraw's managerial performance was highly praised by baseball men, but the National League decided to eliminate its four weakest franchises, and Baltimore was one of the four clubs to go.

McGraw moved to St. Louis of the National League as a player, along with his longtime friend and teammate Wilbert Robinson. At first McGraw refused to report to St. Louis, as he and Robinson were the proprietors of a thriving Baltimore saloon. But he joined St. Louis after receiving a salary of $10,000, becoming the highest paid player in the game. McGraw played well for manager Patsy Tebeau, but the club did poorly and there were rumors that Tebeau would be replaced by McGraw. But McGraw insisted that he would not take over the manager's job in order to prove that he had not undermined Tebeau. But he aided Tebeau's figurehead replacement by taking charge of the team on the field without being officially designated as its manager.

In 1901 McGraw, accompanied by Robinson, took over the Baltimore franchise in Ban Johnson's newly-formed American League. Beginning in November 1900, McGraw traveled the eastern half of the country intensively attempting to sign players, particularly National League players who had not yet signed contracts. He picked up a number of promising players, most notably pitcher Joe McGinnity; Fred Clarke's second baseman, Jimmy Williams; and outfielder Mike Donlin.

But the season was barely under way before the rough-and-ready McGraw clashed with Ban Johnson, mostly because Johnson backed up his umpires in their constant ejections of McGraw and his equally aggressive players. As many baseball men had predicted, McGraw and Johnson simply could not get along. Third baseman–manager McGraw played well, with a .349 batting average and 71 runs scored in only 73 games, before serious knee injuries in August ended his playing season. McGraw's club slipped badly after he had to leave the field, finishing fifth in the eight-team league.

Outfielder Mike Donlin, expected to lead McGraw's offense in 1902, was expelled from the league by Johnson after a drunken brawl. In a game against Boston, McGraw disputed a call by umpire Jack Sheridan in sending a runner home safely after McGraw had bumped the runner as he rounded third base. The next day McGraw was hit by pitches five times, but each time Sheridan refused to wave him to first base, claiming that McGraw had intentionally let pitches hit him. After the last call, McGraw sat down in the batters box, refusing to remove himself until Sheridan ordered him out of the game. As a result, Ban Johnson suspended McGraw for five days.

McGraw's next major mishap as a player-manager came a month later in a game witnessed by his horrified wife. Playing against Detroit in Baltimore, McGraw was spiked flagrantly and viciously by Detroit outfielder Dick Harley. Trapped well off third base, Harley leaped feet first into McGraw, ripping open the manager's left knee. McGraw responded by leaping on top of Harley, and the two men rolled around in the dirt fighting and kicking each other. McGraw developed a bad infection from his open wound, forcing him out of the lineup for several weeks.

The ugly incidents between McGraw and Johnson's umpires continued as McGraw stated publicly that Johnson wanted to have Baltimore thrown out of the league. Many observers were of the opinion that McGraw antagonized the umpires in an attempt to discredit Johnson. Actually, it was learned later that McGraw was in the process of removing himself from Baltimore because he wanted to leave before Johnson removed him by dropping the Baltimore franchise. McGraw met with officials representing New York Giants president Andrew Freedman and, on July 8, he became the Giants' player-manager. His contract called for a salary of $11,000 a year for four years, which made him the highest salaried player or manager in the game. Shortly after, Freedman became the controlling stockholder of the Baltimore club and he directed the release of Orioles players who McGraw wanted for the Giants. They included righthanders Joe McGinnity and Jack Cronin, first baseman Dan McGann, and Roger Bresnahan.

The Giants played their first game under player-manager McGraw at the Polo Grounds on July 19, 1902. They lost to the Phillies as shortstop McGraw had a putout, two assists, and a single in three official at-bats, plus a walk and a sacrifice bunt. The *New York Evening World* account stated: "John McGraw, the new manager of the Giants, and his Baltimore recruits made their local debut today before nearly 10,000 people, who gave them a warm welcome. They also were pleased with the showing of the team, although disappointed over the result." But although the new players from Baltimore gave McGraw the nucleus of an improved team in the future, it was only a nucleus. The Giants finished last, a full 53½ games off the pace. The injury-plagued McGraw played in a total of 55 games during the season, 20 of them with Baltimore, failing to hit .300 with the Orioles or the Giants.

McGraw felt that his days as a regular player were very likely over as he began to test his injured right knee in a workout in spring training in Savannah the following spring. His ailing knee gave way, he lost his agility, and his playing career was essentially over. He played in a total of 24 games over the next four seasons before removing himself from the playing roster.

McGraw was such a dynamic, commanding presence on the field throughout his playing career that in many ways he was a de facto player-manager before being given the title of manager. Years later McGraw expressed the view that a manager could do a better overall job of running his team from the bench than from the field as a player, or coach, for that matter. During a crisis situation, player-manager McGraw frequently left the field and directed his team from the bench. When he left the field in such a situation, Christy Mathewson told a writer that opposing fans and players rode him mercilessly. Many of them called him a quitter. Mathewson said, "McGraw never knew the meaning of the word fear. He knew he could pull the team through from the bench, concentrate better, and see more of what was going on. And he missed nothing."

McGraw's brilliant managerial career after he left the playing field has been well documented. Overall, he managed the Giants for 30 years and won 10 pennants and three World Series, and his clubs finished in second place 11 times. And his profound impact upon the game continued long after he retired in June 1932, as many of his players served as managers in subsequent years. He was widely admired and respected for his achievements and his unpublicized generosity to former players who were down on their luck. But he was disliked just as intensely by others who could not abide his tyrannical style. He was willing to do anything to fulfill his most famous quote: "The idea is to win."

Most knowledgeable baseball men considered McGraw the greatest manager of the first half of the twentieth century. When asked how he rated the managers he had known, no less an authority than Connie Mack commented, "There is only one manager and that's John McGraw." McGraw also was a great player, with a lifetime average of .334 and an on-base percentage of .466, below only Babe Ruth and Ted Williams on the all-time list. Over his 33-year managerial career, his teams had a remarkable 2763–1948 (.586) record. "The Little Napoleon" was elected to the Hall of Fame in 1937, a member of the first group inducted into the Hall two years later. McGraw died in New Rochelle, New York, on February 25, 1934.

8

Chance, Jimmy Collins, and Tenney

FRANK CHANCE

Frank Chance, along with Fred Clarke and Jimmy Collins, was one of the most successful of the player-managers of the early 1900s. Frank Leroy Chance was born in Fresno, California, on September 9, 1877, the son of a banker. He was a catcher with the Fresno High School team and subsequently caught for the University of California while playing for an independent team in Fresno. He studied dentistry briefly before signing with the Chicago Cubs when he was 21, on the recommendation of Cubs outfielder Bill Lange.

Hall of Fame second baseman Johnny Evers recalled: "The real beginning of the Chicago Cubs was in March 1898 when a big, bow-legged, rather awkward young player came from the Pacific Coast to be tried as a catcher. Quiet, good-natured, rather retiring off the field, serious, and in deadly earnest while playing, honest and sincere in everything, ... Chance reported at training quarters in West Baden, Indiana, carrying a bunch of gnarled and wrecked fingers.... While awkward and unfinished, pitchers who worked with him declared that Chance from the first showed his genius for leadership and great skill in handling pitchers and watching batters."

"Husk," as Chance was called because of his solid, 6 foot, 190-pound frame, caught and played in the outfield for the Cubs in his first several years with the club until 1903, when Cubs manager Frank Selee convinced him to shift to first base. Chance insisted that he could not play first base. He threatened to quit playing until a salary increase induced him to make the change. Chance, a speedy runner for a big man, led the league in stolen bases and hit a career-high .327 in 1903. Meanwhile, Selee, with Chance's advice, was forming the foundation of a championship club. The Cubs'

acquisition of rifle-armed catcher Johnny Kling dictated Chance's move to first base. Next Selee transferred third baseman Joe Tinker to shortstop, and acquired second baseman Johnny Evers, outfielders Jimmy Slagle and Frank "Wildfire" Schulte, and righthanders Mordecai "Three Finger" Brown and Ed Reulbach.

Chance established a reputation as a fearless player who crowded the plate, practically daring the pitcher to pitch him inside. As a result, he was hit frequently by pitches. In a doubleheader in May 1904 he was hit a record three times in the first game and twice in the second game. He was hit in the head a number of times during his career, eventually causing deafness in one ear and severe headaches.

In 1905 Selee's illness forced him to leave the club in mid-season. Chance became the club's player-manager, and the Cubs finished third. After the season, Chance reinforced his pitching staff by picking up lefthander Jack Pfiester, leftfielder Jimmy Sheckard,

Frank Chance was a solid first baseman who hit .296 in 17 seasons as a player. His Cubs won four pennants and two World Championships when he was their player-manager.

and third baseman Harry Steinfeldt. The Cubs were ready to compete for the pennant with McGraw's and Clarke's teams.

The Cubs put it all together in 1906. The club won the pennant by 20 games over the second place Giants, with a magnificent 116–36 record. Chance's club played at a still-existing record .800 (60–15) pace on the road, with a 56–21 record at home. Chance himself had a splendid year, hitting .319, and Brown (26–6), Reulbach (19–8), and Pfiester (20–8) were the standouts on a pitching staff, which boasted a 1.76 ERA.

Chance gained early recognition as a brilliant strategist and field leader, and his players impressed as much with their mental acuity and team effort as with their playing exploits. Most of the Cubs' victories were low-scoring affairs. At Chance's insistence, his players excelled at moving runners up and stealing bases, following the lead of their player-manager, who led the league with 57 steals.

Dynamic little second baseman Johnny Evers and tough shortstop Joe Tinker were an effective keystone combination who, with their player-manager, later gained fame as the well-publicized double play combination of "Tinker to Evers to Chance." The three men played together for the first time on September 13, 1902, and pulled off their first double play two days later. In retrospect, their double play statistics are not impressive, as there were only a total of 25 Tinker-to-Evers-to-Chance twin killings during their prime four years, from 1906 through 1909. Actually, Tinker and Evers, neither of whom was a sweetheart, disliked each other intensely, and yet the two men played together effectively for 11 years.

The World Series between the all-conquering Cubs and the Chicago White Sox, known as "The Hitless Wonders," provided a classic example of baseball's unpredictability. The Cubs were prohibitive favorites as the Series opened. The two teams split the first four games but the White Sox took the last two games with relative ease. None of the Cubs performed well in the Series, and Chance hit a mere .238. Yet, despite their surprise World Series defeat, baseball men considered the 1906 Cubs one of the best teams ever.

Chance gained an early reputation as an authoritarian man whose orders were to be followed without question. One of his young pitchers allowed batters to hog the plate until Chance corrected the problem by directing his pitcher to hit a batter in the first inning of each game until the hitters abandoned that practice. One of his players asked Chance whether he could get married in mid–September in the midst of a close pennant race, and Chance ordered him to not marry until after the season. One Cubs pitcher was sent home from a road trip to get in shape to pitch an important game, but he did not follow Chance's instructions to work out at home. The pitcher was released unconditionally. Chance was a notoriously hard loser. There was the story, probably apocryphal but nevertheless illustrative, about the time the Cubs suffered a tough, one-run loss in an extra-inning game. The bitter player-manager returned home to his wife, who tried to console him. She said, "Well, anyhow dear, you still have me." Chance looked at her bitterly and groused, "Yeah, I know, but I'd have traded you for a clutch hit there in the tenth inning." Cubs catcher Jimmy Archer talked of Chance's difficulty in dealing with defeat even when his club was playing well. Archer said: "One time we won 13 straight, then lost the next game in the tenth inning, 2–1. He came in, threw his bat through the piano, and threw all the tables out of the clubhouse."

The Cubs repeated in 1907 with virtually the same team in the same dominating manner. This time they won 107 games and won the pennant by 17 games over Fred Clarke's Pirates. Chance, who hit a team-leading .293, Steinfeldt, and Sheckard provided much of the offense, and Brown and Reulbach carried much of the pitching load. The Cubs won the World Series decisively over the Detroit Tigers, tying the Tigers in the first game but winning the next four games with relative ease. Steinfeldt and Evers led the hitters. And each of the four starting pitchers—Brown, Vierall, Pfiester, and Reulbach—won a game while holding Ty Cobb to a .200 average.

The Cubs won a third straight pennant in 1908, but this one did not come without a struggle. Chance's team was six games behind the Pirates and three in back of the Giants as late as the middle of August. By late August the Cubs fought back, narrowing the gap behind the Giants as the Pirates slipped to third place. Chicago fans were at fever pitch as the Cubs took two of three from the Giants in Chicago to move to within ½ game of the lead. The Giants led by a game and a half on September 23 as the clubs met at the Polo Grounds in one of the most controversial games ever played—the "Merkle boner" game.

With Christy Mathewson matched against Three Finger Brown, the game was tied at one in the bottom of the ninth. With the Giants' Harry McCormick on third base and 19-year-old Fred Merkle on first, Giants shortstop Al Bridwell singled to center, scoring McCormick. With the game apparently over, Merkle ran halfway to second base before turning and heading for the center field clubhouse. Johnny Evers grabbed a ball (very likely not the game ball) and touched second base as the crowd swarmed all over the field. Umpire Hank O'Day ruled that the run did not count since the force play at second was the third out, nullifying the run, and the game ended in a 1–1 tie.

Ironically, the Cubs had been involved in an identical play against the Pirates a few weeks earlier, and the run had been allowed. The Cubs' protest was denied, but they learned a lesson which would prove invaluable a few weeks later. John McGraw was furious. "If Merkle was out," he bellowed, "then the game was tied and O'Day should have ordered the field cleared and the game resumed. But he wasn't out and we won the game and they can't take it away from us!" But they could and they did.

The league president ruled that it was a tie game, but denied Chance's demand that the game be forfeited to the Cubs. It was ruled that the game would be replayed if it became necessary to decide the pennant race. The Cubs and the Giants finished the regular season dead even and prepared for the playoff game. Chance always had hit well against Mathewson, who was matched against Lefty Jack Pfiester in the deciding game. Giants outfielder Fred Snodgrass described McGraw's strategy for eliminating Chance from the game:

> Before the game we talked it over in the clubhouse how in the world we could get Chance thrown out of the game. Matty was to pitch for us, and Frank always hit Matty pretty well. We felt if we could get him out, in some way, that we had a better chance of winning…. Besides, we thought the call on Merkle was a raw deal, and any means of redressing the grievance was legitimate. So it was cooked up that Joe McGinnity was to pick a fight with Chance early in the game. They were to have a knockdown, drag-out fight … and both would get thrown out of the game. Of course, we didn't need McGinnity, but they needed Chance. McGinnity did just what he was supposed to. He called Chance some names on some pretext or other, stepped on his shoes, pushed him, actually spit on him. But Frank wouldn't fight. He was too smart.

The Giants scored a run on Pfiester in the first inning on a double by Mike Donlin. With two on and two out, Chance brought in Brown, who stopped the Giants cold. The game actually was decided in the third inning when Tinker came up with two runners on. Mathewson waved centerfielder Cy Seymour back deeper, and Seymour move back to the spot Mathewson had indicated. But after the pitcher turned his attention back to Tinker, Seymour, feeling that he knew the hitter better, moved closer to his original spot. Tinker drove a long fly ball to the deeper point where Mathewson had signaled Seymour to play. The ball soared over Seymour's head, and two runs came in on the triple. Johnny Kling drove Tinker in, and the Cubs led 3–1. Chance doubled in the fourth run, and that was all the Cubs needed for a 4–2 victory and the pennant. The key to the Cubs' pennant win was their superb pitching and defense. Chance had a fair season personally, hitting .272, and Evers and Tinker, celebrated for their fielding skills, had good seasons offensively.

The Cubs took on the Tigers for the second year in a row in the World Series. In the first game the Tigers had a 6–5 lead going into the top of the ninth. But the Cubs came back with six straight singles and a double steal to win the game for Brown. The Cubs took the second game behind Overall, but the Tigers came back and battered Pfiester for 10 hits in an 8–3 win. Despite returning to their home field, Detroit could do little in the last two games, as they were shut out in both games, first by Brown and then by Overall. By the last game the Detroit fans had given up on the Tigers, as only 6,210 attended the game. Chance led his players with a .421 average and eight hits, followed by Johnny Evers, who hit .350, duplicating his performance in the1907 Series. The brilliant Cobb was the only effective Tiger hitter, with a .368 average.

The Cubs won 104 games the following season, six more than in 1908, but were beaten out by Fred Clarke's Pirates. As usual, the pitching staff was excellent, with an ERA under 2.00 for the third time in the last four seasons. Three Finger Brown led the league with 27 wins, 32 complete games, and seven saves. Chance had a mediocre season, slowed by a number of injuries, forcing him to miss 40 percent of his club's games. The outclassed Cubs finished 6½ games behind the Pirates.

Chance's club won 104 games again in 1910, but this time they beat out the Giants by 13 games as the Pirates fell back. Again the Cubs won because of effective pitching, great defense, and a career year by centerfielder Solly Hofman. But the Cubs suffered a serious setback in August when Evers broke his leg, a loss that affected the club's performance for the rest of the year. Although Chance hit .298, this was the last season in which he was a significant factor as a player. At 33 he had become injury prone and had lost much of his speed and agility in the field. But as a manager he was still the razor-sharp leader the players had known since he took over the club in 1905.

The Cubs were outplayed in the World Series by Connie Mack's Philadelphia Athletics. They missed the presence of Evers, but even the lantern-jawed little second baseman would have made no real difference. The Cubs lost the first game to star righthander Chief Bender, and powerful righthander Jack Coombs won the other three games. The Cubs were competitive only in the fourth game when they tied the game in the last of the ninth and won it with a tenth inning run. Chance hit .353 in his last hurrah as a player. A veteran reporter wrote after the last game: "The Cubs seemed to have lost the confidence and dash that was theirs in the days of 1906 to 1908." Chance's success on the field had taken their toll on the man, who had been as hard on himself as he had been on his players. Johnny Evers wrote of Chance:

> One evening after Frank Chance had won two World Series Championships, he sat gloomily silent for a long time. The big, hearty, joyous boy who had come from California a dozen years before was battered, grizzled, careworn and weary. Still young, his fine face showed lines of care and worry, and a few gray hairs streaked through his head. He was thirty-two and looked old. For a long time he sat musing. Then he looked up and smiled grimly. "This business is making a crab out of me," he remarked.

The Cubs played well in 1911 but they could do no better than second place, 7½ games behind McGraw's club, which had a number of young, up-and-coming players and, of course, Christy Mathewson. Brown was a 20-game winner for his last time, and little righthander Lew Richie pitched well. Evers was only a shadow of the player who had sparked the Cubs in their glory years, and only Frank Schulte and Jimmy Sheckard played well. Chance's playing career essentially was over.

Chance's men slipped to third place in 1912, and he was fired after the season while he was in the hospital for an operation to remove blood clots that had caused continual headaches. Johnny Evers became the Cubs' new player-manager. Chance was hired as the bench manager of the New York Highlanders, lasting only two seasons of second division finishes before retiring. He remained out of the game for two years until 1916, when he became part owner and manager of Los Angeles in the Pacific Coast League. He returned to the big leagues in 1923 to manage the Red Sox, but his club finished last and he retired from the game after that season. In ill health after that, Chance died in Los Angeles on December 15,1924, when he was only 47.

Chance ranks thirteenth in the number of games played by player-managers. The righthand hitting and throwing Chance had a decent .296 batting average over his 17 years as a player. During his career as a manager his teams won 946 and lost only 648, for a .593 average. In 11 years his clubs won four pennants and two World Championships, finished in second place twice, and in the first division eight times. In addition to his accomplishments as a manager and a player, he is remembered for his honesty and integrity. Chance was inducted into the Hall of Fame in 1946.

JIMMY COLLINS

Jimmy Collins was born in Niagara Falls, New York, on January 16,

1870, but his family moved to Buffalo when he was two. He played local sandlot ball before entering St. Joseph's Collegiate Institute in Buffalo, and worked for the Lackawanna Railroad while he was in school and after his graduation. He began playing professional baseball in 1893, at the advanced age of 23, with the Buffalo club of the Eastern League. He played the outfield before moving to third base with Louisville in 1895. The Boston Beaneaters, of the National League, called him up, and within two years he was recognized as the premier third baseman of his era.

Expert baseball men like John McGraw, Connie Mack, and Honus Wagner considered him the greatest fielding third baseman in the game's first 75 years before Pie Traynor of the Pirates came along. Before Collins, most third basemen played close to the bag. But Collins played in or back depending upon the hitter or the situation. He was a master at performing the prettiest play a third baseman can make—charging slow hit balls and bunts, scooping them up barehanded, and rifling the ball to first or second base with no wasted motion.

Although Collins is best remembered as a brilliant defensive third baseman, he was a powerful hitter. In his second full season with Boston, the compactly-built Collins had 132 RBI, along with a fine .346 average, and in 1898 he led the league with 15 home runs. He was a standout on Boston Beaneaters teams, which won consecutive pennants in the twelve-team National League in 1897–8. Collins had two more good years until he jumped at the opportunity to become the player-manager of the Boston Somersets in the newly-formed American League, which began operation in 1901.

Collins began his managerial career with three excellent players who jumped from the National League. Legendary righthander Cy Young, already the winner of 286 games with Cleveland and St. Louis, had come over from the Cardinals. First baseman Buck Freeman and centerfielder Chick Stahl also joined the Beaneaters. The season started well as Young defeated the Athletics, the first of the league-leading 33 games he would win, as he also led the league with a 1.62 ERA. Behind Young's "Cy Young" year and fine seasons by player-manager Collins, Freeman, and Stahl, the Somersets finished in second place, four games behind Clark Griffith's White Stockings. Young was the winner in 41.8 percent of the Somersets' victories, a post–1900 record that would stand until lefthander Steve Carlton won 45.8 percent of the Phillies' 59 victories in 1972. There was one day during that season that rookie player-manager Collins pulled a boner, causing him considerable embarrassment. It seems that the Somersets pulled into Philadelphia for a game against the Athletics. The only problem was that the schedule called for Collins' club to play at home against

John McGraw's Baltimore Orioles. Collins had misread the schedule, and it was some time before he heard the end of it.

Young had another overpowering season in 1902, although the club slipped to third place. But it was a different story in 1903. Collins' players had little competition, winning the pennant by 14½ games over Connie Mack's A's. Cy Young led the league in wins for the third consecutive time, this time with 28. Collins, now recognized as one of the best player-field bosses, hit .296. To top off a great year, Collins's club defeated Clarke's Pittsburgh Pirates in the first World Series, five games to three.

Collins's team, now called the Pilgrims, won the pennant again in 1904, but this time it was not a cakewalk. Young had another great year with 26 wins, including the second of his three career no-hitters, this one a perfect game. Righthander Bill Dineen came close to matching Young with 23 wins, followed by lefty Jesse Tannehill who won 21. With these three pitchers leading the way, Pilgrims pitchers set a Boston team record low of 1.5 walks per nine innings. The Pilgrims did not clinch the pennant until the next-to-last day of the season. Playing the New York Highlanders in a doubleheader, and needing a split to win the pennant, Collins' club broke a 2–2 tie in the top of the ninth when Highlanders ace pitcher, Jack Chesbro, threw a wild pitch on a misguided spitball. During the season, Pilgrim pitchers had 148 complete games out of the club's 157 games, setting an American League record. There was no World Series that year because the National League pennant-winning Giants refused to play "a bunch of minor leaguers," a reflection of their disdain for the upstart American League—but one displaying an element of fear (worried, perhaps, that they might lose to Collins' team). These two pennants would prove to be the high points of his managerial career.

Boston's 1905 team slipped down to fourth place, and the next year's club fell apart completely, finishing last. The combination of advancing age and nagging injuries restricted Collins to playing in only 37 games for the newly-named Red Sox in 1906. He began to manage the club in street clothes, à la Connie Mack, which led the irritated club's owners to remove him as manager with one quarter of the 1906 season remaining. Collins never again managed in the majors. He returned to play 41 games that season under outfielder Chick Stahl, who replaced him as manager for the rest of the season.

Stahl committed suicide in March 1907 and Cy Young replaced him. But Young lasted only six games before being replaced. Collins was put in the uncomfortable position of playing under men whom he had managed. But an unhappy Collins was traded to the Athletics in June, and he played the rest of the season for Connie Mack, hitting .278 over the full season at the age of 37. He played for the A's in 1908 to complete his major league career, then played with minor league teams for the next three years before retiring from the game in 1911.

Collins left baseball with the reputation as the best fielding third baseman to play the game up to that time, and one of the best offensive players of his era, with 983 RBI, 194 stolen bases, and a .294 batting average. He wound up with a respectable career managerial record of 455–376 (.548). Only 13 other men were regular players and managers in more games than the 663 games in which Collins filled that role.

After his retirement, Collins went into the real estate business. He did well financially during the 1920s but fell onto hard times, and most of his savings and his business were wiped out during the Great Depression of the 1930s. He went to work with the city government and headed the city's large municipal baseball program before World War II. Collins died in Buffalo in 1943, two years before his election to the Hall of Fame.

FRED TENNEY

Frederick Tenney was born in Georgetown, Massachusetts, on November 26, 1871. He graduated from Brown University, joining the Boston Beaneaters directly after his graduation in June 1894. Despite being a lefthanded thrower, Tenney was used primarily as a catcher in his first three years with Boston until Manager Frank Selee shifted the small (5 foot 9 inch, 155 pound) Tenney to first base. He became one of the most dependable first basemen in the game over the rest of his playing career, especially adept at two plays many first basemen have had difficulty mastering. One is charging a bunt on a sacrifice play and cutting down the advancing runner at second base; the other is the first to second to first double play.

In 1897 Tenney hit .318 as a member of the pennant-winning Beaneaters' stellar infield, along with second baseman Bobby Lowe, shortstop Herman Long, and Jimmy Collins. He was a solid player through the 1904 season, hitting over .300 in six seasons before he took over as the club's first baseman–manager in 1905. He inherited a weak club, finishing seventh in an eight-team league, and his 1905 club duplicated that finish with a 51–103 record. Tenney led his club in hitting, with a modest .288 average, and four of his pitchers lost over 20 games. His 1906 club, with a virtually new cast of players, was even worse, finishing an incredible 66½ games off the pace.

It was the same story in 1907—a weak start until things became even worse after mid-season. Still, Tenney's undermanned club won nine more games than in the previous season. The team needed a complete revamping, and Tenney left the club after the season to join the Giants as John McGraw's regular first baseman. Although he hit only .256 and .235 for the Giants in 1908–9, the lefthand-hitting Tenney served McGraw well, leading the league in runs scored in 1908 and preparing Fred Merkle to take over as the Giants' regular first baseman. Merkle was substituting for Tenney when he committed the historic "Merkle boner" late in the 1908 season.

Although it can be difficult for a player-manager to revert back to being only a player, Tenney fit in well with the Giants. In his *My Thirty Years in Baseball*, John McGraw wrote of Tenney: "[The public] wondered why I wanted Tenney, who was then getting old and had been manager of the Boston club. Despite his age, Tenney had kept wonderful care of himself and knew the game. He was particularly willing to work for me as a player, notwithstanding the fact that he had been a manager. I want to say right here, too, that Fred Tenney gave his whole heart and soul to the Giants. He was a big help." Tenney returned to the Braves as their first baseman–manager in 1911. But he could do no better this time than he had done in his last player-manager stint. His club again finished last, despite the presence of such well-known players as Buck Herzog, Harry Steinfeldt, Mike Donlin, Al Bridwell, and Cy Young. The problem was that these players were either not ready to excel in the big leagues or were well over the hill. Tenney himself hit .263 and closed out his major league career.

Over his 17-year playing career, Tenney hit .294, with 2231 hits and 688 RBI. Although not of Hall of Fame caliber, he was one of the most consistent and dependable players of his time. His managerial record was a very poor 202–402 (.334), with two seventh place and two last place finishes in the four years he was a manager. And yet he ranks 20th in the number of games in which he was a player-manager, an indication of the respect baseball people had for him, especially significant since the Boston club asked him back again as a player-manager even after three unsuccessful seasons. After leaving baseball, the urbane, well-spoken Tenney became a correspondent for *The New York Times*, specializing in pre-season assessments of pennant races and of World Series competitors. Tenney died in Boston on July 3, 1952.

9

Lajoie and Jones

NAPOLEON LAJOIE

Napoleon "Larry" Lajoie was born in Woonsocket, Rhode Island, on September 5, 1875, the youngest of eight children born to a French-Canadian couple. After finishing grade school he worked in local cotton mills and drove a hack for a livery stable. He also played semipro ball as a catcher and first baseman before the Fall River club of the New England League hired him for $100 a month when he was 20. The righthand-hitting Lajoie burned up the league with a .429 average, and by late summer he joined the Philadelphia Phillies, hitting .326 in 39 games.

He became the Phillies' regular first baseman in 1897 because of his sizeable (6 foot 1, 195 pound) frame and his hitting ability, demonstrated when he hit .361. Manager George Stallings moved Lajoie to second base in 1898, and the big Frenchman made the move effortlessly, fielding gracefully and leading the National League with 43 doubles and 127 RBI. Despite injuries, he played brilliantly over the next two seasons before moving to Connie Mack's Athletics in the new American League in 1901 for a small pay increase. He was the most coveted player of the 100 National Leaguers who jumped to the new league. Lajoie responded beautifully for Mack, hitting an out-of-sight .426, still the highest batting average an American Leaguer has ever had. Lajoie had the league's pitchers so terrified that White Stockings Manager Clark Griffith ordered him walked intentionally with the bases loaded.

Lajoie's move to the new American League triggered a legal controversy lasting a year. The Phillies filed suit in March 1901, and the Pennsylvania Supreme Court ruled in favor of the Phillies on the grounds that his loss would cause "irreparable injury" to them. A year later, on Opening

Napoleon Lajoie was one of the most graceful and best-hitting second basemen in baseball history, with 3242 hits and a lifetime .338 batting average. The popular player-manager of the Cleveland club over five seasons, he was unhappy as a manager and he stepped down in 1909 and continued as a player.

Day in 1902, just after Lajoie singled off Baltimore's Joe McGinnity, he was notified that the Phillies had obtained an injunction restraining him from playing in Pennsylvania. American League President Ban Johnson sidestepped the ruling by having Lajoie transferred to Cleveland and ordering that he not play in Philadelphia. As a result, a reluctant Connie Mack sold Lajoie to Cleveland, for whom he hit .378.

Before squaring off against a pitcher, Lajoie's batting style was to draw a line in the dirt alongside home plate before choking up on the bat. He stood deep in the batter's box and stood well off the plate before stepping into the pitch. Lajoie was a handsome man with sharp features who carried himself with the same grace off the field that he exhibited when playing. He had thick, wavy, jet-black hair and wore his cap cocked on the side of his head in a characteristically sporty style. In his *Super Stars of Baseball*, Bob Broeg wrote that one of Lajoie's admiring fans described him as follows: "Old Nap Lajoie was the only man I ever saw who could chew scrap tobacco in such a way as to give a jaunty refinement to a habit vulgar and untidy in so many others."

Lajoie played brilliantly over the next three seasons, leading the American League in hitting in each year, beginning in 1902 with a .378 average and following with averages of .344 and .376. Considering this was the dead ball era, his hitting performance could be considered the best of the century. He became the toast of the town almost immediately after joining Cleveland, and his popularity increased each year as fans were taken by his powerful and consistent hitting, extremely graceful fielding, and his quiet, pleasant demeanor.

Lajoie was highly respected by the other players. Former Yankees pitcher and manager Bob Shawkey said, "Lajoie was something to watch out there. He was a big man, and for his size the most graceful man I ever saw. Up at the plate he was murder. He wouldn't swing at the ball unless it was a strike, wouldn't budge that bat." Pittsburgh Pirates Tommy Leach commented, "What a ballplayer that man was! Every play he made was executed so gracefully that it looked like the easiest thing in the world. He was a pleasure to play against, too, always laughing and joking. Even when the son of a gun was blocking you off a base, he was smiling and kidding with you. You just *had* to like the guy." Hall of Fame spitballer Ed Walsh remembered, "If you pitched inside to him, he'd tear a hand off the third baseman, and if you pitched outside he'd knock down the second baseman." Famed sportswriter Grantland Rice wrote: "If Lajoie had Ty Cobb's speed he might have batted .500."

Lajoie's ability to pull vicious shots down the third base line was the primary reason for his 657 career doubles. One day against Detroit he pulled a slow pitch so savagely that the drive handcuffed third baseman George Moriarty, bruised his shoulder, and bounded into left field for a hit. The next time up, the pitcher, still convinced that he could fool Lajoie with a slow pitch, threw Larry a changeup. The big second baseman smoked a drive down the third base line, again handcuffing Moriarty, who was lucky to escape being skulled as the drive whizzed past him. The white-faced Moriarty walked to the mound and hissed angrily, "If you give that Frenchman another slow one, so help me, I'll kill you—unless Lajoie gets me first."

Lajoie became the player-manager of the Cleveland club after the 1904 season, and the team was renamed the "Naps" in his honor. Lajoie took over a fourth place club. His key players, in addition to the player-manager himself, were third baseman Bill Bradley, rightfielder Elmer Flick, and righthander Adrian "Addie" Joss. Flick, a future Hall of Famer, had taken the same path to Cleveland from Philadelphia as Lajoie. Joss, another Hall of Famer, was a tall, lanky righthander who pitched with an exaggerated pinwheel motion, making it difficult for hitters to pick up the ball. He had won 49 games in his first three years with Cleveland and was on his way to a great career.

Cleveland had a mediocre season in 1905, Lajoie's first managerial season, finishing fifth, 19 games off the pace. Flick led the league with a low .308 batting average and in triples and slugging average. Joss had a 20–12 record and a 2.01 ERA. Hampered by injuries and the new burden of playing and managing, Lajoie hit .329, but he played in less than half of the club's games. The 1906 season was a brighter one for Lajoie, as his club moved up to third place. He rebounded to hit .355 and lead the league with 214 hits. Flick had another great year, and the accomplished Joss pitched superbly.

The normally calm and easygoing Lajoie showed some of the strain of managing one day in Cleveland, protesting that a discolored and misshapen baseball should be discarded from a game. Ty Cobb described Lajoie's out-of-character belligerence in a colorful anecdote in his *Ty Cobb—My Life in Baseball*:

"Lajoie ... protested to umpire Tommy Connolly, demanding a new ball. 'You'll hit against the same ball as the Tigers did,' answered Connolly.... 'Now stand in there and give me no more of your tongue.'

"'Why, you Irish immigrant!' yelled Lajoie. 'I remember you when you couldn't say "ball." You just said "B-r-r" and we had to guess what you meant!'

"'You French chowderhead!' roared Connolly. 'I remember you when you carried everything you owned in a paper suitcase!'

"Lajoie and Connolly were now wrestling for the ball.

"'Out it goes!'

"'It stays in!'

"With a sudden wrench, Lajoie got possession, rared back and heaved with all his might. Over the grandstand into the gloom sailed the horse-hide—so discolored you could hardly follow its flight.

"'Now it's out!' cried Lajoie triumphantly.

"'And so are you!' said Connolly, jerking his thumb."

Lajoie's club slipped to fourth place in 1907 as only Flick and Joss played up to form. Player-manager Lajoie hit .299, the first time he had fallen below .300 in his major league career. The high point in the Naps' season came on September 4th when the Cleveland fans showed their appreciation of Lajoie by presenting him with a wagonload of gifts plus a live black sheep. After the presentation Addie Joss paid his respects to his boss in his own way, pitching a one-hitter against the Tigers.

Lajoie was an understanding manager who was considered extremely lenient with his players. He reached a new high in forgiveness on one occasion during the season. First baseman George Stovall went into a slump and Lajoie decided to move him to a lower place in the batting order. Stovall responded by arguing with his manager and emphasizing his annoyance by hitting Lajoie over the head with a chair. The sports-writers assumed this would be curtains for the irate Stovall. The French-man was asked if he would keep Stovall on the club. Lajoie shrugged and replied, "Why not? He's a good player and we need him. That chair business was just one of those things."

Lajoie earlier had shown his ability to let bygones be bygones. He got along well with his star outfielder, Elmer Flick, although that had not always been the case. Researcher Al Kermisch reported the following in SABR's 1996 publication *The Baseball Research Journal*:

> Hall of Famers Nap Lajoie and Elmer Flick were hardhitters with the Philadelphia Phillies from 1898 through 1900. On May 31, 1900, Lajoie and Flick were missing from the Phils lineup and the club issued a statement that they were injured in morning practice. It finally came out that they had engaged in a fist fight and that Lajoie had broken his thumb and received a black eye. After the fight Flick left the clubhouse, vowing he would not play again with the team.

Lajoie's 1908 club was his best, even though neither he nor any of his players had especially good offensive seasons. Lajoie hit only .289, and first baseman George Stovall led the team with an unspectacular .292. The Naps' offensive weakness was offset by its remarkable pitching, as the staff led the league with a 2.02 ERA, led by Addie Joss' sparkling 1.16 ERA. The Naps were in fourth place as late as August, but they rose to second place behind Detroit on the strength of a ten-game winning streak. The teams were tied for first place on October 2 as the teams' aces, Chicago's workhorse righthander Ed Walsh and Joss, met in a classic pitching duel.

The game was scoreless until the third inning when Walsh wild-pitched in a run. Walsh recovered to strike out Lajoie's men, one after another. But Joss was even more impressive. Protecting a one run lead with the pennant at stake, he did not give up a hit, and he induced so many ground balls that Stovall had 16 putouts at first base. Walsh finished with 15 strikeouts, allowing only four singles and a walk. Three pinch hitters came up in the ninth, and Joss sent the first two men down with ease. The third hitter, pull hitting Brian Anderson, sent a hard bouncer over third base, ordinarily a base hit. But Bill Bradley, stationing himself behind third base on his own initiative, threw Anderson out, saving Joss' perfect game. The no-hitter was only the second perfect game in the modern era.

Both teams won their season finales, but the Tigers, because they had not made up a rained-out game, won the pennant by ½ game. Lajoie protested, with considerable justification, that had the Tigers played the rained-out game and lost, the teams would have tied for the pennant and a playoff would have been necessary. But this was the time before the current rule requiring that such games be played or replayed if their outcome could determine the pennant winner.

The Naps of 1909 lacked the pitching excellence of the previous year, despite the addition of the aging Cy Young, and the club was no longer competitive. Lajoie, never happy as a player-manager, stepped down in August with his club playing .500 ball and languishing in fourth place. Lajoie told writers that he was relieved at leaving the running of the club to someone else, and that he felt that his play had suffered because of the demands of managing. Relieved of his burdens, he returned to the lineup after a wrist injury and hit .324, third in the league in hitting behind Ty Cobb and Eddie Collins.

Lajoie came back in 1910 with a vintage performance. He led the league in hits and doubles and barely lost the batting title to Ty Cobb in a famous season-ending controversy. The season ended with Cobb officially credited with a .3848 average to Lajoie's .3841. On the last day of the season, in a doubleheader, Larry had eight "hits" in eight trips. Six of the safeties were outright gifts on bunt singles on which St. Louis Browns rookie third baseman John "Red" Corriden was unable to make a play. He had been ordered to play so deep at third that he was unable to throw out Lajoie, who was not a fast runner.

On one of Lajoie's other at-bats he hit a sharp grounder to shortstop Bobby Wallace, and Wallace threw wild to first base. The official scorer properly ruled the play an error. Shortly after the ruling, the official scorer received an unsigned note offering him a suit of clothes if he changed the error to what would have been Lajoie's ninth hit. The scorer refused to change his call and Cobb was awarded the title. Ty received a luxury car given by the Chalmers Auto Company. Ban Johnson ordered the firing of the Browns' manager, who had turned the game into a farce, and the Chalmers Company awarded a second car to Lajoie. In a final twist to the story, subsequent research by *The Sporting News* revealed that Cobb's official average was inflated because one of his games mistakenly was counted twice. This would have given Lajoie a higher average.

Lajoie hit .365 in 1911 but played in only 90 games because of an injury. His boss that year was another player-manager, first baseman George Stovall, he of the flying chair incident. The unflappable Lajoie got along beautifully with the man who had originally played under his direction, never asking to be traded. Lajoie played well in 1912, but he missed many games with recurring back problems. He hit a respectable .335 in 1913 but slowed down significantly in the field, and the Indians released him after the season. Larry finished his major league career with Connie Mack's Athletics. He still loved to play, and in 1917, when he was 43, the stylish Lajoie hit .380 over a full season with Toronto in the International League.

Lajoie hit over .300 in 16 of his 21 major league seasons, with a lifetime .338 batting average. He had 3,242 hits (tenth highest all-time), 657 doubles (sixth highest all-time), and 1599 RBI. He led second basemen in fielding in six seasons. Lajoie had a managerial record of 377–309 (for a .550 percentage). He ranks 16th among player-managers, with 639 games in which he both played and managed. Lajoie died in Daytona Beach, Florida, on February 7, 1959. He was elected to the Hall of Fame in 1937.

FIELDER JONES

Fielder Allison Jones was born on August 13, 1871, in Shinglehouse, Pennsylvania. He played on a local baseball team until he was 21, and began playing professionally in 1893 in the Ohio-Pennsylvania League as a catcher-outfielder. He also played with teams in Corning, New York, and Springfield, Massachusetts, before catching on in the National League in 1896 with the Brooklyn Bridegrooms. Jones made good immediately as a slap-hitting rightfielder when he hit .354 in 104 games. Over the next four

Fielder Jones was a tough, strong-willed outfielder whose weak-hitting Chicago White Sox finished in the first division—even winning one World Championship—in each of his five years as their player-manager. A brilliant field leader and tactician, he was one of the best fielding outfielders of his era.

seasons the 5 foot, 11 inch, 180-pound, left-hand-hitting Jones established himself as one of the better players in the league, hitting around .300 consistently. He set the table for the harder hitters following him in the lineup, and he fielded his position so effectively that some fans thought the name "Fielder" was a description of his play rather than his given name.

Jones was one of the 100 National Leaguers who jumped to the new American League in 1901. He signed with the Chicago White Stockings and became an immediate favorite of the fans with his aggressive, alert play. He was especially adept at getting on base, ranking second in the league to Nap Lajoie in walks and on base percentage, and fourth with 38 stolen bases. He continued his steady play in the next two years, and in 1904, 42 games into the season, he replaced leftfielder-manager Jim "Nixey" Callahan.

Player-manager Jones took over a fourth place team, and he improved it sufficiently to finish in third place, six games behind Jimmy Collins' pennant-winning Pilgrims. Jones started his managerial career with a team largely dependent on its pitching staff. The only players of proven hitting ability were shortstop George Davis, who had come over from the Giants; third baseman Lee Tannehill; and Jones himself, but the club had no power hitters. The most effective pitchers were righthanders Frank Owen and Frank Smith, and lefties Nick Altrock and Doc White. Of the four, only White and Altrock would have notable careers. Righthander Ed Walsh, a future Hall of Famer, was a 20-year-old rookie. Jones' club had a great start under their new boss, moving briefly into the lead before reality set in and the club slipped back to third place. Jones' performance at the plate suffered, as his batting average slipped more than 44 points after he took over as manager.

Jones' club moved up to second place in 1905 with virtually the same lineup, playing at essentially the same level as in the previous season. The difference was that the Pilgrims and the Highlanders flopped, and Connie Mack's Athletics were greatly improved. The A's took a seven game lead into early September and held on to win the pennant by two games after two crucial wins over the White Stockings. The A's were led by the eccentric lefthander Rube Waddell and a very normal threesome; lefthander Eddie Plank and righthanders Andy Coakley and Chief Bender. The White Stockings pitching staff led the league, with a 1.99 ERA, with the same standouts—Altrock, Owen, White, and Smith. The pitching highlight of the season came on July 1 when Frank Owen just missed becoming the first man to pitch a doubleheader shutout, as the St. Louis Browns scored one run off him in the two games. Player-manager Jones was second in the league in scoring runs, despite an undistinguished .245 batting average.

Jones by that time had become widely recognized as a master at squeezing out runs with a weak-hitting team while putting together a club with an exceptionally tight defense. Baseball historians also credit him with devising innovative defenses. But, on the down side, Jones had a sullen manner and he was one of the most vicious umpire-baiters of his time. He was famous for his habit of racing in frequently from his center field post and being ejected for kicking dirt on umpires and abusing them with violent language. Jones was a strict taskmaster with his players, suspending them frequently for drinking or not staying in playing condition, and he fined his underlings for their mental mistakes more often than most managers.

Jones' 1906 club is one of the most famous teams in the game's history. The weak-hitting Sox got off to a slow start, falling to five games under .500 by June 1. But they improved and rose to fourth place by August 1. On the following day, Doc White pitched a 3–0 win over Boston and the club went off on a tear, winning close games consistently as Owen, Altrock, White, and Ed Walsh pitched brilliantly. Over the next three weeks the White Sox ran off a winning streak of 19 straight games (still the longest in American League history), and ended the streak in first place.

The 1906 season would prove to be the highlight of Jones' baseball career, despite his career-low .230 batting average and his team's league-lowest .230 batting average and 570 runs scored. A Chicago reporter summed up the White Sox offensive effort with the comment, "A typical rally included a base on balls, a sacrifice, a passed ball, and a long fly." George Davis had the club's only mildly impressive offensive season, leading the club with a .277 batting average and finishing third in the league in RBI. Again, it was the pitching staff that carried the club, as nearly one-third of the its wins were won by only one run. Owen (22–13 and a league-best 1.52 ERA), Altrock (20–13), White (18–6), and young Ed Walsh were superb. Walsh had his breakthrough year with 17 wins and 10 shutouts. The 1906 club has gone down in history as "The Hitless Wonders."

The White Sox took on Frank Chance's powerful, overwhelmingly favored Cubs in the only all–Chicago World Series. The Cubs had won 116 games to the White Stockings' 93. The first game was a pitchers' duel between the Cubs' Three Finger Brown and Nick Altrock. The White Sox won 2–1, scoring the winning run in the sixth inning on Brown's error. Ed Reulbach won the second game 7–1, and Walsh returned the favor with a two-hit shutout victory over Jack Pfiester. The White Stockings' three runs came on a sixth inning, bases-loaded triple by lightly-regarded White Sox reserve infielder George Rohe, a last minute replacement for George Davis. In the fourth game Brown outpitched Altrock to win a 1–0 shutout and even the Series at two-all. But, in the key fifth game, Jones' weak-hitting club surprised by attacking Cub pitchers with 12 hits to win an 8–6 victory for Walsh over Pfiester. Doc White clinched the Series with a relatively easy 8–3 victory. As a Chicago writer put it, "David had beaten Goliath."

Jones personally managed only two hits in the six games, but his club's offense was adequate, led unexpectedly by Rohe and second baseman Frank Isbell. But, as Ed Reulbach pointed out, Jones' "... adroit method of matching his weakest points against the enemies' strongest, and his own strongest against their weakness, that he hoped to make a relatively inferior pitching staff show up as effectively as possible against an admittedly stronger one ... was entirely successful."

After his great season, Jones hit owner Charles Comiskey up for a raise. Commy, never known as a big spender, haggled with Jones for some time before agreeing to a $10,000 salary for 1907. Before signing the contract, Jones wrote a piece for the *Saturday Evening Post* which reads like an early day Curt Flood argument, to wit:

> There are salaries of more than $6,000 per man paid under these [baseball] contracts, and that for a short season of 154 ball games is not a bad rate of compensation…. From the ballplayers' standpoint, I am practically a slave. So is every ballplayer in the 31 [major and minor] leagues…. We are 'commercial chattels' in the sense that we cannot sell our ability … in any market to which we may elect….

In 1907 Jones' club, essentially unchanged from the previous year, was outclassed by the Ty Cobb–led Tigers and by the improved Athletics. It was the same old White Sox story—good pitching and defense but weak hitting. The Sox led the league well into the first half of the season but fell back to finish in third place, 5½ games behind the pennant-winning Tigers. White tied Addie Joss for the league lead with 27 wins, and Walsh, then in his prime, pitched magnificently. But Altrock, Owen, and Smith had aged and lost their effectiveness. 1908 was a carbon copy of 1907 as the Sox finished in third place, 1½ games behind the Tigers. It took a superhuman season by Ed Walsh to keep them that close. On October 5 Walsh beat Detroit for his 40th win, and the White Sox were only half a game behind the Tigers as the season moved into its last day. But on that final day the bone-tired Walsh, having worked in 13 of the club's previous 16 games, was unable to pitch. Jones selected Doc White to pitch the big game, but White was ineffective and the Tigers won 7–0 to clinch the pennant.

Jones retired after the season "to earn some money for a change." He went into the lumber business in Seattle until 1914 when the seventh place St. Louis Terriers, of the Federal League, hired him with only 40 games left in the season. Jones placed himself on the active list and became a player-manager again at 43. He played in only five games, and this crowd-pleasing gesture had no effect on the sad-sack Terriers, who finished dead last. Federal League officials shuffled their clubs in an attempt to strengthen teams in key cities, and St. Louis was one of those key cities. As a result, the St. Louis, Chicago, and Pittsburgh clubs finished the season in a tie. However, Jones' club played two more games than the Chicago Whales and split the games, thereby losing the pennant to the Whales by one percentage point. Jones again was technically a player-manager by virtue of a small number of token appearances in seven games. The Federal League ceased operations after the season and Jones moved back to the American League to become the bench manager of the St. Louis Browns. He managed the Browns unsuccessfully until mid-season of 1918 when he retired from the game and returned to his lumber business.

Tough, strong-willed Fielder Jones had a lifetime .285 batting average and 359 stolen bases in 1788 games. He was rated one of the best fielding centerfielders of his era. Jones is best remembered, though, as a brilliant field leader and tactician. He had a creditable 683–582 (.540) managerial record, and his White Sox teams finished in the first division in each of the five seasons he managed them. Jones succumbed to a heart ailment at age 63 in Portland, Oregon.

10

Catcher-Managers

There have been fewer catcher-managers than their advantageous position on the field would suggest. Buck Ewing was the most important catcher-manager in the 1800s, but, surprisingly, few of the other catchers of the pre–1900 period were player-managers. The notable catcher-managers of the post–1900 era were Mickey Cochrane and Gabby Hartnett (both discussed in Chapter 11), and Roger Bresnahan, Red Dooin, Jimmie Wilson, and Bill Carrigan.

ROGER BRESNAHAN

Roger Philip Bresnahan was born in Toledo, Ohio, on June 11, 1879, the son of parents born in Tralee, County Kerry, Ireland. The stocky (5 foot 9 inch, 200 pound) youngster played all positions on the Toledo sandlots. He began his professional career at 16 as a righthand pitcher with Lima in the Ohio State League, and later that season he signed with the Washington Statesmen of the National League. He made his debut on August 27, 1897, limiting St. Louis to six hits in a 3–0 shutout win. The sturdy teenager won three of his next five starts and finished with a 4–0 record. Flushed with success, the cocky youngster held out for more money, and the club responded by releasing him. He remained in the high minors for the next two seasons until the Chicago Colts brought him up for the traditional "cup of coffee." Baltimore Orioles playing manager John McGraw picked him up in 1901. After Bresnahan proved ineffective in two starts, McGraw played him in the infield and outfield, and then behind the plate after veteran catcher Wilbert Robinson was injured. When McGraw moved to the Giants in July 1902, he brought Bresnahan with him.

Over the next two seasons the versatile Bresnahan excelled wherever McGraw needed him, mostly in center field, but also at first base and behind the plate. In 1903 he established himself as a fine offensive player, finishing fourth in the league in hitting, with a .350 average, and ranking second in on-base percentage. By 1905 he became the Giants' first-string catcher. He had become a close friend of McGraw, no surprise because the two men were identical in personality, temperament, and approach to the game. They were physically and mentally tough on themselves and everyone else with whom they came in contact. Both men were completely capable of doing anything to win. Like his boss, Bresnahan was a hard-drinking brawler who baited umpires unmercifully and found himself in constant hot water with league officials and his employers.

In 1905 the Giants won their second straight pennant, with Bresnahan skillfully handling the Giants' star righthanders Christy Mathewson, Leon "Red" Ames, Joe McGinnity, and Luther "Dummy" Taylor, and left-hander George "Hooks" Wiltse. Bresnahan sparked the club, hitting .302 during the season and .313 in the Giants' World Series over the Athletics. That Series is remembered best for Mathewson's three shutout wins, all caught by Bresnahan. He continued to excel over the next three years, though the Giants were outplayed by the Cubs. During this period, base-ball writers gave Bresnahan the colorful nickname "The Duke of Tralee," although he never visited his parents' birthplace.

Bresnahan's reputation as a resourceful player was enhanced by his innovative use of protective equipment. In 1905, after being beaned and hospitalized with a head injury, he was the first player to experiment with a batting helmet manufactured by the A. J. Reach Company. This helmet resembled the leather football helmets used at the time, cut vertically down the center with each half covering a side of the player's head. On April 11, 1907, Bresnahan was overwhelmingly ridiculed when he became the first catcher to wear guards over his pants. Bresnahan devised bulky, rudi-mentary catcher's shin guards with a flap that covered the leg up to the thigh. The following year Bresnahan improved the flimsy wire catcher's mask then in use with leather-bound padding to better cushion the shock of balls tipped back into the mask.

Bresnahan had made no secret of his interest in becoming a man-ager. After the 1908 season McGraw arranged a trade with the struggling St. Louis Cardinals. He convinced Cardinals president M. Stanley Robi-son that Bresnahan was the man he needed as catcher-manager. Robison was so convinced that he gave up promising righthander Arthur "Bugs" Raymond and outfielder Jack "Red" Murray, and agreed to give Bresna-han a completely free hand in directing the team. So playing-manager

Bresnahan took over a moribund, last-place club, which had the weakest pitching staff and hitting attack in the league. Bresnahan improved the club marginally in his first managerial year, as the Cards moved up a notch to seventh place while winning five more games than in the previous season. He had little to work with, as powerful first baseman Ed Konetchy was his only productive hitter and he had a mediocre pitching staff. Bresnahan, his best playing days clearly behind him, hit .244. But the enthusiastic catcher-manager injected life into the club.

Bresnahan's team finished seventh again in 1910. Konetchy was the only potent offensive performer, although little second baseman Miller Huggins set the table for Konetchy, leading the league in walks and tying for second place in runs scored. The fiery player-manager caught about one-half of the Cards' games, hitting .278, and was constantly warned by the league office for baiting umpires. There was more excitement in Bresnahan's third season as player-manager. In March 1911 Cardinals president Robison died unexpectedly and left the club to his niece, Mrs. Helene Hathaway Britton, making her the first female major league club owner. The improved Cardinals were only three games out of first place in July when they barely escaped a catastrophic tragedy. A New York, New Haven, and Hartford Railroad train transporting the club to Boston plunged down an embankment near Bridgeport, Connecticut, killing 14 passengers. The team's Pullman car was originally hooked on immediately behind the baggage coaches and, when the noise kept his players awake, Bresnahan requested to have his players placed in another car. The car vacated by the Cardinals players was crushed in the wreck; none of the players were injured.

The Cardinals went on to finish in fifth place, finishing just over .500 in what would prove to be their best season under Bresnahan. Konetchy led the attack and Bresnahan duplicated his 1910 performance with a .278 batting average. The season marked the end of the harmonious relationship between Bresnahan and Mrs. Britton. She felt she had a good understanding of baseball, an opinion that Bresnahan did not share. And she made matters worse by criticizing him in the press.

The 1912 Cardinals reverted to their incompetent ways, slipping back to sixth place. Bresnahan hit .333, but injuries restricted his playing time. The frustrations of dealing with his mediocre team were made worse by his frequent arguments with Mrs. Britton. Fred Lieb wrote in his *The St. Louis Cardinals*, "[Bresnahan] was as truculent and as much a battler of umpires and rival players as was [McGraw].... Bresnahan, reared by McGraw in a tough baseball school, wasn't particular about his language. He talked to Lady Lee Britton as he would have talked to ... Stanley Robison." Predictably, Bresnahan's profanity-laced exchanges with her led to his firing at the end of the 1912 season. Bresnahan insisted that the club pay him both as a catcher and a manager under the terms of a five-year contract he had signed just before M. Stanley Robison's death. Eventually, the Cardinals paid Bresnahan a $20,000 settlement.

The Cardinals sold Bresnahan to the Cubs, who utilized him as a backup catcher under second baseman–manager Johnny Evers. He remained with the Cubs as a player until the 1915 season when he replaced Cubs manager Hank O'Day and returned to his old catcher-manager role. But Bresnahan's Cubs bore little resemblance to the crackerjack Cubs of former years. They offered mediocre hitting, average defense, and inconsistent pitching, except for king-sized lefthander James "Hippo" Vaughn. Burdened by his club's inadequacies, Bresnahan did well to manage the team to a fourth place finish, 17½ games off the pace. 1915 was Bresnahan's last season, both as an active player and as a major league manager.

After leaving the Cubs, Bresnahan managed his hometown Toledo club for several years before rejoining his old friend McGraw. He coached for the Giants from 1925 through 1928, helping develop many of McGraw's young stars, most notably Carl Hubbell and Mel Ott. After leaving McGraw, he coached for the Detroit Tigers before retiring from the game in 1932. Upon leaving the game, he worked for the Toledo city government and ran unsuccessfully for county commissioner in 1944.

Bresnahan had a .279 batting average in 1448 games, 324 of which he managed. His teams had an unimpressive 328–432 (.432) record. But Bresnahan's career statistics do not reflect his versatility, colorful personality, or contribution to the game. John McGraw wrote in his *My Thirty Years in Baseball*: "Bresnahan was about the best catcher of all times. The only other catcher that I would rank alongside him is Buck Ewing.... Bresnahan was possessed of as much catching brains as any man I ever saw.... Roger seemed to do everything right by intuition. It was never necessary to tell him anything twice." Bresnahan was voted into the Hall of Fame just a few weeks after his death in Toledo on December 4, 1944.

DOOIN AND WILSON

The Philadelphia Phillies have had two catcher-managers, both not well remembered despite having been field managers for a significant number of games. Charles "Red" Dooin was the Phillies' field manager in 354 games (the most by any catcher), and Jimmie Wilson played in 269 games as the club's manager.

Dooin was born in Cincinnati on June 12, 1879. The compact, right-hand-hitting redhead did not play any position except catcher from the time he began playing on local sandlots, through the minors, and then on to the Phillies, who signed him in 1902. He was regarded as a competent receiver and handler of pitchers from the start, but his weakness as a hitter prevented him from taking over as the club's regular catcher until his third year with the Phillies in 1904. He was appointed manager in 1910, and he led the Phillies into a fourth place finish that year, largely on the strength of a career offensive year by leftfielder Sherry Magee.

The most important story in 1911 was the marvelous performance of rookie righthander Grover Cleveland Alexander, purchased from the Syracuse Chiefs of the International League. Pitching in the Phillies' tiny ballpark, the future Hall of Famer was a finished pitcher at 23 with an effortless, graceful pitching style, good fastball and curve, and superb control. He had a spectacular season, with 28 wins, four consecutive shutouts and 10 in all, 31 complete games, 367 innings pitched, and a 2.57 ERA. With Alexander earning more than one-third of their wins, and newly-acquired first baseman Fred Luderus, Magee, and rightfielder Clifford "Gavvy" Cravath having good seasons, catcher-manager Dooin's club again finished in fourth place.

The Phillies slipped in 1912, finishing in the second division, as Alexander was unable to duplicate his rookie year. Dooin had a poor year himself, hitting only .234 in 58 games. The only positive development for Dooin in the year came when the National League banished Phillies president Horace Fogel for publicly charging that Roger Bresnahan had told his Cardinals to "take it easy" when playing against Bresnahan's old team, the Giants. Dooin and Fogel had clashed repeatedly over player trades and team discipline, so Dooin was greatly relieved when Fogel was given the boot by the National League Board of Directors.

Dooin's team came back in 1913 to finish in second place, well behind McGraw's Giants, although the Phillies were in first place through late June before they faded. The Phillies were carried by Cravath's powerful hitting, and excellent pitching by second year righthander Tom Seaton and by Alexander. But Dooin's managerial career came to a disappointing end in 1914 as his pitching staff disintegrated, with the exception of the brilliant Alexander, who won 27 games. Most telling, the club's home attendance dropped 70 percent from the previous year. Dooin himself was essentially finished as a player, as his feeble .178 average in 53 games indicated, and he was fired after the season ended. The 37-year-old veteran played sparingly for Cincinnati and the Giants before leaving the playing field for good in 1916.

Dooin's final impact on the major league scene came in a 1920 investigation of gambling, triggered by the 1919 Black Sox scandal. Dooin claimed that he and a number of his 1908 teammates were offered more cash to throw games to the Giants that year than the White Sox players were promised if they would throw the 1919 World Series to the Reds. Dooin reflected the dilemma faced by many of the relatively low-salaried players in those years who were offered bribes. In a remorseful statement he said, "I have never said anything about this before now because the other players and myself believed it would be in the best interests of baseball not to say anything, as none of us accepted any of the bribes." Dooin, who died at age 71 in Rochester, New York, finished with a 392–370 (.514) average as a manager and a .240 career batting average.

JIMMIE WILSON

Jimmie Wilson was a native Philadelphian who played and managed much of his career with the Phillies. Born on July 23, 1900, the strapping (6 foot 1 inch, 200 pound) youngster made a name for himself as a local soccer star before beginning his professional career at 19 with a four year stint in the high minors. The Phillies brought him up before the 1923 season, and he took over as the regular catcher in 1925, hitting .328 and catching skillfully. The Phillies traded him to the Cardinals early in the 1928 campaign, where he became one of the Cards' most important players. He handled such starters as lefthander Bill Sherdel and righthanders Jesse Haines and Grover Cleveland Alexander, as the Cardinals won the pennant. Wilson hit .325 the next year and .318 in 1930 as St. Louis bounced back to win the pennant. The Cards won the pennant again in 1931, and Wilson, his catching and leadership skills now well recognized, finished sixth in the MVP National League voting, despite hitting a modest .274 in 115 games.

After the 1933 season the Cardinals traded Wilson to the Phillies, where he became the club's catcher-manager. In his *Rowdy Richard*, Dick Bartell wrote: "Wilson and [Frankie] Frisch had been rivals for the Cards' managing job when Gabby Street was fired halfway through the 1933 season.... So when Frankie got the job, there's no way Wilson could stay." Wilson had an early indication of the tribulations that lay ahead when the Phillies, who had finished seventh in 1933 and, as usual, were cash poor, traded star rightfielder Chuck Klein to the Cubs before the season for three lackluster players and $125,000. The Phillies had lost a good deal of money because of dwindling home attendance, and new Phillies President Gerald P. Nugent needed the money to keep the financially strapped franchise afloat. Klein was only one of many Phillies stars sold to keep Nugent's team afloat; others included Dick Bartell, Dolph Camilli, Bucky Walters, Lou Chiozza, Curt Davis, Claude Passeau, Kirbe Higbe, and Morrie Arnovich.

Wilson inherited a seventh place team, and the writers saw little hope for improvement. The Phils started the season with a young infield of Dolph Camilli at first, Lou Chiozza at second, Bartell at short, and future pitching star Bucky Walters at third. The outfielders were veterans Ethan Allen, George "Kiddo" Davis, and Johnny Moore. Wilson and Al Todd split the catching duties. The pitching staff was a collection of used-up veterans and untried youngsters, and the club was never in the running, finishing in seventh place, 37 games off the pace. The stars of the club were Bartell, who hit .310 and fielded brilliantly at short, and righthanded sidearmer Curt Davis, a 31-year-old rookie who had a 19–17 record and a commendable 2.95 ERA. Player-manager Wilson hit .292.

Bartell, a highly opinionated man, especially when it came to evaluating his managers, described Wilson as a man he liked and respected as a player but the "worst manager" he ever played for. He wrote that Wilson was "high strung, noisy, and openly critical" of his players, although a good developer of pitchers. Other players described Wilson as a manager who had little to say to them and who rarely called club meetings.

The story was the same in 1935, another seventh place team hurt by the loss of Bartell, who was traded to the Giants. It was a Phillies season notable only for the Phillies' participation in the first major league night game in Cincinnati. By this time, Wilson had developed a clear understanding of the term "Phillies player," which was used widely. It was a derogatory term indicating that some Phillies players tended to be more concerned about their own statistics than the welfare of their club. Baseball men had the feeling that Phillies players' offensive statistics were enhanced by tiny Baker Bowl, and that players did not perform as well when they were traded to clubs contending for pennants. Critics often cited Chuck Klein as a prime example of a "Phillies player," as Klein did not play nearly as well with the contending Cubs as he had with the Phillies.

Dick Bartell used himself as an example of a player who played selfishly when he was with the Phillies. He wrote that Phillies players tended to be much more concerned with their own statistics rather than that of the team. An example of that selfish attitude occurred when a player sacrificed a runner on his own in the hope that he would obtain a single if he beat the bunt out but would not be charged with a time at bat if he were thrown out at first. This was the player mentality faced by player-manager Wilson.

Wilson continued as a part-time catcher for the Phils in 1936 and 1937, hitting nearly .280 in both years as his playing career wound down. He played in only a few games in 1938 with the last place club and was dismissed after that season. He coached for Cincinnati in 1939 and 1940, although the Reds returned the 40-year-old to their playing roster after regular catcher Willard Hershberger committed suicide in early August 1940. After playing in 16 games as a backup catcher, Wilson ended his playing career in style in the Reds' World Series win over Detroit, catching six of the seven games, hitting .353, and stealing a base.

Wilson was the bench manager of the Cubs during the 1941–43 seasons. He had only slightly more success in Chicago, finishing in sixth place twice and fifth once. He left the Cubs after they lost nine of their first 10 games in 1944 and completed his career as a Reds coach.

Wilson had a .284 batting average over his 18 seasons as a player, although he had little power. But he was one of the best defensive catchers of his time and a good handler of pitchers. He retired with a very poor overall 493–735 (.401) managerial record, with no first division finishes and two last place finishes in his eight full years as a manager. Wilson retired from baseball in 1947 and died later that year in Bradenton, Florida.

BILL CARRIGAN

William Francis Carrigan was one of the most successful player-managers of the pre–World War I era. Born in Lewiston, Maine, on October 22, 1883, he played local baseball when he was not working on nearby farms. He was a catcher on several minor league teams until he was recommended to Boston Red Sox player-manager Jimmy Collins before the 1906 season. The righthand-hitting, 5 foot 9 inch, 175-pounder joined the Boston club in mid-season of that year, playing in 37 games and hitting .211. The stocky, 23-year-old Carrigan impressed with his catching and throwing, but he did not have an extra-base hit among his 23 hits. Over the next five years Carrigan shared the catching duties, except for two years when he caught most of the club's games. He was a tough-minded man who insisted upon calling every pitch of every game he caught, his firmness earning him the nickname "Rough."

The 1912 Red Sox won the World Championship under first baseman Jake Stahl, but the club slipped badly in 1913 and, in mid-season, the 29-year-old Carrigan became the Sox's player-manager. He took over an under-performing fifth place team which had the magnificent Harry Hooper-Tris Speaker-Duffy Lewis outfield, a fair infield, and several decent pitchers who were performing well below their previous season's performances. After a marvelous 34–5 year in 1912, righthander Smoky Joe Wood broke his thumb in the spring and lost velocity on his pitches. Righthanders Hugh Bedient, Charley Hall, and Buck O'Brien also had lost their effectiveness. The club perked up a bit after Carrigan took over, led by the brilliant Speaker, and managed to move up to fourth place as the season ended.

The 1914 Red Sox reacted favorably to Carrigan's steady leadership and finished second behind Connie Mack's powerful club, which featured his famous "100,000 infield" of Stuffy McInnis, Eddie Collins, Jack Barry, and Frank "Home Run" Baker. Carrigan's club was sparked by the incomparable Speaker and the best pitching staff in the league. Lefthander George "Babe" Ruth, purchased from the Baltimore Orioles, made his major league debut on July 11 against the Indians, leaving with the game tied 3–3 after pitching seven innings. The Red Sox were in sixth place in early July but they recovered, playing at a 51–24 pace to finish in second place. Player-manager Carrigan hit .253 in 82 games.

Ruth's presence was hardly a catalyst for the Sox's improved performance, as Carrigan used him infrequently, apparently feeling that the 19-year-old youngster needed more time on the bench to become acclimated to big league baseball. Robert W. Creamer, in his *Babe— The Legend Comes to Life*, wrote: "The problem may have been one of behavior.... Ruth was the 1914 equivalent of a 'hot dog,' and the veteran players resented him." In August Red Sox owner Joseph J. Lannin arranged for Ruth to be sent to Providence in the International League, where he remained for the rest of the season. Years later Carrigan said, "I've read many times that Ruth was sent down for more seasoning, but that's not true. He was already a finished pitcher, good enough for us. But we were out of the pennant race, and Lannin sent Ruth down to help Providence win theirs."

Carrigan was a civil, well-mannered man who came from a middle-class, New England background. He had a pleasant, ruggedly-tough face and he projected an unmistakable air of authority. Corrigan was a demanding manager but he treated his players with affection and respect. He was profane but was never known to curse his players or humiliate them in public. He was a natural leader who demanded and received the respect of his players.

Carrigan was high on the pitchers he had in spring training in 1915. Babe Ruth had returned, but righthanders Ernie Shore and George "Rube" Foster, and lefthanders Dutch Leonard and Ray Collins, were Carrigan's projected starters. After the season got under way, these starters faltered, and by late May the Red Sox were well below .500, far behind the contending White Sox and Tigers. But in June, after Ruth was inserted into the starting rotation, player-manager Carrigan's club came alive. The team went on a sustained winning streak, took the lead, and clinched the pennant on September 30, winning 101 games. The runner-up Tigers became the first team to finish in second place despite winning 100 games. Consistently good pitching was the key to the Sox's success. The club was led by Ray Foster's 19 wins, Ernie Shore's and Ruth's 18 victories, and 15 wins apiece for Joe Wood and Dutch Leonard. And submarining righthander Carl Mays was the best reliever in the league, providing Carrigan with a beautifully balanced pitching staff. Carrigan caught 44 games and hit .200.

Babe Ruth's off-field behavior (despite his recent marriage) and his uncontrolled spending habits were a continuing concern to Carrigan, who was fully appreciative of Ruth's potential as a hitter as well as a pitcher. Carrigan said, "He [Ruth] had no idea whatsoever of money. You've got to remember his background. He'd buy anything and everything. So I would draw Babe's pay and give him a little every day to spend."

The World Series was a matchup between the Sox's "scratch-out-runs" style and their sound pitching staff against the Phillies, who were propelled by rightfielder Gavvy Cravath, the dominant National League power hitter, and Grover Cleveland Alexander, the league's top pitcher. Alexander outpitched Shore to win the first game 3–1. Ruth made his only appearance in the Series when he pinch hit in the ninth inning and bounced out harmlessly. But the Red Sox rebounded to win the next four games, all by one-run margins, to become the Worlds Champions. Rube Foster won twice, and Ernie Shore and Dutch Leonard each won a game. Holding the dangerous Cravath to two hits in the Series was the key to the Sox win, along with the hitting of Duffy Lewis and Harry Hooper, who accounted for all of the club's three home runs and eight of its 11 RBI. Carrigan went hitless in the only game he caught.

The folding of the Federal League after the 1915 season made available a large number of former Federal League players. As a result, the owners had the opportunity to slash player salaries. Tris Speaker, the only Red Sox player to hit .300 in 1914 and 1915, and acknowledged to be the best defensive outfielder in the game, was offered a contract calling for a 50 percent cut from the annual $18,000 he had been paid the previous two years. Speaker held out for $15,000 the entire 1916 spring training season while training with the team. Just three days before the season opener, Lannin surprised everyone by announcing that he had sold Speaker to the Cleveland Indians for a record $50,000. Carrigan and his players were stunned by the deal but, always the resolute leader, Carrigan told his team, "All right, we've lost Speaker. We're not going to score as many runs but we're still a good team. We'll win again if you guys just get down to business."

With the team also losing Joe Wood, because of his salary cut, the otherwise unchanged Red Sox opened the season with four straight wins. But the club's offense stalled and Carrigan's club struggled along, playing no better than .500 ball through the first two months of the season. In late June the Red Sox rebounded with a vengeance. Foster pitched a no-hitter, and the rest of the starters—Ruth, Shore, Mays, and Leonard—regained their top form. The Sox took over first place from the Indians a month later. They widened the lead to six games and appeared to be running away with the pennant until they slumped badly in August. By early September the Red Sox were in a desperate fight for first place with the White Sox and the Tigers.

On September 12, as the club was leaving on its last western swing of the season, Carrigan announced he would retire after the season. On the western trip the Red Sox swept three games in Detroit and, after taking three of four in Cleveland, clinched the pennant. Ruth led the staff with 23 wins, nine shutouts, and a 1.75 ERA. Leonard and Mays both won 18 games, Shore collected 16, and Foster won 14. With a team batting average of .248 and without a potent power hitter, the Red Sox win again was built on a solid, well-rounded pitching staff.

The Red Sox faced the Brooklyn Robins in the Series. The first three games of the Series were tightly contested, each game decided by one run. Shore and lefthander Rube Marquard were tied 1–1 until the Sox moved into a 6–1 lead in the top of the ninth. The Robins fought back with four runs until Mays shut them down in relief, and the Sox won 6–5. In the second game, with the Robins leading 1–0, Babe Ruth tripled in the tying run and held the Robins scoreless to win 2–1 in 14 innings. Brooklyn won the third game, but Leonard and Shore won the next two games and the Sox were Worlds Champions again. In his last appearance as a player, Carrigan caught only one game in the Series, getting two hits in three at-bats. After the last game, Carrigan went out on the field to wave goodbye to the fans, and they applauded him loudly for several minutes.

Carrigan returned home to Lewiston, Maine, where he had a banking business. The Sox finished deep in the second division from 1922 through 1926, and Carrigan agreed to return as bench manager in 1927. But the conservative Carrigan could not help the club, finishing in last place from 1927 to 1929. His inability to improve his teams was attributed not only to his club's inferior talent, but also to his difficulty in adjusting

Bill Carrigan (left) and Bucky Harris were successful player-managers. Carrigan, a weak-hitting journeyman catcher, led the Boston Red Sox to World Championships in 1915 and 1916. Harris, a feisty second baseman, managed the Washington Senators to the World Championship in 1924, his first year as player-manager, and to a pennant win the following year. Carrigan retired after the 1916 season but returned in the late 1920s to manage (unsuccessfully) the Red Sox. Harris, who hit .274, managed 27 more seasons with the Senators and several other clubs, including the 1947 World Champion Yankees.

to the free-swinging, high-scoring game that major league baseball had become in the 1920s, influenced in large part by Carrigan's old problem child, Babe Ruth. Carrigan retired after the 1929 season to devote full-time to his banking business. He left the game with a 489–500 career managerial record (.494) but with an excellent 323–205 (.612) winning percentage during his years as a player-manager. He had a .257 lifetime batting average. Carrigan died at age 85 in his hometown.

11

Cochrane and Hartnett

Mickey Cochrane and Gabby Hartnett were two of the greatest catchers ever to play in the majors. Both Hall of Famers earned their selection to the Hall as players but also made their marks as player-managers.

MICKEY COCHRANE

Gordon Stanley "Mickey" Cochrane was born on April 6, 1903, in Bridgewater, Massachusetts, the son of Scotch-Irish immigrants. His father was employed as a coachman and caretaker for a wealthy Boston family. The dark-haired, well-built young man entered Boston University, where he worked his way through college by playing in bands and washing dishes. His most important sports activity at college was in football, where he starred at quarterback, running back, and kicker, and was the team captain in his senior year. Cochrane attracted national attention with a 53-yard dropkick against Tufts University. He also excelled in baseball, basketball, track, and boxing.

Cochrane began his professional career at 20 in 1923 with Dover, Delaware, of the Eastern Shore League, playing under the name "Frank King" to protect his amateur status. Cochrane wrote in his *Baseball— The Fan's Game* that he signed with the agreement that he would be made a free agent at the end of the season. The green young man, who had not caught before, was pressed into service as a catcher in an emergency. He broke in with four hits but with two muffed foul flies and two wild throws. Still, he hit .322 and gained enough familiarity with the catching position to be promoted in 1924 to Portland, Oregon, in the Pacific Coast League, where he hit .333.

The Philadelphia Athletics bought his contract after the season, and Connie Mack had his regular catcher, Cy Perkins, work with the young man during spring training in 1925. A fast learner, the lefthand-hitting Cochrane was an immediate sensation, starting on Opening Day, when he broke into the lineup by pinch hitting for Perkins. Mickey singled and his teammates told him that Perkins commented at the time, "There goes Perkins' job." He was right, as Mickey took over immediately as the A's regular catcher. Cochrane had his best game of that rookie season on May 21 when he hit three home runs in a game en route to a .331 average for the season.

The kid with the thick, matted black hair, ever-present five o'clock shadow, bright red face, and blazing blue eyes showed early signs of his characteristic fiery leadership and will to win. In his *Super Stars of Baseball*, sportswriter Bob Broeg wrote (perhaps with some exaggeration) of Cochrane's willingness to assert himself as soon as he became a regular:

> One time [in Cochrane's rookie year] when [lefthander] Rube Walberg hit a wild spell, walking the bases loaded and forcing in a run, Black Mike called time, stormed out to the mound, grabbed the pitcher by the shoulders and spun him around. To Walberg's surprise, Cochrane kicked him right in the seat of the pants and said, " Damn-it, Rube, settle down." Walberg, though startled, chuckled at the direct parental approach and did settle down to win the game."

Cochrane played well over the next three seasons as Mack put together a dominant team. In 1928 Cochrane was voted MVP by the league (this preceded the MVP awards that were awarded by the Baseball Writers' Association beginning in 1931), more for his leadership qualities than for his modest .293 batting average. From 1929 through 1931 the Athletics interrupted the Yankees' domination of the American League with three straight pennant wins. The 1929 club featured an infield of Jimmie Foxx, Max Bishop, Joe Boley, and Jimmy Dykes. Al Simmons was in left, George "Mule" Haas in center, and Edmund "Bing" Miller in right. Cochrane, then in his prime, was the catcher. The starters included left-handers Robert "Lefty" Grove and Rube Walberg, and righthanders George Earnshaw and Ed Rommel. This overpowering club led the league from start to finish in 1929, beating the Yankees by a whopping 18 games. Mack's club whipped the Cubs in a five-game World Series, remembered because the A's surprise first-game starter, righthander Howard Ehmke, beat the Cubs 3–1 and struck out a record 13 hitters. Cochrane, who had hit .331 during the regular season, hit .400 and drew seven of the 13 walks collected by the A's.

It was an acrimonious Series, and Commissioner Kenesaw M. Landis heard so much salty language from his box seat that he issued a cease-and-desist order before the last game. Cochrane recalled that before that game he walked over to the Cubs' bench and yelled, "Hello, sweethearts, we're going to serve tea this afternoon, come on out and get your share." Judge Landis, sitting in a nearby box, showed no sign of having heard Mickey's remark. After the game Landis came into the A's locker room to congratulate the winners. He spoke with several of the players but paid no attention to Cochrane, who thought that Landis had deliberately ignored him in apparent annoyance over Cochrane's remark. But just as Landis was leaving, he stopped in front of Cochrane and said, "Hello, sweetheart, I came in after my tea; will you pour?"

The A's repeated in 1930, beating out the second-place Senators by eight games. Simmons and Foxx again were the big hitters, and Grove had another magnificent year, leading the league in wins, winning percentage, strikeouts, saves, and ERA. Cochrane ranked fifth in the league, with a .357 average. Grove and Earnshaw were dominant as the A's defeated the Cardinals in the Series, four games to two. Cochrane, although held to a .222 average in the Series, made his hits count, with two homers and four RBI.

The 1931 season was a carbon copy of the two previous years as the A's won their third straight pennant, this time by a 13½ game margin over the second place Yankees. Simmons was again Connie Mack's biggest offensive star, and Grove had the best year of his career with an out-of-sight 31–4 record and a league-leading 2.06 ERA. Grove won 16 straight games and lost his bid for a 17th consecutive win 1–0 when a substitute leftfielder misplayed a routine fly ball. Cochrane had a fine .349 average, but he was most proud of having caught each of Grove's 16 consecutive wins. Although Cochrane and Grove worked well together, both of these extremely hot-tempered, volatile men had their differences. There was one occasion when they almost came to blows during a game. It seems that the peppery Cochrane fired the ball back to Grove on the mound too hard for Lefty's taste, and he cussed out Cochrane. Mickey became so aroused that it took the combined efforts of infielders Jimmy Foxx and Jimmy Dykes to keep Black Mike from a fist fight with his own pitcher before a good-sized crowd.

The Cardinals took on the Athletics again, favored to win their third Series in a row. The story of the Series was the spectacular play of Cards' rookie centerfielder Pepper Martin. Grove defeated Cardinals righthander Paul Derringer 6–2 in the first game, despite three hits by Martin. But in the second game Martin singled and doubled and scored both runs as the Cards' won 2–0 to overcome a great effort by Earnshaw. In the third game

Martin again had a single and double to score twice as righthanded spit-baller Burleigh Grimes beat Grove 5–2. In the next game Earnshaw held St. Louis to two hits, both by Martin, in shutting out the Cards 3–0. In the pivotal fifth game the irrepressible Martin drove in four runs as Hallahan beat righthander Waite Hoyt 5–1. In the sixth game the A's tied the Series as Grove again outpitched Derringer in an 8–1 Athletics' victory. In the tense deciding game Martin walked and stole his fifth base of the Series as Grimes beat Earnshaw 4–2. Losing 4–0 in the top of the ninth, the A's came close to pulling the game out. They scored twice and loaded the bases with two men out. But Hallahan, who had won two games, induced Max Bishop to hit a high pop foul that first baseman Jim Bottomley caught near the box seats to give the Cardinals the Series.

It was an especially tough Series for Cochrane, hampered by sinus problems and bruised legs. He was held to a mere .160 average, but his main problem was his inability to keep Martin under control. Mickey was widely criticized for being victimized eight times by Cardinals' stolen bases, five of them by Martin. Pepper absolved Cochrane, feeling that he had stolen successfully because Grove and Earnshaw had not held him close enough to the bag.

The Athletics' reign ended as the A's finished well behind the pennant-winning Yankees in 1932, and even further behind the first place Senators the following year. Mack found it necessary to sell some of his stars because of the serious financial inroads of the deepening Depression. After the 1933 season he reluctantly sold Cochrane, one of his favorites, to Detroit for $100,000. H.G. Salsinger, the sports editor of the *Detroit News*, urged principal Tigers stockholder Navin to obtain Cochrane to have a star player, still in his prime, run the Tigers on the field. And so Mickey Cochrane became the Tigers' player-manager in 1934.

Cochrane took over a team that included four future Hall of Famers. Big first baseman Hank Greenberg was on the verge of becoming a great power hitter. Second baseman Charley Gehringer was the most accomplished hitter and fielder at his position. Leftfielder Leon "Goose" Goslin was a prolific hitter and sound outfielder. And Cochrane was rated among the top two or three catchers in the game. Curveballing righthander Tommy Bridges and veteran righthand reliever Fred "Firpo" Marberry were the best of the pitchers. Shortstop Billy Rogell was an underrated player, perfectly suited to complement the great Gehringer. Player-manager Cochrane was a hyper, driven man, but he was not a martinet who robbed his players of their individuality. Rogell recalled, "Mickey was a good guy. I'll tell you one thing. You played [your own kind of] baseball when you played for him. He never second-guessed you. I used to say to him when he was catching and he'd come out to the mound to talk to the pitcher, 'Get back and do your catching. We're having enough trouble out here.'"

The Tigers started slowly but by mid-season they moved ahead of the Yankees to take over the lead for good. Cochrane's club (101–53) finished seven games in front of the second place Yankees, carried offensively by superb seasons from Greenberg and Gehringer, and a decent season by Goslin. Playing-manager Cochrane hit .320 in 129 games. Second-year righthander Lynwood "Schoolboy" Rowe had a marvelous 24–8 season, topped off on August 25 when he defeated the Senators, his 16th win in a row. This tied the American League record held by Walter Johnson, Smoky Joe Wood, and Lefty Grove. In his moment of triumph, the tall, lanky Rowe had a radio interview during which he crowed exuberantly to his wife, "How am I doin', Edna?" After that he was constantly ribbed by opposing players for the remark. Righthanders Bridges (22–11) and Marberry (15–5), and submarining righthander Eldon Auker (15-7), rounded out the starting staff.

The Tigers met the rambunctious St. Louis Cardinals in the Series. Second baseman–manager Frankie Frisch was the leader of the Cardinals, who had a colorful variety of players—brothers Dizzy and Paul Dean, Joe Medwick, Leo Durocher, and the inimitable Pepper Martin. The Cardinals had beaten out Bill Terry's World Championship Giants by two games in the last few days of the season, led by righthander Dizzy Dean's brilliant 30 wins and a career season by first baseman Jimmy "Ripper" Collins.

As described in Chapter 17, it was a completely unhappy Series for player-manager Cochrane. His club lost in seven games to a cocky team that he especially wanted to beat. He was bothered again by his inability to control Pepper Martin on the bases. And Cochrane was a negative factor in his team's performance, hitting only .214. It was a great letdown after the superb season he had given Detroit fans, a year for which he was named American League MVP for the second time in his career.

The Tigers squad gathered at Lakeland, Florida, in 1935 was identical to that of the previous season. After another slow start, the Tigers rebounded to take the lead, and they were far enough ahead of the Yankees to withstand a September slump and win the pennant by three games. Greenberg was the team's offensive star, leading the league in RBI and total bases, tying for the home run lead with Jimmy Foxx, and finishing in the top five in runs scored, hits, doubles, triples, and slugging average. He was voted the American League MVP. Gehringer, Goslin, and Cochrane, who hit .319 during the season, carried the rest of the offensive load, and Bridges (21–10), Rowe (19–13), Eldon Auker (18–7), and Alvin Crowder (16–10) were the leading pitchers.

Cochrane's club faced the Chicago Cubs in the World Series. The Cubs had beaten out the Giants and Cardinals with a sensational 21-game winning streak in September. The Cubs' most important position players were catcher Gabby Hartnett, second baseman Billy Herman, shortstop Billy Jurges, third baseman Stan Hack, and leftfielder Augie Galan. The leading Cubs pitchers were 20-game winning righthanders Lon Warneke and Bill Lee, lefthander Larry French, and veteran righthander Charlie Root.

The Cubs won the first game as Warneke outpitched Schoolboy Rowe, giving up only four hits in shutting out the Tigers 3–0. The Tigers evened the Series in the second game, beginning with a four-run outburst off Charlie Root in the first inning and Hank Greenberg's two-run homer. Tommy Bridges kept the Cubs under control to win easily, 8–3. The

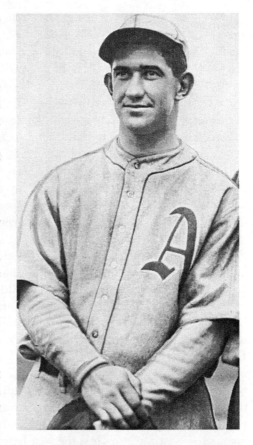

Mickey Cochrane was a highly successful catcher-manager for the Detroit Tigers in 1934 and 1935, winning the pennant in 1934 and the World Championship the following year. The fiery Cochrane, whose playing career ended after he was beaned in 1937, hit .320 and .319 in both years, matching his .320 career batting average.

Tigers sustained a serious blow when Greenberg's left wrist was broken by a pitched ball. In the third game the Cubs took a 3–1 lead into the seventh inning. The Tigers rallied in the top of the inning with four runs on a walk and four hits to go ahead 5–3 after the top of the ninth. But the Cubs came back with two runs in the bottom of the inning to tie the game at five. The Tigers won the game for reliever Schoolboy Rowe with a run in the 11th inning on two hits and an error.

In the fourth game Alvin Crowder yielded only a home run by Hartnett as he outpitched the Cubs' Tex Carleton 2–1. For the second day in a row, Cub errors gave the Tigers the deciding run. Facing elimination in the fifth game, the Cubs fought back with a 3–1 victory on excellent pitching by Warneke and Lee. Back in Detroit the teams went into the ninth inning of the extremely tense sixth game tied 3–3 as Bridges and French dueled before a frenzied crowd of over 48,000. Stan Hack opened the top of the ninth, and the fans braced for the tie-breaker as Billy Jurges, a decent contact hitter, came up to bat. Cochrane trotted out to the mound and instructed Bridges, an accomplished curve ball specialist, "Breaking balls, nothing except breaking stuff." Cochrane blocked the second pitch to Jurges, a biting curve that bounced in the dirt two feet in front of Cochrane. Then the cool Bridges threw six of the most puzzling, hard-to-hit curves that Cochrane said he had ever seen, and Jurges went down swinging. Charlie Grimm left pitcher French in the game to hit, and he bounced back to the box for the second out as Hack was forced to hold at third. Then Bridges threw his first fast ball of the inning and Galan flied out, as the relieved Tiger fans cheered wildly.

In the bottom of the ninth Cochrane, who had singled in the first inning to set up the first Detroit run, singled again. Gehringer followed with a drive down the first baseline, on which young Phil Cavaretta made a great diving stop to retire Gehringer, as Cochrane slid safely into second. Goslin stepped up and lined a 2-and-2 pitch into right center for a hit, and Cochrane scored the winning run. He jumped up and down on the plate exultantly as his players raced out on the field to embrace him. He had accomplished the goal he had set for himself, to overcome his team's devastating Series loss the year before.

Cochrane's club was never really a serious contender for the 1936 pennant, even though it finished in second place, a distant 19½ games off the pace set by the Yankees. Joe McCarthy's club had rookie Joe DiMaggio to complement other future Hall of Famers Lou Gehrig, Tony Lazzeri, Bill Dickey, Red Ruffing, and Lefty Gomez. The Tigers' chance to repeat as winners ended 12 games into the season when Hank Greenberg, hitting .348, was lost for the rest of the season after Washington outfielder Jake Powell crashed into him, breaking the same wrist injured in the 1935 Series. Gehringer, Bridges, and Rowe played up to form, but the rest of the Tigers did not play well. This included high-strung player-manager Cochrane, who hit only .270 and played in only 44 games because of a nervous breakdown and other ailments.

In 1937 Cochrane's club was in third place on May 25 when the Tigers played the first place Yankees at Yankee Stadium. On Cochrane's first at-bat he homered off righthander Irving "Bump" Hadley. In his second time at the plate, with a runner at first, he crowded the plate in an attempt to hit behind the runner. Hadley's 3–1 pitch came in high and tight and Cochrane lost sight of it. The pitch struck him just above his right eyebrow with a sickening sound. Cochrane was knocked cold. He revived briefly in the clubhouse but then lost consciousness for several days. His skull had been fractured in three places and doctors forbade him to play again.

Mickey returned to manage the club later in the season. But as a bench manager he resembled a caged animal, moving restlessly and completely unable to spark the Tigers with his characteristic, inspired leadership. Many years later Gehringer said, "After he [Cochrane] became a bench manager, it seemed like he weighed everything a little more, and you can't do that in baseball.... He never seemed to be wrong when he was playing, but he was not as good when he wasn't playing. He knew when a pitcher needed to come out, which was something they would never tell you." Eldon Auker, who had several decent years under Cochrane, thought that Mickey was a good pitcher's manager. Auker commented to a SABR group in 2000, "Mickey treated you like a man. He told me, 'Don't hesitate to shake me off if you don't like the pitch I call. If the guy hits a homer, it's your fault, but if you strike him out, I was wrong.'" Cochrane finished his last season as a player-manager in 1937, hitting .306 in 27 games as his club again finished in second place behind the powerful Yankees. Cochrane managed the Tigers in 1938 through August when it became apparent that he was much less effective managing from the bench. He was relieved of the job on August 8, with his club in fifth place and playing under .500 ball.

Cochrane had a career batting average of .320 in his 13 years as a player. He had an excellent career on-base percentage of .419 and was considered one of the best field generals of his era. He had a successful managerial career, with a 348–250 (.582) record. Black Mike, who played in 315 of the games he managed, was inducted into the Hall of Fame in 1947.

Cochrane spent World War II as an officer in the Navy's fitness program, running the athletic program at the Great Lakes Naval Training Station and coaching the base team, which included a number of prominent major leaguers who had entered the service. After the war Cochrane worked in the trucking industry and operated a dude ranch. He returned to baseball in 1950 as a coach, then general manager of the Athletics, and he scouted for the Yankees and the Tigers before becoming vice-president of the Tigers. He held that position until his death on June 28, 1962.

GABBY HARTNETT

Charles Leo "Gabby" Hartnett was born in Woonsocket, Rhode Island, on December 20, 1900, the eldest of 14 children. He grew up in Millville, Massachusetts, 26 miles from Woonsocket, where his father, Fred, was a streetcar conductor. Fred Hartnett had been a semipro catcher, and he taught the game to his large brood. Gabby began playing baseball at a local academy, and, at 16, he began playing for a local semipro team while he worked at the American Steel and Wire mill in Woonsocket. When he was 20 he signed with Worcester, of the Eastern League, where he hit .264 and impressed with his catching skills.

The Cubs purchased Hartnett's contract for $2500 after the 1921 season. During his first training camp in 1922 Hartnett said nothing to reporters, who called him "Gabby" as a gag. Actually, the nickname fit his personality perfectly because he was normally an outgoing, talkative individual who would often be described later as a "beefy man with a tomato face who talked a lot." Hartnett made his major league debut on April 12, 1922, catching the great Grover Cleveland Alexander. The strapping 6 foot 1, 200-pounder became the Cubs' regular catcher two years later. By that time, he was one of the best catchers and handler of pitchers in the National League, and its hardest hitting catcher. In 1925 the righthand-hitting Hartnett hit 24 home runs, finishing second in the league to Rogers Hornsby.

Hartnett had decent years from 1924 through 1928, and, with the livelier ball in use in 1929, he appeared ready for the biggest offensive season of his career. But he suffered a serious setback in spring training that season when he injured his extremely strong throwing arm. As a result, Hartnett played in only 25 games in 1929. The Cubs never revealed what happened to cause Hartnett's throwing problem, but, more than 60 years later, shortstop Woody English, who played with Hartnett, gave the explanation. English said, "In 1929, Gabby had a sore arm all season, and I can tell you how that happened. Nobody ever knew about it. He did it by shooting clay pigeons over in Lincoln Park in Chicago. The recoil from the gun shooting clay pigeons, that's what hurt his arm. They didn't want the news media to know about it."

Hartnett came back in 1930 with his offensive career year. He hit .339, with 37 homers and 122 RBI. But it was wasted when the Cardinals beat out the Cubs for the pennant by two games. Hartnett had some memorable moments and achievements over the next several years. He was the Cubs' indispensable spark plug when the club won the pennant in 1932, and he was the man behind the plate on Babe Ruth's "called' home run during that year's World Series. Gabby was the National League catcher in the first All-Star game in 1933, and the receiver in the 1934 All-Star game when Carl Hubbell struck out Ruth, Gehrig, Foxx, Simmons, and Cronin in succession. He was the National League MVP in 1935, testimony to the vital role he played as the Cubs came from behind with a 21-game winning streak to win the pennant. And he played well in the Cubs' losses in the 1932 and 1935 World Series.

The 1938 Cubs had their slowest start in several years and, with the club playing sluggishly (although it was in third place), manager Charlie Grimm stepped down on July 26. Hartnett replaced him. The Cubs improved under their catcher-manager and scrapped their way into a dogfight with the Pirates by mid–September, helped along by several clutch wins by Dizzy Dean, obtained

Gabby Hartnett was the best National League catcher for many years before becoming the player-manager of the Chicago Cubs in mid-season of 1938. His short player-manager career is remembered for his dramatic homer that keyed the Cubs' pennant win that year.

from the Cardinals. Hartnett's club charged into a virtual tie with the Pirates after a ten-game winning streak during the last two weeks of the season. On September 27 the Pirates came into Wrigley Field, leading the Cubs by 1½ games, for the series that would decide the pennant. The courageous Dean, who had not pitched in two weeks because of a sore arm, held the Pirates scoreless until the ninth inning when he gave up a couple of hits. Righthander Bill Lee came in and got the last man out for a 2–1 win, and the Cubs were only half a game out.

In the second game the score was tied at five after eight innings, and the umpires informed Hartnett and Pirates manager Pie Traynor that the ninth inning would be the last because it was growing dark (Wrigley Field did not have lights at the time). The Pirates did not score in the top of the inning off reliever Charley Root, and Pirates righthander Mace Brown disposed of the first two Cubs hitters in the bottom of the ninth. Hartnett stepped up to hit in the gathering darkness as the tense crowd of 34,465 watched. The Cubs' Phil Cavaretta described it in Peter Golenbock's *Wrigleyville*:

> The first pitch, Mace threw Gabby a slider, and Gabby swung and missed. I figured, oh well, two more and that's the game. And the next pitch he threw a fastball, a waste pitch for a ball.... The next pitch [a slider] was up, and Gabby was a good high-ball hitter.... Gabby hit the ball, a line drive. It looked like it was going to hit the bottom of the bleachers, two bases ... but the ball went into the first row of the bleachers, just made it.

That would be Hartnett's most famous contribution to the game—his miraculous "homer in the gloamin." Lee beat the devastated Pirates the next day, and the Cubs clinched the pennant the day before the season ended as the Pirates lost to the Reds. Player-manager Hartnett took the last game off, completely hung over but happy after a pennant-clinching celebration.

In a complete anti-climax, the Cubs lost four straight in the World Series to the overpowering Yankees. Righthander Charlie "Red" Ruffing outpitched Lee to win the first game. The next day Dizzy Dean, pitching on guile alone, held the Yanks to two runs in seven innings. But with a 3–2 lead in the eighth, Dean gave up home runs to Frank Crosetti and Joe DiMaggio for four runs, and Lefty Gomez won the game, 6–3. Righthander Clay Bryant lost 5–2 to righthander Monte Pearson, and Ruffing polished off the Cubs easily to complete the sweep. The 37-year-old Hartnett showed his age, with only one hit in the three games he caught.

After the Series there were changes in the Cubs lineup. Dick Bartell, Hank Leiber, and Gus Mancuso arrived from the Giants in exchange for Billy Jurges, Frank Demaree, and Ken O'Dea. But the trade did not help the Cubs. They slipped to fourth place in 1939, finishing 13 games off the pace in Hartnett's last year as their regular catcher. The fading Cubs were even worse in 1940, finishing fifth, 25½ games out of first, and Gabby was released after the season.

Few people could fault Hartnett as a player, but he was criticized as a player-manager. Despite his jolly exterior, Hartnett had a strong temper and he could be moody. Still, although he issued only two fines (both to Dizzy Dean), Gabby had his detractors among the players. Phil Cavaretta and Billy Rogell had their problems with Gabby, and Dick Bartell was quoted by Peter Golenbock as follows: "I came to Chicago respecting him as a player. But I lost my respect for him as a manager.... He was very difficult to get along with. He was just as noisy in the dugout [as when he was catching] but it wasn't positive noise.... He was high-strung [sic] and would get into arguments with players.... Gabby had an ego that wouldn't quit. It got in the way of his managing.... He made life miserable for Gus Mancuso, because Gus didn't handle the catching job the way Gabby did."

Regardless of the players' criticism of him, Hartnett was always a fan favorite. The Wrigley Field faithful loved him, and not just for his greatness as a player. They liked the way the big Irishman carried himself and the way he chatted with them. His friendly chattiness got him into trouble one day in the late 'twenties when he was called over to a box seat in the Cubs' park to talk with underworld boss Al Capone. The next day a photo of the visit was published and a deeply concerned Commissioner Kenesaw M. Landis immediately issued a non-fraternizing ban on such meetings with fans. This was a bitter pill for Hartnett, who enjoyed talking to fans, whether they were important people or not. Landis was reported to have reprimanded Hartnett, and the gregarious Irishman responded, "If you don't want anybody to talk to the Big Guy, Judge, you tell that to Capone."

Hartnett was a special favorite when the Cubs played the Giants at the Polo Grounds. The clubhouses at the Polo Grounds were located some 480 feet from the plate in deep center field. At the end of a game players usually raced from the dugout to their clubhouse in order to minimize contact with the fans, who were allowed on the field after the game. Hartnett was one of the few players who walked casually through the crowded field on the way to the clubhouse, chatting all the way. The fans loved to talk to the big catcher with the face the color of rare roast beef, and he reciprocated in kind.

Hartnett caught on with the Giants as a player-coach in 1941. He hit .300 in 64 games amid rumors that the Giants planned to appoint him to replace manager Bill Terry. Instead, Gabby left the Giants after the season. He managed in the minors in Indianapolis, Jersey City, and Buffalo through the World War II years before retiring from baseball after the 1946 season. After leaving the game, Hartnett went into the insurance business and operated a bowling alley. He returned to the game briefly as a coach for the Kansas City Athletics in 1965.

Hall of Fame Manager Joe McCarthy, who saw a lot of Mickey Cochrane and managed both Bill Dickey and Hartnett, called Gabby the perfect catcher, a manager's dream. McCarthy said, "He had everything except speed and he was far from slow. He was super-smart. Nobody ever had more hustle. Nobody could throw like him…. I must take Hartnett as the best clutch-hitter." He batted .297 over his 20-year career and, at one time, his 236 homers were the most by any catcher. Hartnett led the National League in fielding in six different years, four of them in a row. The big fellow was not rated highly as a manager, although his clubs had a 203–176 (.536) record. But he was an important player-manager if only because of that one unforgettable swing of his bat in 1938. Elected to the Hall of Fame in 1955, Hartnett died in Park Ridge, Illinois, on his 72nd birthday.

12

Harris and Bancroft

Second basemen and shortstops often have been selected as player-managers not for their hitting prowess but because of their leadership skills. There have been a number of excellent hitting middle infielders, notably Eddie Collins, Rogers Hornsby, Joe Cronin, and Lou Boudreau. These players are discussed in later chapters. This chapter deals with Bucky Harris and Dave Bancroft, who were noted more for their mental sharpness and field leadership than for their hitting.

BUCKY HARRIS

Stanley Raymond "Bucky" Harris was born in Port Jarvis, New York, on November 8, 1896. His parents, of Swiss-Welsh descent, moved to Pittston, Pennsylvania, where his father became a coal miner. After completing sixth grade, 13-year-old Bucky began work in the mines as a "breaker boy," where his onerous job was to separate slate from coal as it moved down the chutes. He worked in the mines and played on local baseball teams until he was 19. In 1916 the tough 5 foot, 9½ inch, 156-pound second baseman played for Muskegon, Michigan, in the Central League. In the next three seasons he moved up, with stops at Norfolk, Reading, and Buffalo, in the International League.

In 1919 Washington Senators manager Clark Griffith sent scout Joe Engel to Buffalo to look over one of the club's pitchers. Engel instead was impressed by Harris, the Buffalo club's little second baseman. At Engel's urging, Griffith came to Buffalo to see the young man play a doubleheader. Harris impressed Griffith with six hits in the two games, and Griffith was even more impressed to learn that Harris had insisted upon playing despite a broken finger. As a result, Harris joined the Senators after the International League season, making his major league debut on August 28.

Bucky became the Senators' regular second baseman in 1920, hitting a career-high .300. Over the next three years he established himself as one of the best fielding second basemen in the league. He was a good offensive player, although he did not possess extra-base power. But Harris could do the important things—hitting behind the runner, bunting and running bases effectively, and hitting in the pinch.

Harris had been the Senators' captain in 1923, nevertheless, it was a big surprise when he became the Senators' player-manager in 1924. Henry W. Thomas, Walter Johnson's grandson, described the situation in his *Walter Johnson—Baseball's Big Train*:

> Except for [outfielder] Goose Goslin, Harris was the youngest starter on the team.... The responsibilities and demands of the job held no fear for Harris, and his tough play at second base had long since earned him the respect of his teammates—his players now. He also was smart enough to assuage any hard feelings among the older veterans.... Harris went to Johnson and [first baseman Joe] Judge and asked for their support. Not only were they behind him 100 percent, they told him, but they would make sure that it went for the rest of the team also.... For his part Harris expressed to the players his feeling that his success depended on them, not the other way around. They appreciated his honor system with regard to training rules, eliminating bed checks and other restrictions.

Harris took over a fourth place team with a sub-.500 winning percentage in 1923. His infield had Judge at first, the new player-manager at second, veteran Roger Peckinpaugh at short, and Ossie Bluege at third. The veteran Sam Rice was in right, little journeyman Nemo Leibold was the centerfielder, and slugging Leon "Goose" Goslin was in left. Catcher Herold "Muddy" Ruel was in his prime. The starting pitchers were Johnson, lefthanders George Mogridge and Tom Zachary, and righthander Fred Marberry.

Harris's club began poorly, in seventh place four weeks into the season. But the club took off and was in first place by mid-season. When the Senators played the Tigers in Detroit, Tigers player-manager Ty Cobb tried to rattle Harris, rather boorishly calling him "Baby face" and "Snookums," and shouting out to Bucky "Boot it! Boot it!" every time a ground ball headed towards second base. Harris laughed and ignored Cobb. *Baseball Magazine*, which had picked the Senators to finish seventh, lauded Harris' leadership. Veteran baseball man and clown Al

Schacht said of Harris years later, "I think Bucky Harris was the best of all the player-managers. He was smart, aggressive; he made the right moves."

Through late July and early August the Senators, the Yankees, and the Tigers fought for first place, but the Senators pulled ahead of the Tigers for good after beating Cobb's club decisively in a mid–August series. The Senators were helped greatly by the acquisition of outfielder Earl McNeely, purchased from Sacramento, to replace the slumping Leibold. The fast, smallish McNeely hit .330 over the season and provided the team with an excellent leadoff man.

The Senators struggled with the Yankees, who had won the previous three pennants, for the lead through September and clinched a tie for the pennant on September 27. They won the pennant two days later, beating the Red Sox 4–2 on a three-run double by unknown rookie outfielder Wade Lefler, who had just been brought up from the Eastern League. This would prove to be his one sip of a cup of coffee, as he did not play another big league game after 1924. The Senators' win was truly a team effort, although there were standouts. Johnson was voted league MVP, Goslin led the league with 129 RBI, and Sam Rice had a league-leading 216 hits. Player-manager Harris hit .268.

The Senators prepared for the World Series against John McGraw's Giants, who were playing in their fourth straight Series. First baseman George "Highpockets" Kelly and second baseman Frankie Frisch were the brightest stars on a club featuring other future Hall of Famers, including rightfielder Ross Youngs, first baseman Bill Terry, shortstop Travis Jackson, and third baseman Freddy Lindstrom. The Giants' pitching leaders were lefthanders Art Nehf (14–4) and Jack Bentley (16–5), and righthanders Virgil Barnes (16–10), and Hugh McQuillan (14–8).

The teams played an exciting seven-game Series, with four of the games decided by one run. Walter Johnson, in his first World Series after 17 seasons and 377 wins, opened against Art Nehf in Washington. The game was tied two-all after 11 innings. The Giants broke through on Johnson with two runs in the top of the 12th, and the Senators drew within a run in the bottom of the inning when Harris drove in a run. But Kelly made a one-handed pickup on Goslin's smash to save the game for Nehf. The next day Zachary beat Jack Bentley 4–3, helped by home runs by Goslin and player-manager Harris, and a clutch hit by Roger Peckinpaugh in the ninth inning. The clubs split the next two games and the Series was tied at two.

The Giants defeated Johnson again in the fifth game, 6–2, as winning pitcher lefty Jack Bentley hit a home run to put the Giants ahead for good.

In the sixth game the Giants moved ahead with a first-inning run on a hit by Kelly, but Zachary held them scoreless for the rest of the game. With men on second and third in the fifth inning, Harris drove in two runs with a single, all the runs Zachary needed in a 2–1 win. The Series was knotted at three games apiece.

The Senators had picked up righthander Warren "Curly" Ogden in mid-season, hardly a likely choice to start in the deciding game of the World Series. Regardless, Harris picked him to start the final game, and John McGraw predictably packed his lineup with lefthand hitters, most notably Bill Terry, who already had six hits in the Series as a part-time player. Ogden struck out Giants leadoff man Freddy Lindstrom and walked Frisch, and then Harris replaced him with lefthander George Mogridge in a successful attempt to have McGraw remove his lefthand hitters. Many baseball men saw Clark Griffith's fine hand in Harris' maneuver.

The game was scoreless until the bottom of the fourth when Harris drove a three-and- two pitch from Giants starter Virgil Barnes into the temporary bleachers in left field for a 1–0 Washington lead. It was Harris' second home run of the Series, one more than he had hit in the regular season. In the top of the sixth the Giants scored three before Firpo Marberry came in and put out the fire. Down two runs, the Senators came back in the eighth and loaded the bases with two out. Harris hit an apparently easy bounder to 18-year-old third baseman Freddy Lindstrom. Just as he prepared to grab the ball, it took a crazy hop over his head and two runs came in to tie the game. Walter Johnson started the ninth inning and gave up a triple to Frisch but retired Kelly and the equally dangerous Meusel to end the inning. Johnson held the Giants scoreless through the next three innings.

In the Senators' half of the twelfth inning, with one out, catcher Muddy Ruel popped an easy foul ball behind the plate. Giants catcher Hank Gowdy started back to make the catch, pulling his mask off and discarding it as he moved back. Incredibly, his left foot came down squarely inside the mask and he stumbled to one knee as the ball bounced out of his mitt. Given that opportunity, Ruel doubled and, with two out, Earl McNeely drove a hard bouncer directly at Lindstrom. The ball again hit a pebble and bounced high over Lindstrom's head. Ruel, a notoriously slow runner, chugged towards the plate. He prepared to slide in but the jubilant Harris, the on-deck hitter, gave him a hands-up motion, indicating that a slide was unnecessary. The Senators were the Worlds Champions.

After the celebration in the Senators' clubhouse had subsided, Harris showered and, not taking the time to put his clothes on, walked around the clubhouse, still overcome by his team's victory. The club trainer felt that Harris was in a daze and tried to calm him down, despite Bucky's protests that he was fine and was completely under control. With that, Harris moved over in front of a mirror, carefully combed his black hair into a neat part, and started to leave the clubhouse—apparently completely unaware that he didn't have a stitch on.

Harris continued to savor his triumph. He lauded the team effort, especially on the part of his veteran players who had so unselfishly supported the "boy wonder manager," as the writers referred to Harris. He expressed his pleasure at playing so well in the Series, during which he hit .333, with 11 hits. And he spoke of his special satisfaction that Walter Johnson had won the final game. In the Giants clubhouse, pitcher Jack Bentley, who lost the final game, was philosophical. He said, "Walter Johnson is such a lovable character that the good Lord didn't want to see him get beat again."

Harris relaxed in the off-season, enjoying his status as a highly eligible bachelor. He was unmarried, well-spoken, good-looking, and a major league baseball hero at a time when no other professional sport compared with baseball in popularity. So it was natural that Harris could often be seen dating attractive young women, many of them members of prominent Washington business and political families. Two years later Harris married Washington socialite Elizabeth Sutherland, a complete transition from the former coal mine breaker boy to the higher levels of Washington, D.C. society.

Harris' club did fairly well in the first month of the 1925 season, although the Senators were several games behind the blazing Athletics by the end of May. The two teams met in the first important series of the season in late June, and the Senators took four out of the five games to move into first place. The clubs fought on even terms until August 20, but Connie Mack's team ran out of gas after Labor Day and the Senators won the pennant by 8½ games.

Johnson, former Cleveland Indians righthander Stan Coveleski, Marberry, Goslin, Rice, Roger Peckinpaugh, and player-manager Harris were the most important contributors in the Senators' repeat win. Johnson had a 20–7 record, despite missing starts because of illness. A good hitting pitcher, Johnson hit a remarkable .433 during the season, still the record for pitchers. Coveleski, a spitball specialist, recaptured the form he had shown with the Indians several years before. For the second year in a row Marberry led the league in games and in saves. Goslin had another splendid year, leading the league in triples and stolen bases, and ranking within the top five in runs, RBI, and total bases. Rice hit .350, with 227 base hits.

Peckinpaugh was a surprise MVP choice for his clutch hitting and brilliant fielding. And Harris duplicated the field leadership and excellent defensive play he had displayed the previous year.

Harris was a tough competitor, but he admitted he could overdo it. In Sport Magazine's *All-Time All Stars*, Harris told writer Jack Sher:

> [Lou] Gehrig was crucifying us.... The next day, with the score tied 2–2 in the eighth inning and a man on third, I bunted down the first base line. Lou fielded it and ran for the bag. I came down [intentionally] hard on his toe. I've never seen a man so surprised and hurt. When the man on third broke for home, Gehrig threw the ball way over the catcher's head and we won the game ... but he never said a word. Every time I came down to first [after that] he just looked at me as though to ask me how I could do such a thing to him. I got to feeling so ashamed of myself that I finally apologized to him. You should have seen him light up!

The Senators faced the Pirates in the World Series. Approaching his 38th birthday, Walter Johnson outpitched righthander Lee Meadows in Pittsburgh to win the first game. Johnson had great stuff, yielding only a home run to third baseman Pie Traynor. In the outdated writing style of the day, a reporter wrote, "Johnson did it so easily, with so little grunting and wrenching, with such casual grace, that the baffled young athletes of the resident squad are still wondering how, and are willing to believe the Swede was doing parlor magic." The Pirates evened the Series the following day as Stan Coveleski lost to righthander Vic Aldridge when outfielder Kiki Cuyler hit a two-run home run in the bottom of the eighth.

The Senators won the third game on Goose Goslin's home run. The game is remembered for a play in the eighth inning. Two men were out in the top the eighth inning, with the Senators leading 4–3. After two men were retired, Pirates catcher Earl Smith smoked a drive towards the temporary bleachers in deep right center field. Sam Rice raced after it until he ran out of room at the barrier and his momentum carried him over it just as the ball arrived at the same spot. Both outfielder and baseball disappeared simultaneously into the seats for a few seconds until Rice popped up out of the crowd holding the ball in his glove. Umpire Cy Rigler called Smith out, and the Pirates argued long and loud that Rice had not made the catch but had picked up the loose ball in the seats. The umpire's call stood, and the Senators won to take a lead in the Series.

After the game, Commissioner Landis asked Rice, "Sam, did you catch that ball?" Rice answered, "Judge, the umpire called Smith out." Landis, anxious to protect the integrity of the game, responded, "That's just what I wanted you to say, and that's the way I want you to answer anybody else who asks you that question." After Rice died, his widow reported that her husband had shown her a letter to be opened after his death. Rice wrote that he had made the catch and that "at no time did I lose possession of the ball."

The Senators won the fourth game, as the indomitable Johnson pitched a 4–0 shutout and Goslin hit a three-run homer. The Senators led three to one in games and appeared on the way to their second straight Series win. But the Pirates won the fifth game as Coveleski again was out-pitched by Aldridge. The teams returned to Pittsburgh for the sixth game, and the Pirates won 3–2 as shortstop Roger Peckinpaugh, playing on heav-ily-bandaged legs, committed a record-tying sixth Series error to let in two runs.

It was the tired Johnson against Vic Aldridge in the seventh game, played on a wet, slippery field. With the Senators leading 6–4 after six innings, the Pirates tied the game with two runs in the seventh as Peck-inpaugh dropped a pop fly, and went ahead for good with three more runs in the eighth on the devastated shortstop's wild throw. The Senators lost the sloppy game 9–7, as Johnson pitched the entire game, yielding 15 hits. But the Series' goat had to be Peckinpaugh who, although he drove in two of the Senators' runs with a single and a home run, made his seventh and eighth errors of the Series. Harris, who hit a pallid .087 during the Series, shrugged off criticism for keeping Johnson in the game so long.

It was a different story in 1926. The Senators played well through mid–May, in second place behind the powerful Yankees. Johnson was his usual effective self, with a 6–1 record, but the aging star pitcher and his teammates slipped badly. Over the next month Johnson lost seven games in a row, and Harris' club dropped into the second division. The club rallied over the last six weeks of the season and barely finished in the first division. Goslin, who tended to take team curfews lightly, nevertheless had another splendid year at the plate, finishing in the top five in runs, hits, triples, and home runs. Manager Harris had a typical year, hitting .283 in spite of the problems of handling his erratic team.

The 1927 season was essentially a repeat of the previous season as the Senators finished in third place, 25 games behind the murderous Yankees. This was Walter Johnson's last season as a player. He had a 5–6 record as the Senators and A's fought in vain to deal with the awesome power of the Yankees. After the season Johnson was released to become the player-manager of the Newark club in the International League. There was one other item of note during the season. The Senators picked up all-time great outfielder Tris Speaker, who hit .327 in 141 games in his only season with the Senators, after his enforced departure as manager of the Cleveland Indians, described in Chapter 14.

The Senators slipped further in 1928, falling hopelessly out of the race before Memorial Day, as the club finished four games under .500. Goslin had a brilliant year, leading the league with a .379 average, and old reliable Sam Rice hit .328. But Harris had slowed up perceptibly. Henry W. Thomas wrote in his *Walter Johnson—Baseball's Big Train*:

> Harris was miserable at the plate, hitting only .204.... At the age of 31 he was washed up as an active player. Rumors circulated that fame, wealth (Griffith had rewarded him after 1925 with a 3-year deal at $30,000, annually), and marriage into a prominent family had gotten Harris caught up in the Washington social scene to the detriment of his duties as team leader. His stunning decline as a player was more the result of prematurely aged legs, though the Washington owner never lost his affection for Harris personally or his admiration for his talents as a manager.

As the season ended, it was apparent that Harris had become unpopular with Senators' fans, and a 28 percent drop in attendance confirmed it. So it came as no surprise that Harris was released on October 15 and Walter Johnson was named to replace him. Shortly after leaving the Senators, Harris was hired as the player-manager of the Tigers. He managed inept Detroit teams for the next five years but played in a total of only 11 games before retiring as a player after the 1930 season. None of his Detroit clubs finished in the first division, and he was replaced by player-manager Mickey Cochrane before the 1934 season. Harris became known as the "Available Man" after leaving the Tigers. Next he managed the Red Sox, and, subsequently, the Senators twice more, again in Detroit, two-thirds of a season with the Phillies in 1943, and finally two years with the Yankees. In New York he won a World Championship in 1947 and came within 2½ games of winning again the following season. Except for the Yankees, he managed weak teams from the bench, but he was credited with getting the most out of his limited material.

Harris played in a total of 1263 games, with a career batting average of .274. He was considered one of the most effective field leaders in the game during his 556 games as a player-manager, ranking 19th in games managed by players. He ranks fourth among all managers, both with his 2157 wins and 2218 losses. Harris was elected to the Hall of Fame in 1975, just two years before his death on his 81st birthday.

DAVE BANCROFT

David James "Beauty" Bancroft was born on April 20, 1891, in Sioux City, Iowa. His father was a truck farmer. Bancroft played baseball at Sioux City Central High School and on local community sandlots. He started his professional career at 18 with Duluth and Superior, both in the Minnesota-Wisconsin League. A weak hitter at the time but a gifted shortstop, he played at Portland in the Pacific Coast League for three years until the Philadelphia Phillies brought him up in 1915. Although he hit only .254, Phillies manager Pat Moran credited Bancroft with sparking the Phils to the 1915 pennant after a sixth place finish the previous year. The smallish (5 foot, 9½ inch, 160-pound) 24-year-old switch-hitter hit .294 as the Phils lost the World Series to the Red Sox.

Bancroft played with Philadelphia through the 1919 season, gaining recognition as the National League's premier fielding shortstop. He had all of the classic shortstop tools. He had a strong arm, sure hands, excellent speed and ground covering ability, was skillful in pivoting on double plays, and nimble in evading sliding runners. Bancroft also had the ability to respond quickly to changing defensive situations. He was an adroit bat handler and bunter whose ability to draw walks made him a valuable leadoff hitter. In addition, he was a loud, encouraging presence in the infield, his nickname "Beauty" deriving from his constant shout after every good pitch, "That was a beauty!"

Bancroft was John McGraw's type of player, and the Giants acquired him in June 1920 for shortstop Art Fletcher, righthander Wilbur Hubbell, and an estimated $100,000. When Bancroft joined the Giants, a coach began to give him the Giants' signs. Bancroft cut the coach off quickly with, "Don't bother, I know them already." McGraw immediately appointed the outgoing, aggressive Bancroft team captain after he joined the Giants.

Over the next three seasons Bancroft was McGraw's most indispensable player, the Giants' field leader as they won pennants each year. These were Bancroft's peak seasons, as he was at the top of his game in the field. He also hit well over .300 in each season, including hitting for the cycle on June 1, 1921. Bancroft was especially skillful at working the cutoff play, not a standard defensive maneuver at the time.

With Travis Jackson ready to take over at shortstop, McGraw traded Bancroft, along with Casey Stengel, to the Boston Braves after the 1923 season. Similar to the deal that sent Roger Bresnahan to the Cardinals, McGraw had been assured that Dave would be named the Braves' player-manager. McGraw told the writers that, although he considered Bancroft the best shortstop in the game, he had made the trade to help out his good friend Christy Mathewson, then the Braves' president. It was thought at the time that the Braves might be on the upswing, as the club had come under new ownership in 1923, headed by Judge Emil Fuchs

Bancroft was as quiet and reserved off the field as he was a ball of fire on it. He took over a highly incompetent team and things worsened immediately. Just before spring training, Tony Boeckel, the Braves' popular third baseman, who hit .298 in 1923, was killed in an automobile accident. The club started well with Casey Stengel hitting third and driving in runs. But Stengel and his new teammates cooled down, and the club fell deep into the second division, finishing in last place, 40 games off the pace. Bancroft's club lost on its merits (or lack of same), with a league-low .256 batting average and a next-to-worst team pitching ERA of 4.46, despite playing in cavernous Braves Field.

Bancroft was of little help as a player because he was sidelined from July 1 until well into September, having sustained a painful injury after being struck in the abdomen by a line drive, which produced appendicitis-like symptoms. An operation indicated that he had developed a small intestinal tumor, and he spent two months recuperating at Judge Fuchs' summer home. In his absence, the Braves fell apart, and by late July the club had plunged deep into the second division. On September 10, the Braves lost to the Giants 22–1 in the first game of a doubleheader. His club's poor pitching and porous infield play were more than Bancroft could stand. Although he was in no condition to play, Banny returned to the lineup in the second game, and he managed to improve his club somewhat—the Braves lost the second game by a mere eight runs.

Things improved for Bancroft in 1925 as he led his club to a fifth place finish, 25 games behind the pennant-winning Pirates. The aggressive player-manager hit for a decent .319 average while playing up to his old form in the field. Journeyman first baseman Dick Burrus was brought up from Atlanta, and he had his career year as he led the club with a .340 average and 200 hits. Leftfielder Eddie Brown, a 1924 pickup whose weak throwing arm earned him the nickname "Glass Arm Eddie," topped the club with 99 RBI. Righthander Larry Benton led the pitchers with a 14–7 record and a creditable 3.09 ERA.

Bancroft's club suffered another critical loss just after the 1925 season ended when club president Christy Mathewson died at age 45 of tuberculosis, the disease triggered after he was gassed during his army service in World War 1. Matty was the only bona fide baseball man in the Boston front office, and his death was a special blow to Bancroft who needed all the expert help he could get in 1926 when his club slipped back into seventh place. The 36-year-old player-manager had slowed up in the field, but he struggled to spark his club, hitting .311 and ranking high among National League players in walks and on-base percentage. But the money- and talent-short Braves were simply unable to compete effectively, and Bancroft, accustomed to playing with McGraw's powerful machines ear- lier in the decade, was a tired, frustrated man as the season ended.

The 1927 club fell even further off the pace, finishing in seventh place again. Bancroft's playing performance slipped, and he missed 40 games with a number of nagging ailments. He was dismissed after the season amid indications of personal difficulties between Bancroft and the Braves' front office; his contract still had another year to run. He signed with Brooklyn, then managed by Wilbert Robinson, in 1928. Sportswriter Frank Graham wrote in *The Brooklyn Dodgers*:

> Robbie sought to jar [his club out of their lethargy] by getting Dave Bancroft.... He was thirty-six years old now, but he still was an agile fielder, still played hard, even desperately, to win, and had had experience handling men as captain of the Giants and manager of the Braves. His contract with Boston still had a year to run, at $40,000 a year.... At any rate, Banny was the highest-salaried player ever to wear a Brooklyn uniform [up to that time].... His chief value, however, lay in the fact that he played 149 games at shortstop and hit .246 (he had been a .280 hitter but had slowed down somewhat in that department). Expected to be helpful also as a lieutenant and sort of assistant manager, he found himself completely thwarted. The players, who by this time were paying little attention to Robbie, paid even less attention to him, and when he looked to Robbie for help in that direction, he got none.

After two frustrating years, Bancroft rejoined the Giants in 1930 as a player-coach. He played in only a handful of games that season before becoming a full-time coach with the Giants until John McGraw retired as the Giants' manager in June 1932. Bancroft had hoped to replace McGraw, but he was dismissed at the end of the season after Bill Terry took over as player-manager.

Bancroft managed in the minors over the next 15 years, until he left the game to work as a warehouse supervisor. He was elected to the Hall of Fame in 1971 on the strength of his magnificent fielding and his aggres- sive field leadership. He ranks among the top five shortstops in total life- time chances, total putouts, and assists and putouts per game. Bancroft had a .279 career batting average. He was a player-manager in 445 games (ranking 26th), with an overall 249–363 (.407) managing record. Ban- croft died at age 81 in Superior, Wisconsin.

13

Cobb and Eddie Collins

TY COBB

Ty Cobb's remarkable career can be examined from several viewpoints. He was so overpowering a player that his career records and playing style leave ample room for analysis. His psychopathic personality and its role in his success provide a fertile field for psychoanalysis. And his methods of carrying out his player-manager responsibilities are another aspect worth reviewing.

Tyrus Raymond Cobb was born in Narrows, in Banks County, Georgia, on December 18, 1886. His well-to-do parents, William and Amanda, moved to Royston, Georgia, where Ty grew up. His domineering father was an important figure in the area, as an educator, mayor, publisher, state senator, and county school commissioner. Ty began his professional baseball career at 17 with Augusta, Georgia, in the South Atlantic League. The aggressive youngster joined the club for a $50 a month salary, if he made the team, with the understanding that he would pay his own expenses. But Ty was released after a few days.

Cobb was depressed at his release, although he remained convinced he could play professionally. Cobb's father, who had objected to his son's playing professionally, surprised Ty by giving him $90 with the stern admonition, "Don't come home a failure." A lefthand-hitting, righthand-throwing outfielder, Cobb fought his way back to the Augusta club, remaining there until August 1905 when he joined the Detroit Tigers. Just before he joined the Tigers, Ty received the shocking news that his father had been shot to death by his mother. It seems that the senior Cobb returned home unexpectedly one night after dark, suspecting he would find his wife with another man. There was no other man there and

142

Ty Cobb and Tris Speaker had remarkably similar careers. Cobb was arguably the best hitter ever, with a 24-year batting average of .366 to Speaker's .345 over 22 seasons. But Speaker was widely considered the most innovative and best defensive outfielder ever. Speaker was a player-manager for eight years, with one World Championship, six first division finishes, and a .543 managerial record. Cobb played and managed in six seasons, with four first division finishes and a .519 record. Their player-manager careers ended after an alleged game-fixing incident involving both men.

Amanda Cobb shot at the shadowy figure in the window, killing her husband.

Cobb hit only .240 in 41 games with the Tigers in 1905, but he improved the following season, despite being hazed unmercifully by his teammates who were repelled by his aggressive, combative nature and who did all they could to force the youngster off the club. He was ostracized, and his teammates tried to prevent him from taking batting practice. Other players jockeyed him into fist fights with older, larger players in attempts to get him in trouble. Cobb, a handy man with his fists who possessed a violent temper to go with it, wrote years later that this hostility did not subside until his third year with the Tigers.

Cobb became established as a great player at the age of 21 in 1907 while leading the American League in hitting, with a .350 average, as the Tigers won the pennant. Over the next 13 years "The Georgia Peach," as Cobb was called, was the predominant hitter in the game. He led the league in hitting in 11 of these seasons, twice hitting over .400. He became the most feared player in the game, both because of his offensive prowess and the unpredictable way he upset opposing teams' defenses.

The 6 foot, one inch, 175-pound Cobb was strong, extremely fast, and a decent outfielder. But the characteristic making him a truly great player was his mental makeup. Larry R. Gerlach discussed Cobb in the *Biographical Dictionary of American Sports* as follows:

> Cobb's brilliance was due more to a careful mastery of skills combined with a maniacal will to succeed than to native talent. His unrelenting quest to be the best featured an aggressive style of play simultaneously admired and abhorred by teammates, opponents, and fans alike. Cobb exhibited in extreme form all the aggressive, extroverted human characteristics—bravery, egotism, ... hypersensitivity. He also [had] a dyspeptic personality, being obstinate, obsessive, paranoid, vituperative, and racist. As a result, he engaged in numerous verbal and physical assaults on and off the field. Some of the ugliest encounters involved blacks, as Cobb, by lineage and upbringing an ardent defender of the Old South, could not abide the lack of "proper" deference shown by northern blacks.

The Tigers won pennants again in 1908–9 under manager Hughie Jennings. In 1910 Cobb won his fourth straight batting title in a controversial finish, described in Chapter 9. But the Tigers were unable to win another pennant again through the 1920 season, and a tired Jennings decided to step down. After the season, Tigers owner Frank Navin approached Cobb about becoming the Tigers' player-manager. Ty, who detested Navin for his miserly policies, turned him down. Cobb had other reasons as well. He felt that few player-managers had been successful since 1900, with the exceptions of Fred Clarke, Fielder Jones, Bill Carrigan, and Tris Speaker. And he was independently wealthy from his investments and didn't need the additional salary.

There were newspaper stories that Jennings' replacement would be Clarence "Pants" Rowland, who had never played big league ball. Rowland had managed the White Sox to a World Series win in 1917, although it was common knowledge that Sox coach and veteran baseball man Kid Gleason had actually run the team. Cobb made it clear that he could not play under Rowland. Influential Detroit sportswriter E. A. Batchelor asked

Ty, "Before you'd play under Rowland, would you take over the management?" Cobb answered, "I'd have to think that over."

With that, Batchelor called Navin to tell him that Cobb could be convinced to manage. As a result, Navin met with Cobb. Ty reluctantly agreed to take over as player-manager in 1921 at a salary increase from $20,000 to $35,000. Cobb later described his decision as "an error I'll always regret" in his *My Life in Baseball*, while also expressing regret that he could not make public his distaste for Rowland as his reason for taking the job. Publicly, Cobb sounded upbeat, telling reporters, "I feel like I've undergone a change of life. I'll expect a hustling club and if I have to crack down on players, I'll get rid of them."

Cobb had some innovative ideas on managing. He abolished morning workouts because he believed most human bodies aren't ready for exercise early in the day. He did not favor team "skull sessions" because he felt that players got more benefit from practicing plays rather than talking about them. Players were forbidden from playing golf. And Cobb forbade his players from fraternizing with opposing players because he felt friendliness between clubs destroyed the "feuding spirit" that made baseball truly competitive. Cobb enforced evening curfews, and he moved his team's bullpen out of open view in order to reduce the distraction to a pitcher of feeling that he "might get the hook at any moment."

Cobb had made a formidable hitter out of righthand-hitting Harry Heilman as early as 1914 by rearranging his stance at the plate and his swing, and Cobb spent much of spring training in his first year as player-manager attempting to improve other players' hitting. The Tigers did reasonably well early in the season, beginning with the opening game on April 14 when they defeated the White Sox 6–5. Cobb doubled in a run and Heilmann smashed a ninth-inning triple to win the game. Cobb recalled: "I was so busy at my new role that I almost forgot to swing that bat…. When we roared into the clubhouse to celebrate the victory, a question crossed my mind. Were my high-average days as a batter ended now that I had the responsibility of governing the actions of almost thirty men?"

Cobb's deft use of such offensive tactics as the hit-and-run, waiting out pitchers, and bunting and stealing unexpectedly kept the Tigers in the first division longer than might have been expected. But the Tigers sank into the second division in late May as their improved offense could not make up for the club's weak infield and pitching staff. Cobb used every psychological ploy he knew. Writer Al Stump described a typical Cobb contrivance in his *The Life and Times of the Meanest Man Who Ever Played Baseball*:

> Outfielder Bobby Veach was too easygoing to suit [Cobb]. Said
> Cobb to Heilmann, "I want you to make him mad. Real mad.
> You are batting behind Veach, so while you're waiting, call him
> a yellow-belly, a quitter, and a dog.... Ride hell out of him.
> Take that smile off Veach's face." Heilmann objected. He liked
> Veach, did not want to lose his good will. Tearing into a team-
> mate was not the amiable Harry's style. "Just do it," ordered
> Cobb. "No arguments."

Heilmann finally agreed to do Cobb's bidding, but only after Ty
promised that at the end of the season he would tell Veach that he had
been set up for his own good. Veach's hitting improved, but he was mad
enough to challenge the burly Heilmann to fight. At season's end Cobb
did not keep his promise to Heilmann, and the coldness between Heilmann and Veach continued for some time. Later in the 1921 season Cobb
tried another cruel stratagem. Stump wrote that Cobb tried to set a fire
under struggling lefthander Dutch Leonard. Cobb left his office door open
deliberately so that Leonard could hear his loud comment, "I'm putting
that damn Dutchman on waivers." Cobb's gambit did not work, as there
was no change in Leonard's performance.

With the Tigers out of the race, questions were raised about Cobb's
ability to handle 23 players of varying temperaments and capabilities.
Detroit Daily News reporter H. G. Salsinger wrote in his column: "Some
weeks ago, Tyrus Raymond Cobb made a flat denial of reports that he
intended to use the iron-clad policy in managing the Tigers. He stated
emphatically that his policy was to use tact and diplomacy, considering
the human element as well as playing ability." If the policy existed, it did
not last long, as proper managerial etiquette was not Cobb's long suit.
During the same week Salsinger's column appeared, lefthander Red Oldham was having a rough outing against the Yankees. Player-manager Cobb
called time from his center field post, raced in to the mound, grabbed the
ball from Oldham, and then proceeded to bawl him out on the spot before
waving in a new pitcher. A few weeks later Cobb derided Dutch Leonard
after Leonard missed two attempts to sacrifice a base runner. Then he
pulled Dutch from the game and sent in a pinch hitter.

Heilmann's .394 average led the league, and Cobb was second with
.389. Cobb also could take some satisfaction from his club's performance.
His club won ten more games than it had the previous year and had
finished one place higher. But he was most satisfied with his club's
improvement in hitting. His team hit a resounding .316, the highest team
batting average in 24 years. The following season began on a disconcert-
ing note when Cobb faced a small mutiny among his troops. Pitcher Dutch

Leonard called Cobb some unpleasant things during spring training and left the club in disgust. Over the next couple of years, some 15 players complained to Navin that Cobb was impossible to play for. They demanded that either the Tigers trade them or get rid of the man none of the players considered a "Georgia Peach." Cobb referred publicly to Navin as a "cheapskate" whose refusal to spend money for good players was the real cause of the team's problems.

The Tigers lost their first nine games in 1922, with Cobb sidelined with leg problems. But the heartily disliked player-manager returned on May 1 and sparked the club with an old-time hitting performance through the summer. By the end of August the Tigers were within five games of the league lead. Cobb was hitting a blistering .415 and proclaiming, "I can taste the pennant." Cobb's taste turned sour in September as his club fell apart. Heilmann broke his collarbone and was out for the season. Cobb was suspended for three days for stepping on an umpire's foot. The team stopped hitting, and two young pitchers, Carl Holling and Lil Stoner, were released after being caught drinking well past the curfew hour. Stoner was probably relieved to get away from Cobb, who had held his nose and waved his glove in disgust after Stoner yielded a clutch home run against the Yankees. The Tigers slumped and finished in third place. Through all the turmoil, Cobb hit .401, an average surpassed only by George Sisler's phenomenal .420.

Cobb had a few favorites among the writers, most notably the famed Grantland Rice, Ring Lardner, and Damon Runyan. But there was a mutual dislike with most other writers, especially those official scorers who the paranoid Cobb felt "stole" base hits from him. He refused to accommodate writers by revealing the name of his starting pitcher in advance of the game, claiming unconvincingly that he was trying to discourage bookmaking. Cobb also felt that the writers favored Babe Ruth over him in their stories.

Cobb nagged Navin into purchasing the contract of young, promising slugger Henry "Heinie" Manush from Omaha. Al Stump wrote that if Navin had not obtained the young lefthand hitter, Cobb almost certainly would have quit the Tigers. In spring training of 1923 Cobb worked hard with Manush, who recalled years later, "Cobb was always on my ass. If I went without a hit, he wouldn't talk to me the following day. He was like a dictator but, as a teacher, he was the best."

When Babe Ruth emerged as a hitting colossus in the early 'twenties, Cobb reacted to the challenge with characteristic pugnacity. He tried several times to precipitate a fight with the easygoing Ruth. There was one game against the Yankees when Cobb tried especially hard to show up the

Babe. At one point Ruth came up with men on second and third. From center field Cobb whistled to pitcher Hooks Dauss to walk Ruth intentionally. Ruth relaxed and Dauss surprised him by firing a strike in the center of the plate. Cobb rushed into the infield, berated Dauss in loud terms, then returned to his position. Dauss poured a second strike over the plate. Cobb raced in again, summoned Dauss and catcher Larry Woodall to the mound, loudly fined them each $100 for disobeying orders, and sent them to the bench. When play resumed everyone expected the intentional walk to be completed. But the relief pitcher whistled the first pitch past the surprised Ruth for a third strike. A gleeful player-manager Cobb had set up the entire charade to fool the Bambino.

The Tigers improved in 1923 and finished in second place behind an excellent Yankee team. Actually, the Tigers appeared hopeless with the season two-thirds over, but they played .640 ball in the last 50 games. Cobb's average fell to .340 but Heilmann picked up the offensive slack, leading the league with a .403 average. Al Stump wrote: "The 1923 season went into the records as the Georgian's finest managerial accomplishment, the product of his willpower, seizing opportunities, goading his men, and playing dirty tricks." Still, the season had taken a lot out of the high-strung Cobb, and the prevailing opinion was that he would quit the manager's role because handling the joint responsibilities of player and manager was adversely affecting his play and his health.

But Cobb was still on the job in 1924. The club was in the running through June. There was a contentious game in mid–June with the Yankees in Detroit. With the Yankees leading 10–6 in the top of the ninth, Ruth fouled out after dodging a pitch aimed at his head. Cobb had triggered the bean ball by whistling in to lefthander Bert Cole. With Bob Meusel up, Cobb whistled in again and Meusel was hit in the back. He charged Cole and the two teams started a free-for-all. Spoiling for a fight with Ruth, Cobb raced in from center field and the two superstars exchanged punches near home plate. The melee went on for nearly half an hour before umpire Billy Evans forfeited the game to the Yankees. Cobb tried to resume his brawl with the Babe but was held back. Meusel shouted at Cobb, "You're a rotten dog. Ruth would kill you if he had the chance." Cobb responded in kind with, "Bring him around to the pass gate and I'll beat the hell out of you and that nigger!" (Cobb, ever the racist, had always insisted that Ruth had some Negroid blood.) The upshot was that Meusel and Cole were suspended and fined, and Ruth was fined. Cobb was completely happy with the affair—he had instigated it and yet had escaped without being punished.

The Tigers continued to play well after the riotous game with the

Yankees, but were closely followed by the Senators and the Yankees. The Tigers fell back after July 4, and the Senators and the Yankees fought a season-long battle for the pennant. Cobb instigated another on-field incident with the New Yorkers later in the season. During a three game series, during which Cobb had clutch hits in each game, he continually hurled insults at the Yanks. He shouted to pocket-sized Yankee manager Miller Huggins, "Hey, who's that midget?" Infuriated by the uncalled-for abuse, husky Lou Gehrig and shortstop Everett Scott raced into the Detroit dugout to take on Cobb. But their wild swings did little damage and both men were ejected. Cobb was allowed to remain in the game because he had not fought back. Later he ignored a note from Ban Johnson asking him to curb his profanity, especially because of the lady fans in the stands. Cobb replied curtly, "Tell the ladies to plug their ears." Years later Ty recalled his club's third place finish with the thought, "We won a lot of games only because we got the other guys too mad to think."

In 1925 the Tigers' hitting, led by Cobb and Heilmann, was not enough to keep the pitching-poor Tigers in the pennant chase, and they finished in fourth place, 16½ games behind the first place Senators. Heilmann led the league with a .393 batting average, while his player-manager stole the hitting laurels with an amazing hitting display in early May. Criticized because he scorned the home run in favor of a more balanced "little ball" style, Cobb called a dozen writers together before a game in St. Louis on May 5. He told them, "Boys, the next two days, I'm going to give you a little demonstration." Cobb proceeded to lead his club to a 14–8 win with a "six" for "six" day, hitting three home runs, a double, and two singles. In an 11–4 victory the next day, he singled in his first time up, giving him nine consecutive base hits, and later in the game he hit two more homers. Cobb had put together the existing record of 25 total bases in two consecutive games. After making the point that he could hit many more home runs if he wanted, Cobb resumed spraying hits to all fields, totaling only 12 homers for the season but hitting .378 at the age of 39.

Pitcher Dutch Leonard sat out the 1922–3 seasons because of his intense dislike for Cobb. He returned to the Tigers in 1924 but had done little. In 1925 he had a better year, with an 11–6 record, but he walked out again in September, returning to his California farm after another dispute with Cobb. He was one of the few Tigers players who stood up to Cobb, and the player-manager referred to Leonard as "a coward and a Bolshevik." In California it was rumored that the furious Leonard "had something" on Cobb.

Just before spring training began in 1926, Cobb had an operation to remove filminess in his eyes. When the Tigers began their spring training in Augusta, there were two new future Hall of Famers in camp, second baseman Charlie Gehringer and lefthander Carl Hubbell. Gehringer would in time become one of the greatest players in the game. Hubbell found greatness elsewhere, as Cobb forbade him from throwing his reverse curve "screwball" because Ty felt it eventually would seriously damage his elbow. (It did, but not before Hubbell became one of the greatest pitchers ever.) Not permitted to throw the pitch, Hubbell was unimpressive, and he never pitched in a Tigers game before being farmed out.

The Tigers finished in sixth place in 1926, and Detroit fans began to call for Cobb's dismissal. A bombshell burst on November 2, 1926, when Cobb unexpectedly resigned his post. Cobb also was leaving as a player, despite his decent .339 batting average in 1926. Cobb's statement was that he had resigned because he was "bone-tired," but Cobb let it be known that the main reason he was leaving was that he could no longer continue to manage for Navin. Then, on November 29, Tris Speaker resigned as the Indians' player-manager, in spite of his club's second place finish and his .304 average.

Stories spread of a thrown game and betting on games by Cobb and Speaker and former Red Sox and Indians star Smoky Joe Wood after Commissioner Landis held a meeting in Chicago with the three men. Cobb's nemesis, Dutch Leonard, had written to Harry Heilmann stating that Leonard had turned over to Landis letters written to him by Wood and Cobb. The letters appeared to indicate that Wood, Cobb, and Speaker had bet on a Tigers-Cleveland game played in Detroit on September 25, 1919, and Leonard contended that Cobb and Speaker had conspired to arrange a Tigers win. At the time, the Tigers were fighting for third place while the Indians had already clinched second place. The vindictive Leonard refused to appear at the meeting with Landis, claiming that, "They've got guys in Chicago who'll bump you off for a price." On January 27, 1927, Landis issued a lengthy decision clearing both men, stating that Leonard had been unwilling to appear at hearings on the matter. But the indication that something underhanded had occurred was too apparent for organized baseball to ignore. As a result, player-managers Cobb and Speaker had to go.

Cobb eventually signed with the Philadelphia Athletics because he was fond of Connie Mack and, not incidentally, because Mack offered him $70,000 in salary and bonus, plus 10 percent of the receipts from all A's exhibition games. The 41-year-old Cobb showed much of his old form in 1927, hitting .357 in 134 games as the A's finished in second place. Ty ended his playing career in 1928, hitting .323 in 95 games. He never again had any involvement with organized baseball, contenting himself thereafter with issuing negative comments on the game and bemoaning the attitudes of players who were incapable of duplicating either his feats or his uncontrollable desire to win at any cost.

Cobb left the game with a marvelous .366 career batting average and some 90 records, most notably his 4189 hits and 892 stolen bases, totals which have been surpassed. Cobb ranks ninth on the all-time player-manager list with 765 games played and managed at the same time. The Georgian had a 479–444 (.519) record as a manager. He was elected to the Hall of Fame in 1936 in the first group of those selected, lacking only four votes from being a unanimous choice.

Cobb was perhaps the wealthiest of all athlete retirees of his time, after years of shrewd investments. He also was one of sports' unhappiest figures after he left the game, frustrated at his departure from the spotlight. Much of Cobb's unhappiness stemmed from his unhappy personal life—two failed marriages, estrangement from his children, physical ailments, and alcoholism. In the final analysis, he was probably the greatest non-pitcher ever to play the game, and yet he remained a selfish, neurotic, egotistical man who was never satisfied with his teammates, players, or anyone else with whom he came into contact. He died in Atlanta on July 17, 1961, and only a few baseball men had enough personal regard for him to attend his funeral.

EDDIE COLLINS

Eddie Collins resembled Ty Cobb in several ways. He was a very fast, bright, and innovative player. Collins had an extremely long major league career during which he accumulated well over 3000 hits. And he played in the deadball era preceding World War I, as well as in the high-scoring years after the war. But the two men also differed. Collins was much better educated and polished, especially off the field. Most importantly, he was a decent man who played within the rules and sought to win games by ability, guile, and mental agility rather than by intimidation.

Edward Trowbridge Collins was born in Millerton, New York, on May 2, 1887, the son of railroad freight agent John Rossman and Mary Meade (Trowbridge) Collins. The 5 foot 9 inch, 175–pounder played semi-pro baseball while the varsity quarterback at Columbia University. Still in college, he signed with the Philadelphia Athletics under the name "Sullivan" to retain his collegiate eligibility, playing in six games for Connie Mack in September 1906. After his graduation in 1907 he played in 14 games for the Athletics under his given name.

Collins was described in the sixth edition of *Total Baseball* as a "wimpy-looking guy, thin but hippy, a generous nose, and a chin that barely clears [sic] his neck." He was the Athletics' regular second baseman by 1909, hitting .347 and leading American League second basemen in fielding. By 1910 Collins was the most prominent member of the Athletics' "$100,000 infield." He was the club leader as the A's dominated the league during the 1910–1914 period, winning three World Series and four pennants during the five years. Over that period the consistently brilliant Collins had an average of .345 during the regular seasons and .347 in the four World Series. Nicknamed "Cocky" because of his confidence on the field, he won the MVP (Chalmers) Award in 1914.

Connie Mack broke up his club after the 1914 season and Collins was sold to the Chicago White Sox for $50,000. Generally regarded as the game's finest position player, Collins signed a five-year, $75,000 contract and joined a club that had not been a serious contender for several years. After the 1914 season, normally penurious Sox owner Charlie Comiskey spent some money. In addition to obtaining Collins, he brought up promising outfielder Oscar "Happy" Felsch from Milwaukee and in midseason obtained slugging outfielder "Shoeless Joe" Jackson from Cleveland. With these players and a decent pitching staff, the White Sox improved. Managed by Clarence "Pants" Rowland, the Sox vacated the second division, finishing third in 1915 and second in 1916. Sparked by Collins, powered by the unlettered Jackson, and featuring an excellent pitching staff led by righthander Eddie Cicotte (28–12), the 1917 White Sox won 100 games and won the pennant by nine games. They faced John McGraw's Giants in the World Series.

The Sox and the Giants split the first four games, and Rowland's club moved ahead by winning the fifth game as McGraw fumed at the thought of losing to that "busher" Rowland. This game produced Collins' signature play. The game was scoreless in the top of the fourth with Collins on second base. He moved to third when Giant rightfielder Dave Robertson muffed Jackson's fly. Happy Felsch hit a bounder to pitcher Rube Benton, and Collins' job was to draw a throw from Benton to the plate to prevent a double play. With Collins starting for the plate, Benton threw home to catcher Bill Rariden. Collins stopped and started back to third base, presumably forcing the Giants to run him down and permit the runners to move up to second and third bases.

As he danced back and forth on the third base line, Collins saw that neither Benton nor first baseman Walter Holke had come in to cover the plate. When the catcher threw to Zimmerman, Collins quickly halted his return towards third and reversed stride. He broke for the uncovered plate with Zimmerman in hot, but futile, pursuit all the way to the plate. That was the unforgettable picture that the crowd of 33,369 would long remember, and Zimmerman appeared to be the goat. After the game, which the Sox won 4–2 to win the Series, McGraw told the writers, "It wasn't Zimmerman's fault; Holke should have been at home plate to take the throw." Zimmerman had an unforgettable response. He told the writers, "Who the hell was I supposed to throw the ball to? [Plate umpire] Bill Klem?" But the quick-thinking Collins, who hit .409 during the Series, had made the deciding play.

The White Sox dropped into the second division in 1918, but the club came back in 1919 to win the pennant. Everything worked well for the Sox, managed by William "Kid" Gleason. Jackson, Collins, third baseman Buck Weaver, righthander Eddie Cicotte (29–7), and Lefty Williams (23–11) played superbly. The heavily-favored Sox played the Reds in the World Series and lost five games to three. There were rumors that the Series had been fixed, but it was almost a year until the scandal came to light. The "Black Sox" scandal has been well documented, but it is worth recalling the views of Collins, who hit a lowly, but honest, .226 in the Series. Bob Broeg wrote in *Super Stars of Baseball*:

> A brusque, honest man, Collins was revolted by the Black Sox scandal in which eight of his Chicago teammates conspired to throw the 1919 World Series to the Cincinnati Reds.... He found it difficult the rest of his life to talk about the episode that infuriated him. When he did, it's worth noting that he showed no compassion for the third baseman, George (Buck) Weaver, who went to a bitter grave contending that he had not participated in the fix and hadn't received a cent, but merely hadn't ratted on the conspirators.

Collins remained the best second baseman in the game through the next several seasons. In early September 1924, with the White Sox mired in last place, Collins replaced crotchety manager Johnny Evers. The Sox improved to play over .500 ball in 27 games under their new player-manager, but finished last. Prospects were not bright for the team Collins took to training camp in 1925. The Sox began the season with several decent players but without any real expectations that the club would be a genuine contender. The stars of the club were second baseman–manager Collins and righthander Ted Lyons, a solid pitcher with a good fastball and curve, and a serviceable knuckleball.

The Sox started the season reasonably well, largely on the strength of strong offensive efforts by first baseman Earl Sheely, centerfielder Johnny Mostil, and Collins, who cracked out his 3000th career hit on June

3. The popular Lyons won a series of well-pitched games, and rookie righthander Tommy Thomas was a pleasant surprise. But in mid-season Collins' club fell back as his pitching faltered, and finished in fifth place. Player-manager Collins did his part, hitting .346, despite missing one-quarter of the season. He also had the satisfaction of having raised the club from its last place finish in 1924 to fifth place, while winning 13 more games.

Collins' 1926 club was virtually identical in personnel and in performance, again finishing fifth. Collins duplicated his previous year with a .344 average in 106 games. But, at 39, he had slowed down in the field, and Comiskey released him after the season, deciding that he could no longer afford to pay $40,000 to a fading player-manager. In 1926 Collins rejoined his mentor, Connie Mack, playing in 95 games for the rebuilding A's, hitting .336. He served as Mack's third base coach and unofficial assistant manager while playing sparingly from 1928 until he retired as a player after the 1930 season. Collins was offered a chance to manage the Yankees near the end of the 1929 season but declined. He had been assured that he would succeed Mack as A's manager, never dreaming that Connie would manage the Athletics for another 20 years. After Tom Yawkey bought the Red Sox in 1933, Collins became the club's vice-president, treasurer, and business manager. He served in these capacities until his death in Boston on March 25, 1951.

Collins had a lifetime batting average of .333 over his 25-year playing career. He also ranks high in career hits, doubles, runs scored, walks, and stolen bases. Collins led all American League second basemen in fielding average nine times, and such authorities as Ty Cobb, Connie Mack, and Frankie Frisch considered him the best second baseman ever. Collins had a managerial record of 174–160 (.521), all of it as a player-manager. Collins' son, Eddie, made his major league debut in 1939, the year that Eddie, Sr. was inducted into the Hall of Fame.

14

Speaker and Sisler

TRIS SPEAKER

Tris Speaker's career was remarkably similar to Ty Cobb's in terms of superior athletic skills and performance, playing longevity, and even in the episode that forced them out of their player-manager jobs. The two men differed, though, in temperament. Speaker was a level-headed man who earned the respect of his players by his authoritative, stable leadership. Cobb was feared and disliked by his players because of his constant threats and reliance on intimidating behavior.

Tristram E. Speaker was born in the small town of Hubbard City, Texas, on April 4, 1888. The son of local merchant Archie and Nancy Jane "Jenny" Speaker, he was the only boy in a family of seven children. Tris was a typical rural Texas youngster of his time, riding horses bareback and, in one instance, breaking his right arm in a fall while bronco-busting a wild horse. Speaker also was a cow puncher and a telegraph linesman. In his spare time he played local baseball after learning to throw accurately with his left hand.

After attending a technical college briefly and pitching for a semipro team in Corsicana, Texas, Speaker joined the Cleburne club of the North Texas League. He signed as a pitcher for $50 a month in 1906 when he was 18. After being switched to the outfield and showing potential as a hitter, the Red Sox bought Speaker's contract for $800. After an unimpressive start with Boston in 1907, Tris was not offered a contract for 1908, but he played well for the Little Rock club and rejoined the Boston club in the 1908 season. Speaker's breakthrough came the following year when the lefthand-hitting and throwing outfielder hit .309. He followed that up with six great years in which his batting averages ranged from a high of .383 in 1912, when he won the Chalmers Award, to a low of .322 in 1915.

Speaker was a stylist at the plate and in the field. He held his bat low, moving it up and down with a twitching motion like a cat's tail as he stared out at the pitcher. Then he cocked his bat at hip level before striding into the pitch. Before Speaker came into the league, centerfielders stationed themselves in medium length center field well out from the infield. In that deadball era, Speaker played in so close to second base that he was virtually a "fifth" infielder. He was willing to risk giving up an occasional extra-base hit over his head in order to reduce the much more frequent singles dropping in front of him. The 6 foot, 195-pound Speaker was a fast, agile man for his size. He cut down on the number of balls hit over his head by accurately judging fly balls as they were hit and, without slowing down to watch the ball, racing to the drive's landing point for the catch.

Speaker's facility in playing a short center field permitted him to rack up a record 35 outfield assists twice during his years with the Red Sox. Later in his career, in April 1918, he twice executed unassisted double plays at second base, snaring low liners on the run and then outracing retreating base runners to second base. On another occasion he played so close to second base that he was the pivot man at second base on a double play started by the second baseman. At other times, with the shortstop and second baseman deliberately playing well off second base, Speaker sneaked in from short center field to take a pickoff throw from the catcher and nail the unsuspecting runner.

The Red Sox won the 1912 World Series from John McGraw's Giants, and Speaker was in the thick of the decisive action. In the deciding game at Boston, with both teams tied at three games apiece, the Giants took a 2–1 lead into the bottom of the ninth with their ace righthander Christy Mathewson on the mound. Sox pinch hitter Clyde Engle took second when Fred Snodgrass muffed his flyball. Harry Hooper belted a long drive to deep left center on which Snodgrass made a fine running catch. The next hitter walked and Speaker popped a short foul ball just off the first base line between home and first. Neither first baseman Fred Merkle nor catcher Chief Meyers made the catch, each expecting the other to make the play. Although Merkle was blamed for not catching the ball, both Speaker and John McGraw faulted Mathewson for not loudly directing Meyers to make the catch. The reprieved Speaker then singled in the tying run. Duffy Lewis walked to fill the bases and Larry Gardner hit a sacrifice fly for the Series win.

The Sox started slowly in 1913, and catcher Bill Carrigan replaced manager Chick Stahl in mid-season. Apparently, there were two religious factions on the 1913 team, causing dissension and contributing to the team's poor performance. Speaker appeared to play an important role in causing the problem. In his *Fenway—An Unexpurgated History of the Boston Red Sox*, Peter Golenbock wrote: "There is evidence that Speaker and Wood may have left the Red Sox [after the 1915 season] because, as non–Catholics, they didn't get along with their Irish Catholic teammates in Irish Boston.... Speaker, a Texan, was a member of the Ku Klux Klan. His close friend, Wood, was an Orangeman. Both were Masons.... According- ing to a close friend of Duffy Lewis, Speaker didn't hide his contempt for his Catholic teammates, including Babe Ruth, Lewis, and Hooper." Golen- bock went on to write that Ruth and Speaker never got along in the years that both men were in the American League, and that Hooper and Lewis hated Speaker.

As discussed in Chapter 10, Speaker was traded to Cleveland after a salary dispute with Sox owner Joe Lannin. Conceivably, Speaker's poor relations with several teammates was also a factor in Lannin's move. The loss of his star centerfielder was a blow to Bill Carrigan, although very likely it was a relief to Hooper, Lewis, and other aggrieved teammates.

If Speaker was disappointed at the trade, his performance in 1916 did not reflect it. He had one of his greatest years, leading the league with a .386 average. Weak pitching held the Indians to a sixth place finish. In 1917 the Indians moved up to third place as Speaker turned in another fine season and two newly-obtained righthanders, Jim Bagby and Stan Coveleski, improved the pitching staff.

Cleveland manager Lee Fohl was an easygoing, colorless plodder who had managed the Indians since 1915. His most successful season came in 1918 when the Indians finished second, 2½ games behind the Red Sox in a season shortened because of U.S. entrance into World War 1. Speaker hit .318 to finish fourth in the league and continued to sparkle in the field. Speaker was something of a co-manager, as the stolid Fohl relied upon Tris' advice in many areas. The Indians were in third place but hard on the heels of the first place White Sox when they faced the Yankees in a mid-season game. With the Indians leading in the ninth, Fohl disregarded Speaker's advice on which relief pitcher to bring into the game to face Babe Ruth. The Babe homered to win the game, and the embattled Fohl was fired the next day, with Speaker replacing him.

Speaker inherited a team with a fair pitching staff, led by Coveleski and Bagby, and adequate hitting, featuring the player-manager himself, third baseman Larry Gardner, and leftfielder Jack Graney. The Indians were particularly well fortified through the middle with catcher Steve

O'Neill, second baseman Bill Wambsganss, shortstop Ray Chapman, and Speaker in center field. The club improved its performance under Speaker's steady direction, playing at a .656 pace after he took over and finishing in second place, only 3½ games behind the crooked, but powerful, White Sox. Speaker may have felt the strain of managing as his batting average dipped to .296, the only time it fell under .300 from 1908 until 1928.

Speaker's first full season as a player-manager was a smashing success, although it also had a tragic side. The Indians took the lead in late April and remained in front through mid–August, locked in a struggle with the Yankees and the White Sox for the pennant. Bagby and Coveleski were the pitching staff leaders, and former Yankee righthander Ray Caldwell regained his old touch with some deft handling by Speaker. Caldwell had an in-and-out career largely because he was one of the game's more enthusiastic drinkers. Speaker arranged for his contract to specify that Caldwell was to *get drunk* after every game he pitched and was not to show up at the ballpark the following day. Speaker assured the pitcher he meant what the contract said. Caldwell pitched effectively thereafter, apparently spoiled by the requirement to drink for one day.

Tragedy struck the club on August 16 at the Polo Grounds. Ray Chapman, the Indians' accomplished shortstop and Speaker's closest friend in baseball, was beaned by Yankees' righthander Carl Mays that afternoon. A righthand batter who crowded the plate, Chapman froze and failed to get out of the way of one of Mays' submarine deliveries. Years later, on-deck hitter Speaker recalled the horrifying scene for *New York World Telegram* sportswriter Joe Williams:

> The ball hit Chappie, bounded back halfway to the pitcher's box and a little to the first base side. Mays rushed over and threw the ball to Wally Pipp at first base, claiming the ball had been hit. I immediately rushed to catch Chappie, since he started to fall almost instantly, but before I could get there he had dropped to the ground. He wasn't unconscious at the moment. In fact, he made an effort to get up and to charge at Mays but it appeared his body was paralyzed. We had him carried out of the park and an ambulance took him to the hospital and he died at 4:50 the following morning.

The grief-stricken Indians seemed to lose their spark after the Chapman tragedy, and the White Sox replaced them in first place after Speaker's club lost a doubleheader to the Yankees. Within a few days the Indians had fallen 3½ games behind the White Sox. Speaker picked up lefthander Walter "Duster" Mails, who had failed in an earlier stint with Brooklyn.

Speaker felt that Mails had two virtues—loads of untapped natural ability and the fact that he had not been on the club during the dreadful Chapman episode. Speaker's judgment was proven right. With Mails' confident personality and immediate success (he won seven straight decisions), and young Joe Sewell a capable replacement for Chapman, the Indians regained the lead within a couple of weeks. They fought off the Yankees, who were carried by the phenomenal hitting of newly-acquired Babe Ruth. The Indians and White Sox were in a virtual tie for the lead until September 28 when a Chicago grand jury indicted eight White Sox players who were charged with participating in throwing the 1919 World Series. The eight players were suspended immediately and, with their loss, the White Sox lost two of their last three games. Speaker's club won the pennant, two games ahead of the White Sox and three in front of the Yankees. Speaker was thrilled at winning the pennant, despite the realization that the White Sox might have won the pennant if the grand jury indictment had come after the season.

Speaker had a marvelous year in 1920, arguably the best season ever turned in by a player-manager. He averaged over .400 through July, and his sensational hitting reached a climax on July 10 when he lined out his eleventh straight hit, a league record at the time. For the season he hit .388, second in the league to George Sisler's .407. Later in the season, in a key deciding game of three played against the White Sox before eight of their players were suspended, Speaker saved the game with a sensational play. The Indians were leading the Sox by a run, with two men on and two out. "Shoeless Joe" Jackson cracked a liner to deep right center. Speaker raced back to the exit gate and, with a frantic leap, made the catch with both feet off the ground, then crashed into the concrete wall. He fell and lay unconscious for several minutes, and the ball had to be pried out of his glove.

But playing-manager Speaker also distinguished himself by the way he ran his club. He was the first manager to platoon his players extensively, although the idea of employing righthand hitters against lefthanders, and vice versa, dated back to the early 1900s. Against lefthand pitchers he often inserted righthand-hitting Joe Evans in left field, George Burns at first base, and Smoky Joe Wood (who had become an outfielder after his pitching arm burned out) in right field. At other times he alternated these players with lefthand-hitting Charlie Jamieson, Doc Johnson, and Elmer Smith. In a far cry from his contentious years with the Red Sox, Speaker was extremely popular with his players. He led his club by his exemplary play but also by the way he treated his players. They understood they would be treated fairly. Speaker was the boss during a game but, unlike most managers, he was one of the boys off the field, rooming with former Red Sox roommate Smoky Joe Wood or catcher Les Nunamaker.

The Indians met the Brooklyn Robins in a best-of-nine World Series. Wilbert Robinson's club had won the National League pennant over the Giants by seven games, led by leftfielder Zack Wheat, centerfielder Hy Myers, and spitballing righthander Burleigh Grimes. Coveleski defeated lefty Rube Marquard 3–1 in the first game, but Grimes threw a 3–0 win against Bagby, and righthander Sherry Smith beat Caldwell 2–1. The Series moved to Cleveland and the Indians tied the Series behind a slick 5–1 Coveleski five-hitter.

Bagby breezed to an 8–1 victory the next day to put the Indians one-up in the Series in one of the most famous World Series games ever. One feature of the game was Elmer Smith's first inning grand slam, the first four-run blast in Series competition up to that time. Bagby became the first pitcher to hit a Series home run, with a three-run drive in the third inning. But the most famous play came in the fifth inning. With none out and runners on first and second, Brooklyn pitcher Clarence Mitchell came to the plate. With both runners moving on a hit-and-run play, Mitchell sliced a low liner toward right center field. Second baseman Bill Wambsganss leaped to make the catch. He spotted the runner, Pete Kilduff, well off second base and beat the runner to the base. Wamby turned to throw to first base but saw the runner, slow-moving catcher Otto Miller, well off the bag. Wamby raced over and tagged Miller to complete the only unassisted triple play in Series history. The Indians won the sixth game when Duster Mails shut out the Robins in a three hit, 1–0 win. And Coveleski came back the next day to win the clincher 3–0, for his third five-hit win of the Series. Player-manager Speaker topped off a brilliant season with a .320 Series average and a team-leading six runs scored.

The 1921 Indians roster was identical to the 1920 roster. By July 4, the race became a two-way duel between the Indians and the Yankees. Speaker's club took the lead from the start and remained in front before a late slump, a knee injury that sidelined Speaker for three weeks, and a Yankee surge gave the Bronx Bombers the flag by 4½ games. Babe Ruth led the Yankees, leading the league by wide margins in home runs (59) and in every other power statistic. Carl Mays had a magnificent 27–9 year to lead a fine Yankees pitching staff. Speaker and Coveleski had excellent years, but the Indians were overmatched by the powerhouse put together by Yankees general manager Ed Barrow.

Speaker treated his players with respect, but he also could be utterly frank with them in discussing their playing drawbacks. The Indians had a third baseman, Walter "Rube" Lutzke, who was with the team under Speaker's managership for several years. Lutzke was an excellent fielder and he occasionally hit well enough to raise hopes that his hitting had come around. But invariably he would fall into a devastating hitting slump that lasted through the rest of the season. After each disappointing season he would seek out the fancied physical problem that had caused his slump. First it was his appendix; its removal would surely help his hitting. The next year he blamed his teeth and they would be removed. Then it was his eyes, so he stopped reading and going to movies. But he remained a .250 hitter regardless of what he tried. His worst year came in 1925 when he hit a pitiful .218. He approached Speaker and said mournfully, "Skip, I've tried everything. I've had my appendix out. I've got rid of my bad teeth. I won't even read a menu without glasses so I won't strain my eyes. What's wrong with me?" Speaker looked at him, thought for a minute, and then responded, "There's only one thing wrong with you, Lutzke, you can't hit."

The Indians fell to fourth place in 1922 as the team suffered a general letdown. Righthander George Uhle (22–16) and Coveleski (17–14) were the leading pitchers, but Bagby was ineffective and the Indians pitching staff had a 4.59 ERA. Speaker had a typical year, hitting .378, but the Cleveland offense was not able to compensate for the club's mediocre pitching. The Indians improved in 1923, finishing in third place, but again they were no match for the overpowering Yankees, despite good years by player-manager Speaker (.380) and Uhle (26–16). The Indians sank into the second division in the next two years, finishing sixth twice as several players showed their age. Speaker had slowed down with advancing age, but he remained the best defensive centerfielder in the league, and he hit .344 in 1924 and .389 the following year.

The club came back in 1926. First baseman George Burns had his career season. And George Uhle led the league with 27 wins. The club started the season well, and in early September Speaker's team was within a game of the league-leading Yankees. But the outgunned Indians were unable to maintain the pace and they finished in second place, three games behind the Yankees. The 38-year-old Speaker hit 52 doubles, although his batting average dipped to .304. His club had done surprisingly well and he had regained the full support of fans unhappy with the Indians' decline in the two preceding seasons.

As discussed in Chapter 13, Speaker resigned on November 29, a month after Cobb was deposed. There was a widely-shared belief that the failure of both Cobb and Speaker to manage again stemmed from a private order by Commissioner Landis forbidding such employment. Bill

James, in *The Bill James Guide to Baseball Managers*, expressed the view that no such order was ever given. James went on to write: "I agree that there is significant evidence ... that [Smoky] Joe Wood bet against his own team and there is some evidence that Cobb may have known that the Indians were laying down for [Detroit's benefit].... But I defy anyone to show me any credible evidence that Tris Speaker was involved."

Speaker played for the Senators in 1927, and the "Grey Eagle" delivered with a decent performance, hitting .327 in 141 games. But his salary was more than Clark Griffith could justify paying a 39-year-old fading superstar. Connie Mack picked up Speaker, where he spent his last season as Ty Cobb's teammate, hitting .267 while playing less than half of the Philadelphia Athletics' schedule. For the next two years "Spoke" was a player-manager for the Newark Bears of the International League. After that he operated the Kansas City club briefly, broadcast games, and then went into business. He was called back by the Indians in 1947 to tutor Larry Doby, and, in subsequent years, coached the Indians and their farm clubs in spring training.

Speaker, elected to the Hall of Fame in 1937, was a major leaguer for 22 years. He ranks fifth in career batting average (.345), first with 792 career doubles, 449 outfield assists, and 139 double plays, and second with 6788 putouts. Tris, with a 617–520 (.543) managerial record, ranks tenth, just behind Ty Cobb, with 741 games played while he was managing. Speaker died of a heart attack at age 70.

GEORGE SISLER

George Harold Sisler was born on March 24, 1893, in Manchester, Ohio. Sisler's father, Cassius, was the supervisor of a coal mine. Young Sisler, an excellent all–around athlete and lefthand pitcher at high school, was offered athletic scholarships at the University of Pennsylvania and Western Reserve. But he turned them down to pay his own way at the University of Michigan in order to attend college with a close friend.

Before leaving for Ann Arbor when he was 17, Sisler, without the consent of his parents, signed an agreement to play for the Akron club of the Ohio-Pennsylvania League, which was affiliated with the Columbus, Ohio, club of the American Association. The University of Michigan permitted Sisler to participate in collegiate sports because he neither had been paid by the Columbus club nor had he played for them. By the time Sisler graduated, Branch Rickey, the manager of the St. Louis Browns, signed him. Prior to that, though, the Pittsburgh Pirates had purchased his contract from Columbus. After considerable legal debate, the Browns were awarded Sisler's contract and he pitched for them a few days after he received his degree in mechanical engineering in June 1915.

The 5 foot 11 inch, 170-pounder pitched three scoreless innings in relief in his major league debut. Two months later he outpitched his idol Walter Johnson and won 2–1. In that first season he pitched in 15 games, with a 4–4 record, and hit .285 in 65 games as a first baseman and outfielder. Sisler played first base almost exclusively in 1916, and hit .305 as an everyday player.

The writers gave the handsome, slick-fielding young first baseman the nickname "Gorgeous George" because of his appearance and good manners. He was obviously well-brought-up, genteel, and well-mannered in a period when there were relatively few college-trained players. But he proved early in his career that he was no patsy. Bob Broeg wrote:

> At a time when he was still a kid freshly converted to first base, he couldn't reach a high throw and by the time he retrieved the ball, the runner was on second base. The Browns' pitcher, Bob Groom, was losing and the mishap did nothing to dampen the fuse of a short temper. "Listen, you … college boy," he said to Sisler in the dugout, "you run harder for those … balls. Where the hell do you think you are, at a … tea party?" No one had ever talked like that to Sisler before, and no one would ever do so again. His face turned white and he stared in disbelief at Groom for an instant, then walked over and decked the startled pitcher with a left hook.

Sisler played brilliantly over the 1917–1922 period, his hitting talents often compared with those of his cross-city rival, Rogers Hornsby. Sisler was widely considered the best fielding, quickest, and most graceful first baseman in the game after the magician-like but infamous Hal Chase retired after the 1919 season. Sisler made an almost unbelievable play in a game against the Senators in 1922, the year when the surprising Browns came within a game of winning the pennant. With Washington's Joe Judge racing for the plate on an attempted squeeze play, Roger Peckinpaugh bunted down the first base line. Sisler anticipated the play and broke for the plate as the ball was pitched. He scooped up Peckinpaugh's bunt about 15 feet from the plate, tagged him as he started down the line, and, in the same motion, flipped the ball to the catcher who tagged out the sliding Judge, completing a breathtaking double play.

From 1920 through 1922 Sisler had averages of .407, .371, and .420, totaling 719 hits for a composite .400 average. Twice during the three-year period he led the American League in base hits, batting average, and stolen bases. His 1922 season, in which he had 246 hits, was especially remarkable because he suffered from chronic eye ailments and a torn arm muscle, causing him to ask his fellow infielders to "throw the ball to me low, boys." During that season Sisler hit in 41 consecutive games.

After the 1922 season, Sisler's eye condition worsened. He suffered from a serious sinus condition which affected his optic nerve, resulting in double vision. As a result, he sat out the 1923 season. After the season the Browns' management approached Sisler about taking over as player-manager. Sisler was reluctant but he relented when he was offered a $25,000 contract, the most he had ever been paid. He took over a fifth place team with two standouts, hard-hitting leftfielder Ken Williams and spitballing righthander Urban Shocker. He had two decent outfielders in centerfielder William "Baby Doll" Jacobson and little rightfielder Jack Tobin. The remaining players were essentially a group of journeymen. And there was one big unknown: How would the new player-manager perform after a year in drydock?

Sisler's first year as manager played out as might have been expected. His club finished in fourth place but was never a factor in the race. Sisler, who hit .305, Williams, and Jacobson were the leading run producers in a modest attack, but the pitching staff had a 4.57 ERA, the second worst in the league. Sisler had lost none of his fielding skill, but he was not the hitter he had been before his layoff. In Donald Honig's *The Man in the Dugout*, Honig quoted pitcher Bob Shawkey: "When he came back, we learned something.... When he was up at the plate, he could watch you for only so long, and then he'd have to look down to get his eyes focused again. So we'd keep him waiting up there until he'd have to look down, and then pitch. He was never the same hitter again after that."

Sisler's club improved in 1925, finishing in third place, a distant 15 games behind the pennant-winning Senators. Sisler led a decent, if not overpowering, attack. He regained his old form with 224 hits, 105 RBI, and a .345 average. But his pitching staff was mediocre, and baseball experts praised the job he had done with such an unimposing club. The Browns found their true level in 1926, falling to seventh place. Advancing age and the strain and frustrations of his managing responsibilities took their toll on Sisler as his batting average dipped to .290. Browns' president Phil Ball agreed with Sisler that it would be best to relieve him of his managerial responsibilities.

George Sisler was not well suited to managing, especially when he was playing. He did as well as possible with the inferior playing material given him and was an excellent instructor, as he would demonstrate later in his career. But the modest, gentlemanly Sisler was not a natural manager and

George Sisler was the best fielding—and most graceful—first basemen of his era, hitting over .400 twice in the early 1920s. He was the St. Louis Browns' player-manager from 1924 to 1926; he stepped down willingly as a manager but remained as a player.

temperamentally unsuited to motivate players by intimidating them, á la McGraw or Cobb.

After being relieved as manager, Sisler had a good season for the seventh place Browns in 1927. But he played well below his standards in 1928 and was traded early in the year to the Boston Braves, then managed by his old friend Rogers Hornsby. After two more seasons with the Braves he played in the minors before retiring in 1932. Ten years later he returned to the majors as a scout and hitting instructor with the Brooklyn Dodgers. Later he went into business and served as commissioner of the National Baseball Congress.

Sisler was named to the Hall of Fame in 1939 on the strength of a .340 career batting average and other impressive offensive and defensive statistics. He had a 218–241 (.475) managerial record, ranking 25th in player-managed games. Two of his three sons were active in baseball. Dick Sisler played in the majors for eight years, and George Jr. was the president of the International League. George Sr., considered by many baseball people as a model baseball player, died at age 80 in 1973.

15

Hornsby and Huggins

The only similarities between Miller Huggins and Rogers Hornsby were that they were player-managers and second basemen. Hornsby was a man whose success was largely due to his playing skills and knowledge of the game, rather than his ability to deal with his employers and players. Huggins was a small, scholarly, tactful man who succeeded as a player by getting the most out of his modest physical skills. He succeeded as a manager by finding and maximizing good managing opportunities and by handling his players with tact and gentle authority.

ROGERS HORNSBY

Rogers Hornsby was born on April 27, 1896, in Winter, Texas, near Austin. Named for his mother's family, he was the youngest of five children born to farmer Aaron Edward Hornsby and Mary Dallas Jones Hornsby. Rogers' father died when the boy was two, and the family moved to Fort Worth. Baseball was Hornsby's raison d'etre from the start. Before he was 13 he was a substitute infielder for a team made up of stockyards and meat packing plant workers, and at 15 he was playing in a Fort Worth city league.

Rogers made his professional debut in 1914 as a shortstop, hitting .232 with the Hugo, Oklahoma, and Denison, Texas, clubs of the Class D Texas-Oklahoma League. Hornsby hit an improved .277 for Denison in 1915, joining the Cardinals in September. The 19-year-old shortstop hit .246, but with little power, in 18 games with the Cards. Miller Huggins, the Cardinals' second baseman–manager, encouraged Hornsby to crowd the plate, use a thick-handled bat, choke up, and concentrate on putting the ball in play. In the field Hornsby was over-anxious and error-prone, and his throwing was erratic.

A St. Louis writer described the righthand-hitting youngster as a scrawny (5 foot 11, 135-pound) "hollow-chested, large-footed, gangling boy with a straight nose, firm mouth, and chin." He was naive, spoke with a high-pitched Texas twang, and used considerable profanity. After the 1915 season ended, Huggins told Hornsby, "Kid, you're a little light, but you have the makings. I think I'll farm you out for a year." Huggins felt the youngster needed more seasoning in the farm system in 1916, but Hornsby thought he was being told to spend the off-season on a farm to build up his body. So he spent the winter building up his body at an uncle's farm in Texas and reported to training camp in 1916, 30 pounds heavier and much stronger. He also displayed a different batting style. Instead of crowding the plate, Rogers returned to his original hitting stance, standing well off the plate, far back in the batters box, with his left foot close to the plate to permit him to reach outside pitches.

The 1916 Cardinals finished 33½ games off the pace in seventh place, although Hornsby played well. He hit his first major league home run at Robison Field in St. Louis on May 14th, an inside-the-park blow which landed behind third base and bounced into the stands, a homer under then-existing rules. By midseason he brought his average up to .300, finishing the year with a .313 average, fourth in the National League. But his fielding remained suspect at shortstop and first base.

The Cardinals rose to third place in 1917, as Hornsby excelled, hitting .327 with power and playing shortstop more confidently. The impact of World War I increased in 1918 but did not affect Hornsby, who was deferred because he was providing sole support for his mother and sister. Hornsby had become the most sought after young player in the league, and his attractiveness had been enhanced by his deferment. As a result, Branch Rickey, who had been hired as the Cardinals' president, signed Hornsby to a two-year contract at $4000 a year.

Miller Huggins resigned before the 1918 season and was replaced by Jack Hendricks. The college-trained Hendricks and Hornsby, a high school dropout who had little use for college men (except Huggins, who was a law school graduate), did not hit it off well. The Cardinals lost most of their regulars to the military and finished in last place. For much of the season the temperamental Hornsby was not on speaking terms with his manager or several of his teammates, who felt that he was not playing hard, as reflected in his sub-par .281 batting average.

In early July Hornsby was reclassified into Class 1 by his draft board under a new "Work or Fight" military directive. This made him subject to the military draft unless he engaged in an essential wartime occupation by August 1. Hornsby was hired by a Wilmington, Delaware, shipyard, spending all of his time playing for the shipyard's baseball team. Presumably to be even safer from the draft, Hornsby sent for Sarah Martin, to whom he had been engaged for a year, and the couple married in late September.

The war ended sooner than expected and Hornsby rejoined the Cardinals in 1919. Branch Rickey had replaced Hendricks as the Cardinals' manager while also serving as a club vice president. But Rickey's cerebral approach to managing did little to help the Cardinals, who finished in seventh place, 40½ games behind the pennant-winning Cubs. Hornsby's play was the Cards' only redeeming feature, as he hit .318, the second highest batting average in the league. At Rickey's insistence, Hornsby learned the techniques of second base play, although he continued to play mostly at third base.

Beginning in 1920, with a livelier baseball in use, Hornsby ran off a string of six straight years as the National League's foremost hitter, leading the league with averages ranging from .370 in 1920 to a magnificent .424 in 1924. During these six years he also led each year in on-base and slugging percentages. In four of the six years he led in base hits, most notably in 1922 when he had 250 hits. During the period, he played exclusively at second base and gained recognition as a steady if unspectacular fielder with just average range and a surprising weakness in handling pop flies. St. Louis writer J. Roy Stockton commented wryly, "Hornsby was unfamiliar with pop flies because he hit so few of them himself."

Hornsby also had another problem during the period, this one off the field. In his book *Rogers Hornsby*, Charles C. Alexander discussed an affair Hornsby had with Jeannette Pennington Hine, a "shapely, strikingly pretty brunette," beginning in mid-season of 1922. Sarah Hornsby responded by moving out of the Hornsby home with their son Rogers Jr. Sarah filed for divorce in June 1923, and Jeannette Hine's husband considered filing an alienation of affections suit. Eventually Hine abandoned the idea and the Hines divorced. After much anguish for all parties, Hornsby married Jeannette Pennington on February 28, 1924, just before departing for spring training for a season in which he would hit .424.

Despite Hornsby's hitting heroics from 1920 through 1924, the money-short Cardinals finished in the first division only twice and did not finish closer than seven games from the pennant winner. On May 29, 1925, after a tough loss in Pittsburgh, the Cardinals languished in last place with a 13–25 record. For some time Cardinals' owner Sam Breadon had discussed with Rickey the possibility of replacing him as manager. Before the season started Breadon had asked Hornsby whether he was interested in managing the club. But Rogers turned him down, saying that he was in his playing prime. But now, with the season one-quarter over and the team doing poorly, a managerial change needed to be made. Hornsby agreed to take the job with no increase in salary—he was being paid $30,000 a year—but he convinced Breadon to assist him in purchasing Rickey's 1167 shares of stock. And so the Texan became the Cardinals' player-manager.

Rogers made some beneficial personnel moves. He brought up short-stop Tommy Thevenow from the Cardinals' Syracuse farm team and made everyday players of leftfielder Ray Blades and rightfielder Chick Hafey, who Rickey had been platooning. And he moved lefthanded reliever Bill "Wee Willie" Sherdel to the starting staff. All of the moves improved the Cardinals, and the club also was helped by solid hitting by first baseman "Sunny Jim" Bottomley and Hornsby, who continued to hit around .400.

Although managing did not affect Hornsby's playing, it did affect his demeanor on the field. Two weeks after he took over, he became involved in a wild scene during a loss to the Phillies in St. Louis. The Phillies got into a rhubarb with plate umpire Cy Pfirman, during which catcher Jimmie Wilson was thrown out of the game. Philadelphia manager Art Fletcher raced to the plate and took up the battle loudly. Hornsby tired of the delay, and he and Fletcher began to shout at each other. Hornsby suddenly landed a punch on Fletcher's jaw and knocked him flat on his back. Rogers was thrown out of the game and fined. Two weeks later Hornsby cursed a home plate umpire who called him out on strikes. He was ejected again and suspended for three days. Several games later Hornsby almost physically attacked umpire Ernie Quigley and had to be pulled away by his players.

Hornsby simplified and shortened his team meetings. His leadership was based upon three "musts." First, he insisted that his pitchers routinely knock down the hitter after going ahead on a no balls-two strikes count. Secondly, the pitcher would be fined $50 if the batter hit an 0 and 2 pitch. And finally, a batter would be fined $50 if he took a third called strike with runners on second and third. Hornsby's first season as a player-manager was successful. His Cards went 64–51 and rose from last place to fourth place. Hornsby played superbly, becoming the only player-manager ever to win the triple crown, with his league-leading .403 batting average, 143 RBI, and 39 home runs. Hornsby was voted the National League MVP, receiving 73 of the 80 votes cast. Now holder of a significant amount of stock in the Cardinals, Rogers became a member of the club's seven-person board of directors. A compulsive bettor, Hornsby was criticized for maintaining friendships with bookmakers, especially Kentuckian Frank A. Moore, who placed bets on horse races and other betting activities. Hornsby shook off all criticism of these friendships.

In 1926 the Cardinals' starting infield included first baseman Jim Bottomley, player-manager Hornsby at second, Tommy Thevenow at short, and Les Bell at third. The outfielders were Clarence "Heinie" Mueller in right, Taylor Douthit in center, and Ray Blades and Chick Hafey sharing left field. Catcher Bob O'Farrell was a solid player. The starting pitchers were lefthanders Bill Sherdel and Art Reinhart, heavy-drinking righthander Flint Rhem, and knuckleballer Jesse Haines.

The club started uncertainly, and in early May Hornsby displaced two vertebrae in a collision at home plate. His back and a

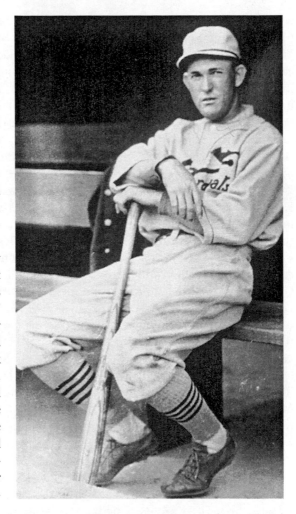

Rogers Hornsby won seven batting titles and had a .358 career batting average, second only to Cobb. He led the Cardinals to their first pennant in 1926 in his second year as their second baseman–manager. The tactless Hornsby continually antagonized his employers and fellow players, a pattern that persisted with the six major league teams he managed.

series of other physical problems hindered him for most of the season. The Cardinals did not reach the .500 mark until late May after making a beneficial move when they traded journeyman Heinie Mueller to the Giants for outfielder Billy Southworth. A week later Hornsby picked up ancient righthander Grover Cleveland Alexander from the Cubs on waivers. In late June the snake-bit Hornsby was hospitalized for 10 days with a leg injury. The Cardinals dueled with the Reds and Pirates through Labor Day, holding a thin lead after the holiday doubleheader. Between games of the doubleheader, Hornsby had a violent argument with Sam Breadon. The owner wanted the Cardinals to play exhibition games during the crucial upcoming eastern trip. Hornsby, feeling that Breadon was taking a chance on injuries to the contending Cardinals, at first would hear none of it. The furious player-manager finally relented, but only after shouting, "All right, but I won't send the first team! Now get the hell out of my clubhouse!"

The Cards went on to win the pennant by two games over the Reds. Hornsby had his least productive year since 1919 because of his physical problems, hitting only .317. But Bottomley picked up the slack, leading the league with 40 doubles and 120 RBI, and Les Bell had an excellent season. Flint Rhem tied for the league lead with 20 wins, Sherdel won 16, and Alexander contributed nine wins and a fine 2.91 ERA in half a season. Catcher Bob O'Farrell, an important member of the 1926 Cardinals, said years later: "Hornsby was a great manager…. He never bothered any of us. Just let you play your own game." St. Louis sportswriter J. Roy Stockton noted that Hornsby had changed from a "colorless ballplayer" to a "dynamic leader."

The Cards faced the highly favored Yankees in the World Series. The day before the Series opener, Hornsby's mother died in Austin. Just before her death, Mrs. Hornsby insisted that Rogers stay with his team to prepare for the World Series. In the first game at Yankee Stadium Herb Pennock outpitched Sherdel in a 2–1 victory as Lou Gehrig drove in Babe Ruth with the game winner. The veteran Alexander tied the Series the next day, striking out 10 Yankees in a 6–2 win. The Series moved to St. Louis, and Jesse Haines shut out the Yankees, punctuating his five-hitter with a two-run homer. The Yankees tied the Series in the fourth game, winning 10–5 as Ruth hit three home runs. Pennock and Sherdel met in the go-ahead fifth game, and again Pennock won a well-pitched game. Returning to New York, Alexander tied the Series with a 10–2 win.

The deciding game drew a small Yankee Stadium crowd of 38,093, Jesse Haines and Waite Hoyt the starters. The Yankees led 1–0 after three innings, but the Cards scored three unearned runs in the top of the fourth to lead 3–1. The Yanks scored their second run in the bottom of the sixth. In the Yankee seventh they had two men on when Haines walked the menacing Gehrig to load the bases with two out. Hornsby hustled in from second to find that Haines had broken a blister on the index finger of his pitching hand. Hornsby waved Alexander into the game.

Grover Cleveland Alexander was one of the heaviest drinkers in major league baseball. After winning his second victory of the Series the day before, he apparently had celebrated in his usual manner, and then some. The old pitcher walked up to the mound as steadily as he could, assured Hornsby that he felt fine, then bent to the task of pitching to the dangerous Tony Lazzeri. The first pitch was a ball. The second delivery caught the inside corner for a strike. The next pitch was a fastball that Lazzeri pulled down the left field line, the drive fair at first but then barely hooking foul. The imperturbable pitcher followed with two curves low and away, and Lazzeri struck out.

Alexander still had to protect the Cards' one run lead for two more innings. He held the Yankees scoreless in the eighth, but in the ninth he walked Ruth with two out and slugging Bob Meusel and Lou Gehrig up next. It was assumed that Ruth would remain close to first base. But, on the first pitch, he amazed everyone by racing for second base in an attempt to put the tying run in scoring position. Catcher Bob O'Farrell rifled the ball to player-manager Hornsby who let the Babe slide into the tag for the final out of the Series. Hornsby, still struggling with his back pain, hit .250 in the Series, but he had four RBI and played an errorless Series. He was on top of the baseball world as he went home to Texas to bury his mother.

Hornsby's salary had not been increased since he had taken over as player-manager. He demanded a new three-year contract at $50,000 a year and, reportedly, the position of first vice president, which would put him in a superior position to Rickey in the event that Breadon left the scene. Breadon reluctantly offered Hornsby a one-year contract for $50,000—but only for one year. He was still furious at Hornsby's insubordination in throwing him out of the clubhouse in September and wanted badly to rid himself of a man who was rude, insulting, and unpleasant to deal with. He admitted before he died that he was afraid that Hornsby would accept the one year contract. To discourage Hornsby even further, Breadon told Rogers that he must never again bet on horse races, go to tracks, or associate with horseracing people. A livid Hornsby told Breadon that his horseplaying was "nobody's damn business" and that Breadon could take his ball club and, as Breadon delicately put it, "perform an utterly impossible act."

A few days later Hornsby was traded to the Giants for star second baseman Frankie Frisch (who had a serious feud going with *his* boss, John McGraw) and righthander Jimmy Ring. As Breadon freely predicted, he "caught hell" in St. Louis for some time after the trade. Many years later Hornsby referred to the trade as his "biggest disappointment." McGraw, who had lost much of his earlier clout in running the Giants, claimed he was unaware of the trade before it was made.

Hornsby signed a two-year contract with the Giants for $36,500 a year plus $500 a year for serving as team captain. There were rumors that Hornsby was in line to succeed McGraw as the Giants' manager after McGraw stepped down. But first there was a conflict of interest to be dealt with. National League president John Heydler announced that Hornsby could not play for the Giants while owning stock in the Cardinals. Hornsby demanded to be paid a handsome profit for his stock, claiming that its large appreciation was attributable to his success as a player-manager. Breadon finally agreed to a price of $100,000, plus another $12,000 to cover Hornsby's legal expenses. Of the total $112,000, Breadon paid $86,000, the other seven National League clubs contributed $2000 each, and the Giants picked up the remaining $12,000. The ever-troubled Hornsby had another legal problem at the same time. Frank A. Moore, his erstwhile bookie, sued him for monies Moore claimed he loaned Hornsby. With Hornsby preparing to join the Giants for spring training, court action was postponed until the Fall. Hornsby eventually won the case.

When John McGraw was away, Hornsby took over the Giants. One day Hornsby harshly criticized third baseman Freddy Lindstrom for a play he made during a practice game. The outspoken Lindstrom responded, "That's the way the Old Man wants us to make it." Hornsby shot back, "Then when he's here, make it that way. When I'm here, make it the way I tell you to." Lindstrom shouted back, "So you know more than the Old Man?" Hornsby looked at Lindstrom and said coldly, "All I'm telling you is that I want it done that way when I'm in charge." Lindstrom said scornfully, "Who the hell do you think you are? When you put that bat down, you're no bargain!"

Despite Hornsby's powerful hitting, the Giants, who had six future Hall of Famers on their team, were not able to win the pennant. They were in fourth place at the end of June. In September McGraw left the team under Hornsby's command when he went on a scouting trip. Hornsby shook up the club and got it up as far as second place. But he couldn't keep them there, and the Giants finished in third place, two games behind the pennant-winning Pirates. The Giants' failure to win was hardly Hornsby's fault. He finished second in the league in hitting, batting .361, and was among the top five in every significant hitting category. To increase Hornsby's frustration, the Cardinals finished half a game ahead of the Giants. And Frankie Frisch had a great season, removing much of the resentment in St. Louis over the Hornsby trade.

True to form, Hornsby got into trouble with his boss on the Giants' last trip to Pittsburgh. Owner Charles A. Stoneham questioned a move Hornsby made in that day's game. In his *McGraw of the Giants*, Frank Graham quoted a reporter who overheard Hornsby's response:

> Hornsby just looked at him and said: "Are you trying to tell me how to run this ball club?".... "Why no, I just thought..." and before he could say any more, Hornsby said: "I don't care what you thought, you _____. If you don't like the way I'm running the club, get somebody else to do it."

And that effectively finished Hornsby's career with the Giants. Out of the blue, on January 10, 1928, Jim Tierney handed reporters a statement signed only by Stoneham. Hornsby had been traded to the Boston Braves "for the best interests of the Giants" for two journeyman players, outfielder Jimmy Welsh and catcher Frank "Shanty" Hogan. McGraw, who was out of town, apparently had nothing to do with the trade, although he was thought to have tacitly agreed with Stoneham that Hornsby had to go. A number of the Giants, such stars as Lindstrom, Edd Roush, Bill Terry, and Travis Jackson, had told Stoneham they wouldn't play for the Giants again if Hornsby continued to do any managing in McGraw's absence.

The Braves had been one of the league doormats for many years. They were owned by genial, but ineffectual, Judge Emil Fuchs, and managed by Jack Slattery, a former second string catcher and Boston College baseball coach. After the Braves lost 20 of their first 31 games, Hornsby replaced Slattery, again assuming his familiar player-manager role. Several of the Braves players criticized Hornsby for undermining Slattery, although it was never clear that Hornsby even wanted the job. Hornsby hit a resounding, league-leading .387. He also led the league in walks, and on base and slugging percentages, and again was voted league MVP. But the Braves did even worse under their player-manager than under Slattery, and Hornsby, within Judge Fuchs' hearing, made no secret of his desire to move to a better team. He got his wish as Fuchs sold him to the Cubs for a record $200,000 and five undistinguished players.

Managed by Joe McCarthy, the 1929 Cubs were a heavy-hitting club in a year with the jackrabbit ball at its liveliest. The Cubs lived up to the experts' expectations. After battling the Pirates for the lead through midseason, the Cubs put the pennant away with a strong surge through July and August, winning the pennant easily. Hornsby had his last great season, hitting .380 with 229 hits and 149 RBI. He played every inning during the season despite a painful heel problem. The Cubs lost the World Series to Connie Mack's Athletics in five games as Hornsby hit a mere .238 with only one RBI in the Series.

Injuries hampered the Cubs early in the 1930 season, and the club was mired in the second division during the first six weeks. There were stories that owner William Wrigley had given Joe McCarthy a win-or-else ultimatum. Hornsby's year also began miserably as his heel problem worsened. He clearly had slowed down in the field and on the bases and lacked much of his old power, hitting a pallid .227 by early May. He managed to reach the .300 level by the end of May but was out for 10 weeks after snapping a bone in his left ankle. To prove that things rarely ever change, there were stories that Hornsby was at odds with McCarthy and several of his teammates. In addition, he was given a warning by Commissioner Landis to quit his betting activities. With the Cubs only 2½ games behind the league-leading Cardinals in late September, Wrigley announced that he had decided to fire McCarthy and replace him with Hornsby. Despite a then-record 171 home runs (56 by Hack Wilson, who batted in a record 191 runs), the Cubs finished in second place, two games behind the Cardinals. New player-manager Hornsby had the worst year of his career, hitting .308 with only two home runs in 42 games.

Hornsby began the 1931 season with a lecture to his team on his strict training rules. Billy Herman, who was a rookie second baseman that season, called Hornsby a "real hard-nosed guy ... who ran the clubhouse like a gestapo camp." Players were not allowed to eat, have a soft drink, smoke, or read a paper. Hornsby was utterly dedicated to the game, and he knew it and its rules completely. But, as Herman told it, Hornsby treated his players so coldly that he sometimes walked by a player for several weeks, appearing to look through him, without saying a word. As a result, many of the younger men feared him, the veterans disliked him, and they performed accordingly. Still, Herman admitted that Hornsby was fair and did a good job of running a game.

It was a disappointing season for the Cubs as most of their players had sub-par years. In mid-season the Cubs were in third place, only five games behind the Cardinals. But by early September Hornsby's club was 15 games off the pace and hopelessly out of the race. Rogers played in most of the club's games in the first third of the season until various ailments forced him out. He regained some of his old batting touch, hitting .331 with 16 homers and 90 RBI in 100 games. But his increasing slowness made him a defensive liability on a team with other serious defensive deficiencies.

By mid-season in 1932 the Cubs were in a three-way pennant fight with the Pirates and the surprising Braves, now managed by Bill McKechnie. In early August new Cubs President William K. Veeck did not hide his annoyance with Hornsby for borrowing money from his players to pay off his debts, but most immediately for failing to hold a clubhouse meeting to talk over pitching strategy against the contending Pirates. When Veeck asked Hornsby about that failure, Hornsby reacted predictably with the defiant response, "If you don't like the way I'm managing, then pay me off." The deeply annoyed Veeck replied, "Not just now, but remember that crack." A few days later the Cubs named first baseman Charlie Grimm to replace Hornsby. The Cubs responded by winning the pennant and failing to vote Hornsby a World Series share, even though he had been with the club for two-thirds of the season. Hornsby appealed to Commissioner Landis for help, but Landis said he could do nothing about the matter.

The following season Hornsby signed a player contract with, of all teams, the Cardinals, who badly needed infield help because shortstop Charley Gelbert had almost blown off a leg in a hunting accident. The Texan swore that he had no intention of replacing Cards manager Gabby Street. With Frankie Frisch moved unhappily from second base to shortstop, Street hoped that Hornsby could do the job at second. But Rogers had too many ailments, playing in only 46 games, hitting .325 but fielding poorly. The Cards traded for shortstop Leo Durocher, Frisch returned happily to second, and Hornsby was relegated to a pinchhitting role. In late July Gabby Street was fired, with the Cardinals in fifth place and playing .500 ball. Frisch was promoted to player-manager, and his first move was to release Hornsby.

The St. Louis Browns picked up Hornsby, and he managed them for their last third of the 1933 season. Hornsby was fond of plainspoken Browns' president Phil Ball, but he could do nothing with the last place club. They drew a total of only 80,932 fans at home over the 77 home games, even with Hornsby remaining on the playing roster as a fan attraction. Ball died after the season. The Browns were sold and a new business manager, Bill DeWitt, was put in charge. Hornsby had his problems getting along with DeWitt, although he improved his overmatched teams enough to finish sixth in 1934 and seventh the following two years, while he remained on the playing roster and made token appearances on the field. But, halfway through the 1937 season, with the Browns deep in the second division, DeWitt called Hornsby into his office and asked, "Have you been playing the horses again?" Hornsby responded, "I have, what about it?" DeWitt told him simply, "You're through." Hornsby was finished, although in his last year as a player-manager he hit .321.

Over the next several years Hornsby was a player-manager at Baltimore and Seattle (then both still minor league teams), Chattanooga, Oklahoma City, Fort Worth, and Beaumont. And during World War II with

Vera Cruz in the Mexican League he hit a game-winning home run when he was 48. The man couldn't run or play the field any longer, but he could still hit. In 1952 William K. Veeck's son Bill hired Hornsby to manage the Browns, and he lasted for half the season before moving to the Reds where he managed through the 1953 season.

Hornsby won seven batting titles and he had a .358 career batting average, second only to Cobb's .367. He led the National League four times in hits (for a career total of 2930), doubles, and RBI. As a manager he had a 701–812 (.463) record, and he ranks 22nd among player-managers in games played while managing. Hornsby, inducted into the Hall of Fame in 1942, died in Chicago on January 5, 1963.

Miller Huggins

Miller Huggins was born in Cincinnati on March 27, 1879. He was the third of four children born to grocer James Thomas, an English émigré, and Sarah Huggins. He played baseball on local sandlots and began his professional baseball career at 20 as a second baseman with the Mansfield, Ohio, club of the Interstate League. His father disapproved of playing baseball on Sunday, so he played under the name "Proctor." An excellent student, Huggins earned a law degree in 1902 to please his parents, but he preferred playing baseball for a living. From 1901 to 1903 the runty young man (he was smaller than his listed 5 foot 6½ inch, 140 pounds) hit over .300 for St. Paul of the American Association.

The Cincinnati Reds purchased Huggins' contract for the 1904 season, and he established himself immediately, fielding competently, hitting .263, and capitalizing on his small stature to draw walks, steal bases, and score runs. Huggins had his most memorable day with the Reds on June 19, 1907, when he hit a leadoff home run off Christy Mathewson. The rare homer (only the third of his career up to that point) excited the Cincinnati fans. They presented the quiet little guy with a pair of shoes, a gold watch, a box of chocolates, a scarf pin, and a Morris chair, a typical haul for an honored player of that time.

Huggins was traded to the Cardinals after an injury-riddled 1909 season. He hit over .300 (.304) for the only time in his career in 1912. By that time he had become recognized as one of the smartest players in the game, and the Cards appointed him their playing manager in 1913. He inherited from Roger Bresnahan a sixth place team without a standout player. Huggins started the 1913 season with essentially the same mediocre cast, and his Cardinals did not even match the performance of Bresnahan's club, finishing last and winning 12 fewer games. Only lefthander Harry "Slim" Sallee (19–15) had a decent season. But in 1914 Huggins' club improved surprisingly, competing with the Giants and the "Miracle" Boston Braves before finishing in third place, 13 games off the pace.

The Cardinals' climb was the result of greatly improved pitching, as the Cardinals' league-worst 4.23 ERA in 1913 improved to the league-best 2.38 ERA in 1914. Spitball-throwing righthander Bill "Spittin' Bill" Doak developed far beyond Huggins' expectations, improving from a 2–8 season to a 19–6 record; and Slim Sallee won 18 games. The offense improved, and Huggins led the league with 105 walks. After the season Huggins was widely acclaimed for his field leadership and effective management of his players.

The Cards reverted to their old form in 1915, slipping down to sixth place. Their only bright spot was produced by rightfielder Tom Long, brought up from the minors after having failed in brief appearances with Washington several years earlier. The speedy Long hit .294 with an unusual batting record, only 21 doubles to go with a league-leading 25 triples. In 1915, his last year as a regular, Huggins hit .241, but he was fourth in the league with 74 walks and a respectable .377 on base percentage. The little guy remained on the playing roster in 1916 but appeared in only 18 games as his club finished in a last place tie. As a bench manager, Huggins led his club to a third place finish in 1917. A successful stock investor, he tried to buy the Cardinals after the season but his offer was turned down.

Huggins became the Yankees' manager in 1918, as Yankees owner Jacob Ruppert hired him on the recommendation of Ban Johnson. The hiring was accomplished over the protests of rough-hewn fellow Yankees owner Cap (Captain Tillinghast L'Hommedieu) Huston, who was with the Army Engineers in Europe. Ruppert hired Huggins despite having an initial negative impression of him. It seems that the two had met informally and Ruppert was surprised at that time by Huggins' appearance—a little man wearing an oversized cap and a perpetually worried look. But Ruppert was impressed by his directness and his thorough baseball knowledge.

Within a few years Ruppert bought out Huston, and Huggins had one less problem. But there was one big headache to come after Huggins convinced Ruppert to buy Babe Ruth from the Red Sox early in 1920. Ruth was the most important factor in the Yankees' unparalleled success in the 1920s, but his well-chronicled escapades off the field and general insubordination drove Huggins to near distraction. He eventually overcame this headache by fining the Babe a hefty $5000 in August of 1925 and making the fine stick. Huggins had successfully established his authority, which lasted for the remainder of his tenure.

Huggins put together a dynasty, winning six pennants and three World Championships from 1921 through 1928. The Yankees' dominance ended in 1929 when Connie Mack's magnificent club beat the second place Yankees by 18 games. Huggins fretted and worried through the season, and the little manager's deep concern took a serious toll on his health. After losing a game on September 22 he was hospitalized, and he died, shockingly, from a form of blood poisoning. Huggins had a career managerial record of 1413–1134 (.555), and as a player-manager he played in 376 games, ranking 28th on the all-time list. The little second baseman had a career .265 batting record, 1003 walks, and 324 stolen bases. Huggins was inducted into the Hall of Fame in 1964.

16

Terry and Grimm

Bill Terry and Charley Grimm were among the most successful player-managers of the 1930s. Terry was one of the all-time best hitting and fielding first basemen, and Grimm was a less talented, but still proficient, player at the position. But both men, although completely different in personality and intensity, were pennant-winning player-managers.

BILL TERRY

William Harold Terry was born in Atlanta on October 30, 1898, to William T. and Bertha (Blackman) Terry. The Terrys were an unstable, unhappy couple, and young Bill was essentially on his own at 13. After his parents separated for the last time, the husky 15-year-old went to work loading heavy sacks of flour.

Terry was a lefthand pitcher in his first few baseball years with a local semipro team. The youngster was wild but very fast when he began his professional career with Newnan, Georgia, in the Georgia-Alabama League in 1915. He played for Shreveport in the Texas League the next two years, impressing as a pitcher and potential power hitter. The good-looking youngster married a Memphis girl after the 1916 season when he was 19. After a mediocre year in 1917, Terry quit organized baseball and went to work for the Standard Oil Company in Memphis where he organized, managed, and pitched for the company team.

The Giants stopped in Memphis on their way north to start the 1922 season. Tom Watkins, an old friend of John McGraw's, told the Giants manager about Terry and arranged for the two to meet. McGraw was in his hotel room the next morning when Terry knocked. Frank Graham described the meeting in *McGraw of the Giants*:

> "Come in," McGraw said. A young fellow walked in—big, broad-shouldered, round-faced, dark-haired, serious-looking. "I'm Bill Terry," he said. [McGraw] noted the easy grace with which Terry moved, the size of his hands, the strength of his grip.... McGraw smiled. "How'd you like to come to New York with me?" he asked. "What for?" [McGraw responded], "Well, to play for the Giants, maybe." "For how much?" McGraw's smile faded. He looked at Terry sharply. "Do you understand what I'm offering you?" he asked. "I'm offering you a chance to play for the Giants—if you're good enough."
>
> Terry took a cigar out of the breast pocket of his coat and lighted it. "Excuse me if I don't fall over myself," he said. "But the Giants don't mean anything to me unless you can make it worth my while. I've got to have a contract with the Giants and for more dough —much more dough—than I'm making around here.... I don't want you to misunderstand me and think I'm just a swell-headed clown.... I'm not. But I have a nice home and I'm in no hurry to leave.... And remember this: I didn't come up here looking for a job." McGraw said, "Well, there's no hurry about it. I'll think it over and let you know later."

McGraw waited a month, then agreed to meet Terry's price, $800 a month. Terry became a New York Giant on May 10, 1922. He was sent to Roger Bresnahan's Toledo Mud Hens. Bill joined the club's pitching rotation, but after several mediocre starts he was transferred to first base in mid–July. He impressed as a hitter, hitting .336 with 61 RBI in 88 games. Playing exclusively at first base in 1923, Bill hit .377 for Toledo and played in a few games for the Giants near the end of the season.

Terry played infrequently in his first half year with the Giants in 1924, hitting only .239. McGraw platooned his players, and during the second half of the season the lefthand-hitting Terry played first base against righthanders while regular first baseman George "Highpockets" Kelly played elsewhere. Terry had a fine World Series as the Giants lost to the Washington Senators four games to three, with the Giants winning the three games in which Terry started. In the first game, against Walter Johnson, he had three hits, including a home run, as the Giants won 4–3. Terry chipped in with a well-stroked triple in the fifth game win over Johnson. But the Senators won the seventh game on Earl McNeely's "pebble hit" over Freddy Lindstrom's head. Terry hit .429 in the Series to lead the Giants hitters. After the season he returned to Memphis to his growing family and his job with Standard Oil.

Terry, a tough bargainer, was the last Giant to sign before the 1925 season. But he proved his value, playing the entire 1925 season as the starting first baseman, hitting .319 and leading all National League first basemen in total chances. The enterprising Terry began to broaden his off-season activities, and when he held out again before the 1926 season, Harry Cross wrote in *The New York Times*:

> Mr. Terry, it would appear, during the past year has developed into an affluent Memphis landlord. He has numerous domiciles for which he exacts rent each month. The arrangements between Landlord Terry and his tenants, so the story goes, is such that Mr. Terry can, without any suffering on his part, assume a somewhat independent attitude in relation to baseball. He doesn't have to make base hits to keep the wolf from the door.

Terry did not sign with the Giants until the end of April. Relations between Terry and McGraw apparently cooled because Kelly was restored to his starting position at first base and Terry played the bag in only 38 games. In 1926 he had a so-so year, hitting only .289 in 98 games as the club slipped below .500 and finished in fifth place. But, beginning in 1927, Terry hit his stride and was widely regarded as the best National League first baseman over the next several years.

As the regular first baseman in 1927, Terry played in an All-Star infield along with newly-acquired Rogers Hornsby, Travis Jackson, and Freddy Lindstrom. Terry hit .326 in each of the next two seasons and climbed to .372 in 1929. Yet these were frustrating years for the Giants. McGraw became increasingly dyspeptic and physically ill as his club finished within two games of the pennant-winning Pirates in 1927 and two games of the Cardinals who won in 1928. There was a strong feeling in New York that the Giants would have won both pennants had they not traded Hornsby to the Braves after the 1927 season. In 1929 McGraw's club lost the 1929 pennant by a wider margin, despite the heavy hitting of Terry and 20-year-old Mel Ott.

The Giants lost out to the Cardinals by five games in 1930, a year for which Terry is best remembered as a player. He hit close to .400 through September 1, and his four hits that day and four more the following day raised his average to .411. He had hit a blistering .446 over the July 8 to September 3 period with, as Peter Williams pointed out, relatively little publicity. This was the last year in which the National League used a baseball with low stitches that favored the hitters. Yet Terry's hitting was still remarkable, a league-leading .401 average, which no National Leaguer has topped since, and 254 hits, which ties Lefty O'Doul's record 1929 total. Terry won the baseball writers' Most Valuable Player award.

Memphis Bill had another magnificent year in 1931 after his usual holdout, losing the batting title by .0003 to the Cardinals' Chick Hafey. The Giants were a listless team as the ill McGraw was unable to energize the club as in past years. Apparently aging prematurely, McGraw had lost much of his mental sharpness, but he still had a vitriolic tongue. Lindstrom and Terry were especially outspoken in their distaste for McGraw's tyrannical tactics. Lindstrom said years later that if a player made a mistake, "McGraw would tear him apart right in front of the team, but Terry, Ott, Hubbell, Jackson, and me were a different breed. We didn't need that and Terry and I wouldn't take it."

Despite their superior talent, the Giants stumbled through the first two months of the 1932 season, in last place on June 3. The Giants' scheduled doubleheader at the Polo Grounds was rained out that day. The *New York World-Telegram*'s Tom Meany headed aimlessly for the Giants clubhouse in search of a story. As he neared the clubhouse, a vendor asked him, "Did you know that McGraw is out and Terry is the new manager?" Meany saw a confirming note in the clubhouse to that effect, and his paper had its "scoop."

Terry had not been on speaking terms with McGraw for two years. When McGraw offered him the job, Terry accepted it on the spot. His first move was to fire the club trainer whom the players considered McGraw's clubhouse spy. Terry's next moves were to move the curfew back to midnight and institute a more relaxed, open door policy towards his players. Player-manager Terry had a successful debut the next day as the Giants took a doubleheader from the Phillies and moved out of last place. With McGraw gone, the Giants played with less tension and improved to finish the season in sixth place. Player-manager Terry performed well in spite of his new responsibilities, hitting .350 with 225 hits, 117 RBI, and 28 home runs.

Terry had a busy off-season. Lindstrom was bitter at not being named manager, and he insisted on being traded, a move he regretted later because the Giants proved to be a better team than his new club, the Pirates, over the next few years. In October Terry traded for Cardinals catcher Gus Mancuso, a solid receiver, and acquired John "Blondy" Ryan, a good-field, weak-hit shortstop.

The Giants, in Los Angeles in March 1933 for spring training, suffered through a major earthquake. Terry considered moving the club to Arizona, but the Giants remained in Los Angeles before breaking camp. The Giants roster differed significantly from that of the previous year. There were three new catchers—Mancuso, Harry Danning, and Paul Richards. The starting infield included holdovers Terry, second baseman Hughie

Critz, and third baseman Johnny Vergez, but Travis Jackson's ailing knees soon forced him to give way to Ryan. Rightfielder Mel Ott and leftfielder Joe Moore were holdovers. George "Kiddo" Davis was the new centerfielder, replacing the departed Lindstrom who had been moved to the outfield in 1931. The starting pitchers included screwballing lefthander Carl Hubbell, knuckleballer Freddy Fitzsimmons, righthander Hal Schumacher, and smoke-throwing righthander LeRoy Parmelee (nicknamed "Tarzan" because of his wildness).

Terry's club figured to finish no better than sixth. The Giants started off the season reasonably well, although Jackson's knee ailments forced him to the bench, and Terry was sidelined for six weeks with a broken wrist. The Giants' pitchers were superb with a deader ball in use. In a doubleheader in May, Hubbell shut out the Reds in the first game 1–0, and Schumacher won the second game 5–0. This was the sort of low-scoring games that Terry, a stickler for defense, had built his team to play. Terry's emphasis on his team's defense was illustrated later in the season after the Giants took a tough 2–1 loss. *New York Daily Mirror* writer Ken Smith tried to console Terry, telling him, "Just another hit there, Bill, and—." Terry cut him short, "Kenny, they shouldn't have scored two runs."

After Terry's wrist healed, he traded first baseman Sam Leslie to the Dodgers for 36-year-old outfielder Lefty O'Doul. The Giants won a memorable doubleheader from the Cardinals on July 2. Hubbell pitched an incredible 18 scoreless innings to win the first game 1–0. The gaunt Oklahoman pitched perfect ball in 12 of the innings, allowing only six hits, with no more than one coming in any inning. He struck out 12 batters and did not walk a man. A single by Hughie Critz off righthander Jesse Haines drove in the only run. In the second game Roy Parmelee, pitching in semi-darkness, also shut out the gun-shy Cardinals 1–0. The only sobering note was a leg injury to Blondy Ryan, forcing Terry to replace him with the gimpy Jackson.

The Giants held a five-game lead over the second-place Cards on July 4, but they lost several games with the crippled Jackson at short. On July 12 Terry received a confident telegram from the irrepressible, injured Blondy Ryan. He returned to the lineup the following day and sparked the quiet, undemonstrative Giants for the rest of the season.

In Terry's club's closing drive to the pennant, Hubbell delivered his tenth shutout of the year. He did not walk a batter, nor was he behind a hitter at any time in ten innings, never even going to a 3 and 2 count. Watching from the press box, famed journalist Heywood Broun marveled at Hubbell's control. He wrote, "Such control in a lefthander is incredible. There must be a skeleton in Hubbell's closet somewhere, perhaps a righthanded maternal grandmother." The Giants clinched the pennant on September 19. Hubbell, voted the league's MVP, led the league with 23 wins, 10 shutouts, and a marvelous 1.66 ERA. Schumacher ranked in the top five in wins, ERA, and shutouts. Ott, in his eighth year with the Giants at 24, was third in home runs and RBI, and player-manager Terry hit .322.

The Giants turned their attention to the World Series and the Washington Senators. Player-manager Joe Cronin had a good offense, a sound defense, and an accomplished pitching staff. Because of their apparent superior strength, the Senators were installed as 10 to 7 favorites to win the Series. A crowd of 46,672 jammed the spruced-up, banner-bedecked Polo Grounds for the first game. The Giants went ahead on Ott's two-run homer and scored two more runs in the third. Ott had a perfect day with four hits, and Hubbell held on for a 4–1 win. In the second game it was righthander Alvin "General" Crowder against Schumacher, and the Giants won again, 6–1, with Lefty O'Doul supplying a two-run single to put the Giants ahead in the sixth inning. Many years later the impish O'Doul admitted, "That was an illegal hit. I actually stepped across the plate and was afraid the umpire would call me out. But he didn't see it, nor did anybody on the Senators."

Back in Washington, the Senators won the third game as Fitzsimmons lost 4–0 to a masterful effort by lefthander Earl Whitehill. With Hubbell pitching the fourth game against righthander Monte Weaver, Terry opened the scoring in the fourth inning with a towering drive into the temporary bleachers in center field. The Senators tied the game in the seventh. Blondy Ryan singled in the go-ahead run in the top of the eleventh. In the bottom of the inning the Senators threatened to tie or win the game against the valiant Hubbell. With the bases loaded and only one out, the Giants beat the percentages when Terry took Ryan's and Critz's advice and played back for the double play. The Giants got it when pinch hitter Cliff Bolton bounced into a double play on a deep bouncer to Ryan to end the thrilling game.

In the fifth game it was Schumacher against Crowder again. The Giants took a three run lead into the sixth inning, but Senators centerfielder Fred Schulte tied the game with a three-run homer off Schumacher. The game settled down to another tense pitching duel as veteran righthanders Dolph Luque and Jack Russell took over the pitching chores and pitched scoreless ball through the ninth inning. In the tenth, Critz and Terry went out and only Ott remained to be retired. The little slugger had fanned his first two times up and hit easy fly balls on the next two. On a 2 and 2 count the lefthand-hitting Ott cocked his right leg high and lifted a high drive toward the center field bleachers. Schulte, moving back at top speed, got his glove on the ball just as it was about to drop into the low, temporary seats. But the ball bounced out of his glove and into the stands, and Ott was awarded a home run. And that was the game as reliever Dolph Luque retired the Senators. Terry, who hit .273 and fielded flawlessly in the Series, had led his surprising Giants to the World Championship.

The only incident of note during the off-season occurred during the winter meetings. *New York Times* writer Roscoe McGowen asked Terry about the prospects for the Dodgers in the upcoming season. Terry responded with the bland remark, "Is Brooklyn still in the league?" The Dodgers had done little since the season ended to improve their sixth place club, and Terry was not deriding the Dodgers but rather reacting to their front office's inaction. All the writers laughed, and they all printed the comment. Terry, never known for his subtlety, had responded lightly, but it didn't come out that way in the writers' stories. Dodger fans took umbrage and flooded the Giants office with angry letters.

In 1934 the Giants were favored to win the pennant. They started well, finding themselves only 1½ games out of first place after defeating the Dodgers twice early in the season before the largest crowd ever at Ebbets Field. The insults and boos aimed at Terry's every move were a reminder of his overblown winter comment about the Dodgers. By July 4 the Giants, hitting on all cylinders, were in first place by three games. Terry managed the National League team in the All-Star game at the Polo Grounds, losing to the American League 9–7 despite Hubbell's classic performance in striking out future Hall of Famers Babe Ruth, Lou Gehrig, Jimmy Foxx, Al Simmons, and Joe Cronin, all in a row. The Giants continued their effective play and led the Cubs and the Cardinals by six games on Labor Day. However, over the next few weeks the pace of the Giants and the Cubs slowed as the Cardinals turned red hot. The Cards were sparked by Dizzy Dean, winning steadily as a starter and pitching effectively in relief. With 10 games left, the league-leading Giants led the Cardinals by only 3½ games. After Dizzy Dean shut out the Reds on September 28, the Giants and Cards were dead even starting the last weekend. The exhausted Giants lost their last two games to the revenge-seeking Dodgers at the Polo Grounds, loaded with Dodger supporters. Meanwhile, the Cardinals won their last two games and took the pennant. A crushed Terry told the press, "I got the credit for last season so I guess I get the blame now." Terry said he was conducting a "garage sale" in which all of the Giants were trade bait except the two untouchables, Hubbell and Ott.

Terry made only one trade over the winter, obtaining shortstop Dick

Billy Terry and Frankie Frisch were important National League player-managers in the 1930s. Terry was the great New York Giants first baseman who succeeded John McGraw and led the club to a World Championship in his first full season as a player-manager in 1933. Terry's club won another pennant in 1936, his last season as a player. Frisch's club won the 1934 World Championship in his first full season as second baseman–manager. Terry, the last National Leaguer to hit .400, had a .341 batting average and a .555 managerial record over ten years. Frisch had a career .316 average and a .514 win-loss record in managing three teams in 16 years.

Bartell from the Phillies. Bartell had earned the nickname "Rowdy Richard" for his peppery play and willingness to take on all comers despite his small stature. The 1935 season resembled the previous season. The Giants started off beautifully, in first place with a seven game lead at the All-Star break. Bartell had breathed new life into his geriatric infield partners—Terry, Critz, and Jackson. Young righthander Clydell "Slick" Castleman pitched impressively enough to be promoted into the Hubbell-Schumacher-Fitzsimmons-Parmelee starting rotation. But Terry's club slipped during the summer and found itself two games behind the first place Cardinals at the start of September. The Giants played themselves out of the race with a poor September, as the Cubs blew out the Giants and the Cardinals with a 21-game winning streak to win the pennant.

Terry hit well over .400 in September in a futile attempt to pull his club to a pennant win. The Giants ended the season in third place, 7½ games off the pace. Terry told the writers, "Our problem is that we have too many old men, and that includes the first baseman. From now on, we're out only for youth and speed." He was satisfied with his three outfielders and several pitchers. But there were three gaping holes in the infield, as Critz, Jackson, and Terry himself were actively considering retiring. Hubbell had another excellent year, going 23–12. Schumacher was third in ERA. Ott had another great year. And Hank Leiber had what would be his best year, batting .331 and driving in 107 runs. And Terry, retirement plans and all, tied for fifth in hitting, with a .341 average.

In the off-season Terry's most important deal was the acquisition of second baseman Burgess Whitehead from the Cardinals. Terry was impressed with Whitehead's speed, agility, and hit-and-run ability, although there were questions about the slim, frail-looking Whitehead's capacity to play a full season. Picked to finish behind the Cubs and Cardinals, the 1936 Giants had a decent start. On Memorial Day they were only a game and a half behind the Cardinals. Terry had manipulated his troops skillfully to remain at that level. He platooned slumping centerfielder Hank Leiber with rookie Jimmy Ripple, and had Jackson share third base with Eddie Mayo, up from Baltimore. Sam Leslie, reclaimed from the Dodgers, also slumped and Terry, still on the roster, took over first base for a few games. Whitehead and Bartell held the infield together with their consistent, sparkling play and, by the All-Star break, the Giants were 5½ games behind the first place Cubs.

Terry, who had a badly ailing knee, was told by his orthopedist that it would be inadvisable for him to continue playing. After losing the first game of a doubleheader to the Pirates on July 15, the Giants' pennant hopes touched bottom. They were 11 games behind the league-leading Cubs and were lodged in fifth place. But they won the second game as player-manager Terry, ignoring his crippled left knee and his doctor's advice, inserted himself into the lineup and led his club to a win with a single, double, and triple.

The Giants won 17 of the next 18 games to pull closer to the lead, and began their final western trip only half a game behind the league-leading Cards. The Polo Grounders moved into first place when Leiber beat the Reds with a late inning hit. In Pittsburgh Terry hobbled off the coaching line to belt a tenth inning game-winning pinch single. The Giants won a doubleheader in Chicago, highlighted by Hubbell's twentieth win and Ott's ninth inning home run, his seventh hit in the doubleheader. The trip ended successfully in St. Louis with Hubbell driving in the winning run in a 2–1 victory over Dizzy Dean. The Giants returned home triumphantly with a four game lead over the second-place Cardinals. Since their shot in the arm from their crippled player-manager on July 15, the Giants had won 39 of 47 games, an .830 pace. Terry's club clinched the pennant on September 24 when Hal Schumacher beat the Braves.

Hubbell was voted the League MVP for the second time. He had 16 consecutive wins as the regular season ended, and led the league with 26 wins. Ott had one of his best years, leading the league with 33 homers and a .588 slugging percentage. Moore and Mancuso played brilliantly, and Bartell and Whitehead were the best second base–shortstop combination the Giants had in many years. And Terry performed heroically, hitting .310 in his last season as a player-manager.

The Giants were overcome in the World Series, losing in six games to one of the greatest Yankee teams, with rookie Joe DiMaggio a teammate of fellow Hall of Famers Lou Gehrig, Bill Dickey, Red Ruffing, Lefty Gomez, and Tony Lazzeri. The Yanks had won the American League pennant by an incredible 19½ games. Hubbell defeated Ruffing 6–1 in the opener, but in the second game the Yankees steamrollered five Giant pitchers in an 18–4 slaughter. Fitzsimmons lost a 2–1 heartbreaker in the third game, and Hubbell lost to righthander Monte Pearson 5–2 in the fourth. After the game Terry talked about his knee ailment. He had been confined to his hotel room except when he was at the ballpark, sleeping at night with pillows under his left leg to reduce the swelling. He told the writers, "I'm playing out this string, but you can bet anything I'll never play after this is over." In his parting shot, Terry drove in the winning run in the tenth inning of a tense 5–4 game, a gutty effort by Schumacher which made it a 3–2 Series.

In the sixth game the Giants were put out of their misery, losing 13–5 as the Yankees broke the game wide open with seven runs in the ninth inning. Pittsburgh Pirates manager Pie Traynor praised Terry, who had played the entire Series as a virtual cripple. Traynor said, "I don't think any other man in baseball could have gotten that team into a World Series. For that matter, he did well to win a game, let alone two games, against a powerhouse like the Yanks."

The 1937 season was something of a replay of the past campaign, with elongated lefthander Cliff Melton the most important of the new players. The Giants started off as if to repeat as pennant winners, led by Hubbell, who won his twenty-fourth straight game. The Giants led the league by a game on Memorial Day as Hubbell lost the first game of the doubleheader, his first defeat in almost 11 months. The last of the epic Hubbell–Dizzy Dean pitching battles came on June 27 when Hubbell, supported by two Ott home runs, outpitched Dean for an 8–1 win. (Hubbell won eight of the 11 head-to-head battles with Dean during their Hall of Fame careers.)

The Giants slumped in July and were seven games behind the first-place Cubs in early August. Terry shook up the lineup, moving the versatile Ott to third base and inserting Jimmy Ripple into the lineup. The change gave the club added punch and new life, and the Giants rebounded to take the league lead. They held on grimly and won the pennant by three games. Experts considered Ott's successful switch to third base, permitting the potent Ripple to play regularly, and Melton's strong (20–9) rookie season as the keys to the Giants' second straight pennant. The Yankees again overpowered the Giants in the World Series. Hubbell won the Giants' only victory, and they were otherwise competitive only in the last game when Gomez, who won twice, beat Melton 4–2. As the *World Telegram*'s Joe Williams summed it up, "The turning point of the Series was when the Yanks suited up for the first game."

The Giants began the 1938 season without Whitehead, who had suffered a nervous breakdown. But, despite his loss, Terry's hopes for another pennant were enhanced when the Giants began the season by winning 18 of their first 21 games. They remained in the lead by 3½ games over the Pirates on July 4 as Ott, still at third base, carried much of the offensive load. But the Giants slipped badly after the All-Star game break and relinquished the lead to the Pirates. Terry's club suffered serious injuries, the worst of which were bone chip conditions developed by Schumacher and Hubbell. Both pitchers underwent operations, ending their seasons prematurely and ending any hope that the Giants could win a third straight pennant. Terry's club did well to finish third.

Terry was popular with his players during his days as a player-manager, but things changed later, especially among the younger men. He remained close to the players who dated back to the McGraw days—Hubbell, Ott, Jackson, Schumacher, and Fitzsimmons—and was helpful to his players in matters involving their business affairs. But even his older players lost close touch with him after he became a bench manager, and even more so when he took on added responsibility as the club's general manager. Peter Williams wrote: "Joe Moore noticed this, surmising it was due to [Terry's] new job as general manager. [Moore said,] 'He went up into the office, and it took lots of his time. You get a little bit far away from your players when you're not close to 'em every day.'" And Hubbell talked of the change in Terry after the 1933 World Series win. He was quoted in Walter M. Langford's *Legends of Baseball*: "That World Series win did a little something for Terry's ego, and after that he got kind of uppity in his managing…. But some of the younger players felt Terry was a cold fish and they didn't like him."

Terry had difficulties with reporters, and vice versa, since shortly after he became the Giants' player-manager. It seems that at that time the *World-Telegram*'s Joe Williams had asked Terry for his home phone number in case Williams needed to check a story. Terry, always protective of his and his family's privacy, had refused Williams' request. From that time on, several of the writers with the 12 daily papers covering the Giants resented Terry's independent attitude toward writers whose living depended upon the accuracy of their stories about the Giants.

Although Terry had some friends in the media, those who resented him wrote stories reflecting their resentment. Upon learning that the businesslike Terry had purchased cattle for investment, Tom Meany wrote sarcastically, "I'll bet Bill buys only white-faced cattle so that he can count their faces at night." Meany also suggested that Terry became "Terrible Terry" in the view of many writers because he was ultra-conservative in the way he ran a game. As one example, they deplored his playing for one run in the early innings of a game. When one of them criticized Bill to his face, Terry told him acidly, "I see you don't like the way I run the club. Maybe we should change jobs." The writer laughed and answered, "That's all right with me as long as we switch salaries." In private, Terry often referred to the writers contemptuously as "a bunch of $25 a week ribbon clerks" and hinted that no writer was competent to second-guess him.

The Giants finished in the second division during the last three seasons of Terry's stewardship. Finishing under .500 in 1940 and 1941, and with attendance also on the decline, Terry agreed to step down as field and general manager and take on the job of farm system director. Mel Ott became the Giants' new player-manager on December 2, 1941.

Terry remained with the Giants for a year before resigning, citing the Giants curtailment of their farm system operations because of World War II. After that he threw himself completely into various businesses. These included farming, cotton manufacturing, and successful Buick franchises, first in West Memphis, Arkansas, and then in Jacksonville. Terry's name cropped up from time to time as a possible manager of baseball clubs, including Brooklyn, but by then Terry's income from his businesses dwarfed the salaries offered him to manage. He also was rumored to be a possible co-purchaser of teams, including the Giants, before the club's move to San Francisco in 1957. However, Terry's only official baseball positions came when he served briefly as president of the South Atlantic (Sally) League in 1955, and a few years later when he bought and ran the Jacksonville Braves of that league.

Terry was one of the great players of his time. A straightaway hitter who hit with power to all fields, he had a .341 batting average over his 14 major league seasons, and his .401 average in 1930 remains the last time a National Leaguer has hit .400. Defensively, he was widely recognized as the best fielding first baseman in the game—graceful, agile, and especially proficient at executing the first-to-second double play. Surprisingly, the 200-pounder also was one of the fastest men in the league.

Terry had a fine managerial record of 823–661 (.555), and in his 10 highly competitive years as a manager, his clubs won a World Championship and three pennants, and had six first division finishes. He played in 614 games while he managed, ranking seventeenth on the all-time player-manager list. Terry, who died at age 89, was voted into the Hall of Fame in 1954, 18 years after his retirement as a player. Typically, after his belated selection to the Hall, the ruggedly independent Terry responded with, "I have nothing to say about it." But, also characteristically, he took the honor seriously and urged Hall of Famers to attend installations of other players as a matter of respect for the game. Terry's businesslike, unvarnished approach to the game could never obscure his love and respect for it.

CHARLIE GRIMM

Charles John Grimm was born in St. Louis on August 28, 1898. He played semipro ball locally until he joined Connie Mack's Philadelphia Athletics in 1916 when he was 18 years old. Mack sent him to Durham in the old Piedmont League, but the team folded when World War I broke out. The young first baseman joined the Cardinals in 1918 and played in about one-third of their games that year before moving to Pittsburgh in 1919. The lefthand-hitting and throwing youngster became the Pirates' regular first baseman in 1920, although he hit only .227 and showed little extra-base power. Grimm hit .274, with 17 triples, the following year as the Pirates played surprisingly well. Behind balanced hitting, sound fielding, and improved pitching, the 1921 club led the Giants by 7½ games with six weeks left in the season. Manager George Gibson's Pirates were a happy, carefree team as they arrived at the Polo Grounds on August 24 to play a five game series that could finish off the second-place Giants. But McGraw's club swept the series, and the stunned Pirates went into a tailspin. The Giants raced past them and took the lead for good, winning the pennant by four games. Grimm remained with Pittsburgh three more years and played with several excellent players, including Hall of Famers Max Carey, Hazen "Kiki" Cuyler, and third baseman Harold "Pie" Traynor. Grimm had his best year in 1923, hitting .345 with 99 RBI. But the Pirates were unable to dislodge the Giants, who won three more pennants during the 1922–24 period.

After the 1924 season, Grimm was traded to the Cubs along with Rabbit Maranville. The Cubs finished last in 1925, but the following year they hired Joe McCarthy and began to rebuild the team. The Cubs moved up to fourth place in 1926 and third place the following year, and won the pennant in 1929. These five seasons were Grimm's most enjoyable years in Chicago. He had picked up the nickname "Jolly Cholly" because of his banjo strumming, his very funny stories told with a heavy German accent, and his warm-hearted antics both on and off the field. Still, there were frustrations because the Cubs tended to under-achieve. They finished second in 1930, two games behind the Cardinals, despite hitting a then-record 171 home runs, and McCarthy was replaced by Rogers Hornsby. Rogers' 1931 club finished 17 games behind the Cardinals. In 1932, with the Cubs in second place two-thirds of the way into the season, player-manager Hornsby was replaced by player-manager Grimm.

Some writers and fans felt that the easygoing Grimm might not be able to control his players. But Grimm's relaxed leadership methods worked perfectly in place of Hornsby's critical, hard-nosed style. His infield included Grimm himself, Billy Herman at second, Mark Koenig replacing regular shortstop Billy Jurges at short (Jurges had been shot by a lady whom he refused to marry), and Woody English at third. The outfielders were Kiki Cuyler in right, Johnny Moore in center, and the veteran Riggs Stephenson in left. The pitching staff, led by starting righthanders Lon Warneke, Guy Bush, Pat Malone, and Charlie Root, was the strongest in the league. Gabby Hartnett was the catcher.

The relaxed Cubs played .673 ball after Grimm took over, winning 18 of 20 games as they overtook the Pirates. They clinched the pennant on September 20 when Cuyler's bases-loaded triple overcame the Pirates. In his second year with the Cubs, Billy Herman became a full-fledged star, with a .314 average, 206 hits, a league-leading 19 triples, and sparkling play at second base. Player-manager Grimm had a good season, hitting .307 with 42 doubles. Peter Golenbock, in his *Wrigleyville*, quoted Woody English on Grimm as a manager: "Charlie was my favorite of all managers to play for—as a man…. Jolly Cholly they called him, and that hit it pretty good. He was always in good humor. Everything was always all right…. Charlie was not the smartest manager, and he knew it. He depended on Hartnett, me, and Billy Herman. Grimm would mostly ask Gabby if the pitcher was losing his stuff. 'What do you think?' and Hartnett would know…. Hartnett would tell him when to change pitchers."

The Cubs precipitated a controversy when they failed to vote World Series shares to either Koenig or Hornsby. Ex-Yankee Koenig had hit .353 in 33 games as Jurges' replacement, and Hornsby had managed the Cubs for most of the season. The Cubs were no match for the Yankees, losing to the Bombers in four straight games as Lou Gehrig and Babe Ruth took the Cubs' pitching apart with five home runs and 14 RBI between them. Grimm personally did well with five hits and a .333 average, but the Cubs never had a chance. Ruth, incensed at the Cubs' failure to reward his former teammate Koenig, harangued them mercilessly during the Series over the matter. The other item of note was Ruth's famous "called shot" home run in the third game off Charley Root. Sportswriter Joe Williams triggered this controversy when he wrote that Ruth had called his homer by gesturing out to the bleachers before hitting the ball. The battle-hardened Root scoffed, "If I thought Ruth had really meant that, I would have set him down on his ass with my next pitch."

The Cubs retooled in the next two years, losing to player-manager Terry's Giants in 1936 and to player-manager Frisch's Cardinals the following year. Floyd "Babe" Herman and Chuck Klein were acquired, but neither man played up to expectations. Third baseman Stan Hack, outfielder Augie Galan, and curveballing righthander Bill Lee established themselves in 1934. Outfielder Frank Demaree and 19-year-old first baseman Phil Cavaretta became regulars in 1935, and righthander Tex Carleton and lefthander Larry French joined the starting pitching staff in 1935. Grimm's playing career essentially ended after the 1934 season, although he remained on the playing roster through the 1936 season. In 1935 a well-balanced offense and superior pitching pulled the Cubs up from fourth place in late June to first place in late September as the club won a remarkable 21 games in a row in the last month of the season. Grimm, with two at-bats during the season, was replaced by Cavaretta. The Cubs lost the World Series to Mickey Cochrane's Tigers, four games to two.

Grimm continued to manage the Cubs from the bench until July 1938 when player-manager Gabby Hartnett replaced him. Jolly Cholly spent the next 2½ seasons in the broadcast booth, then managed Milwaukee before returning to manage the Cubs from 1944 through the first third of 1948. His 1945 club won the pennant but lost the Series. After two years in the minors he returned to manage the Braves for the next five years. His last managerial stint came in 1960 when he started the season as the Cubs' manager. But with the club in seventh place after 17 games, he traded places with Cubs broadcaster Lou Boudreau, who was equally unsuccessful over the rest of the season. Grimm served the Cubs in other positions until he retired in 1981.

Over his 20 years as a player Grimm hit .290 with 2299 hits and 1078 RBI. Grimm was a sound fielder who led the National League's first basemen in fielding average in seven of the 14 years in which he was a regular. He played and managed in 331 games and, in his long managerial career, had a 1287–1067 (.547) record. The always cheerful, popular Grimm died at 85.

17

Frisch and Dykes

Frankie Frisch and Jimmy Dykes were two of the most colorful player-managers of the 1930s, although Frisch was more publicized and more successful because of his colorful and talented "Gashouse Gang" St. Louis Cardinals.

FRANKIE FRISCH

Frank Francis Frisch was born in the Bronx, New York, on September 9, 1898, the son of a prosperous lace linen manufacturer. He was a star athlete at Fordham University where he was a sprinter and captain of the college's baseball, basketball, and football teams. He also was named halfback on the second team All-American football squad in 1918. An extremely fast athlete, the stocky Frisch was nicknamed "The Fordham Flash."

Fordham's baseball coach was Art Devlin, a former Giants third baseman. In May 1919, before his graduation, Frisch had a tryout with the Giants. The switch-hitting Frisch impressed McGraw, who signed him a few days later despite Frisch's unacceptable use of a crosshand style, holding the bat with his left hand on top of his right even when hitting righthanded. McGraw wanted to send him out to the minors for seasoning, but Frisch, with the option of joining his father's thriving business, refused to go, and McGraw reluctantly kept him with the Giants. McGraw worked with him, tutoring him mostly on fielding techniques, sliding, and hitting properly.

Frisch's name intrigued the writers, one of them commenting, "It sounds like something frying." But soon observers were getting used to

197

his name after watching the flashy New Yorker perform. McGraw had decided that Frankie was better suited to play second base rather than third, and he put Frisch in the lineup at second base during a crucial series in September. The first batter smashed a sizzler at Frisch. The ball took a bad hop off his chest and bounced several feet away. Frisch reacted quickly, pouncing on the ball and throwing the runner out. McGraw said later, "That was all I had to see. The average youngster, nervous at starting his first game in a pennant situation like that, would have given up on the play or fumbled the ball."

Frisch established himself as a star in 1921, hitting and fielding brilliantly at second and third, as the Giants won their first of four consecutive pennants. The following year Frankie took over at second base for good. He had his best four seasons during the 1921 through 1924 period, hitting .341, 327, .348, and .328. Frisch also excelled during the four World Series, two of which the Giants won, with averages of .300, .471, .400, and .333.

McGraw rewarded the aggressive New Yorker by appointing him team captain for the 1925 season. The job carried with it an added $500 a year salary. But it also included added responsibilities, especially smoothing relations between the abusive McGraw and the players. It also involved dealing with McGraw's habit of taking out his frustrations on his captains over team misfortunes for which they were not responsible.

As the Giants sank into the second division late in the 1926 season, McGraw bawled out his players after each loss, concentrating on team captain Frisch, whom he referred to as "Krauthead," referring to Frisch's German-American background. After one tough loss in St. Louis, with McGraw's abuse ringing in his ears, Frisch left the team and returned to his home in New York. Although the two men later papered over their differences, and the Fordham Flash returned, it was apparent that Frisch's Giants career would end after the season. This was the case, as Frankie was traded to the Cardinals for Rogers Hornsby.

Frisch's career with the Cardinals (he pronounced it "Cawd'nals' in his New York accent) started off beautifully in 1927, as he hit .337 with 208 hits and a league-leading 48 stolen bases. His play was a great relief to Cardinals owner Sam Breadon, the target of considerable heat from Cardinals rooters for trading player-manager Hornsby. Frisch was the indispensable spark plug as the Cards narrowly missed winning the pennant in 1927, and he was the leader as the Cardinals won pennants in three of the next four years. Former catcher Charles "Gabby" Street managed the Cardinals to the 1930 pennant, and in 1931 to the World Championship, a year when Frisch was voted the National League MVP.

But the 1932 club flopped badly, dropping to a sixth place tie with the Giants.

The Cardinals showed no improvement early in the 1933 season, and on June 24 Frisch became the Cardinals' player-manager. He took over a fifth place team and led it to an improved 36–26 record over the remainder of the season. Frisch's personal high point of the season came in the first All-Star game when he singled off Lefty Gomez and, switching to the lefthand side, homered off righthander Alvin Crowder.

Frisch's colorful 1934 club included Jim "Ripper" Collins at first base, Frisch at second, "Lippy Leo" Durocher at short, and the inimitable Pepper Martin at third. Ernie Orsatti was in center field, flanked by Jack Rothrock in right and slugging Joe "Ducky" Medwick in left. Virgil "Spud" Davis and Bill DeLancey were the catchers. The starting pitchers were righthanders Jerome Herman (or Jay Hanna, depending upon the day) "Dizzy" Dean, Tex Carleton, and rookie Paul Dean. Bill Walker and Bill Hallahan were the lefthand starters.

Three colorful graduates of Branch Rickey's farm system—Dizzy Dean, Martin, and Medwick—were the players who put the most strain on player-manager Frisch. Dean was an overbearing, unlettered Arkansas native with complete confidence in himself and in his uncanny ability to make good on his outrageous boasts. The Cardinals signed the tall, rangy youngster in 1930, and within two years he joined the Cards for good. He had an overpowering fastball, a sharp curve, and an unconquerable will to win. His unpredictable antics kept Frisch on constant edge, and, to make matters worse, his more conventional younger brother Paul idolized him and followed his lead. Martin was a completely uninhibited Oklahoma country boy whose tendency to become involved in zany activities on and off the field did not detract from his spirited play. Medwick was a tough New Jersey native with a murderous bat and an extremely low boiling point.

For much of the 1934 season the Cardinals were barely in striking distance of the Giants and the Cubs, despite fine performances by Collins, Medwick, and the Dean brothers. According to St. Louis writer J. Roy Stockton, the club came together after the Deans were fined and suspended by Frisch for tearing up their uniforms and leaving the team after each brother lost a game in a doubleheader loss on August 12. Frisch's players, resenting a perceived set of privileges granted the Deans, vowed to play harder so the brothers would not be missed. The Cards won seven of their next eight games, and by Labor Day they were within six games of the league-leading Giants. The chastened Deans returned in top form, and they carried the pitching load as the Cards gained on the Giants. Tex

Carleton was pitching with nearly equal effectiveness as the Deans. Medwick, Collins, and Frisch himself carried the offensive load. Durocher was superb at shortstop, and inexperienced catcher Bill DeLancey had developed into an excellent receiver.

The largest turnout in Polo Grounds history watched Frisch's one-two Dean punch conquer the Giants in two games on September 16. Dizzy, with help from Tex Carleton, won the first game, and Paul beat the Giants in 11 innings. The Giants' lead was cut to 3½ games. A few days later Dizzy was scheduled to go against Brooklyn in the first game of a doubleheader, with Paul set to pitch the second game. Frisch began to go over the hitters with Dizzy before the first game. But the cocky Dean cut him short with the response, "Now, Frank, I've already won 26 games and it don't look right for no infielder tellin' a guy like me how to pitch." And with that, Diz, throwing with no apparent effort, held the Dodgers hitless through 7 2/3 innings before relaxing and yielding three hits without a run. Then Frisch watched in amazement as Paul pitched a no-hitter in the second game. Dizzy said after the no-hitter, "Shucks, if I'd a known Paul was gonna no-hit em', I'd a done the same."

After Dizzy Dean whitewashed the Reds on Friday, September 28, the Giants and Cards were in a tie for the lead, with two weekend games remaining. Paul Dean beat the last place Reds easily, and the Giants lost to the revenge-seeking Dodgers at the Polo Grounds before a large contingent of Brooklyn fans. With the Cardinals one game up, Dizzy shut out the Reds (for his thirtieth win) to clinch the pennant. The amazing pitching brothers won seven of the Card's last nine victories. Rip Collins was the club's offensive leader, with powerful assistance from Medwick. Collins hit .333 and finished second in home runs. Medwick, a notorious bad ball hitter, led the league in triples and finished in the top five in most offensive categories. Player-manager Frisch contributed a .305 average in 140 games. Dizzy Dean, voted the league MVP, had a 30–7 record, a league-leading 195 strikeouts and seven shutouts, and a fine 2.66 ERA. Paul Dean (19–11) and Tex Carleton (16–11) were the other pitching stalwarts.

The Cards met Mickey Cochrane's Tigers in the World Series. The Tigers started veteran righthander Alvin "General" Crowder, a 9–11 pitcher with the Senators and the Tigers in 1934, against Dizzy Dean. The results were predictable. Dean was the easy winner, the beneficiary of four Medwick hits and five Tiger errors, giving him a 3–0 lead as he breezed to an 8–3 win. Schoolboy Rowe responded to win the second game 3–2. The physically exhausted Cochrane spent each night in a hospital bed to be certain that he would be able to drag himself out for the next day's game. A Detroit paper carried a picture of Cochrane with the caption referring to him as "Our Stricken Leader," and when Mickey reappeared on the field the following day the Cardinals' dugout kept asking how the "stricken leader" was feeling.

The Series moved to St. Louis for the third game, and Paul Dean hurled a 4–1 victory, yielding the only Tigers run after two were out in the ninth. The next day the Tigers came back to tie the Series at two-all as Eldon Auker held the Cardinals at bay after the Tigers broke a 4–4 tie with a five-run eighth inning. The game was remembered because of a play involving pinch runner Dizzy Dean, who was trying to break up a double play as he neared second base. He was skulled and knocked out by the throw to first. Dizzy was taken to the hospital where X-rays showed no injury other than a bad bruise. The next day the loquacious pitcher was heard explaining to a teammate, "They took a picture of my head but they found nothing."

In the fifth game, with Gehringer and Greenberg doing the offensive damage, the Tigers took the lead in the Series as Tommy Bridges outpitched Dizzy Dean. But Brother Paul came back with his second complete game to win 4–3, as well as driving in the winning run. The deciding game in Detroit was a complete disaster for the Tigers. Dizzy Dean toyed with them, shutting them out as the Cards won an 11–0 laugher. As the Cardinals moved out to a big lead, Dizzy twice handled slugger Hank Greenberg with ease, striking him out on pitches close to the letters. On Greenberg's third at-bat, Dean decided to experiment by pitching Greenberg on the outside. Frisch picked up the sign, raced in from second base, and whispered, "Get serious, Diz, you know he murders that kind of pitch so keep pitching him high and tight." Dean answered stubbornly, "Frank, I don't think he can hit me high and outside." Frisch threw up his hands in disgust and returned to his second base position. Sure enough, Greenberg hit the first high and outside pitch like a bullet past Dean's head for a line single to center. Dean turned around and shouted to his fuming manager, "I guess you were right, Frank." On Greenberg's next at-bat, Dizzy got the big fellow out easily on a high and inside pitch.

The deciding game is remembered for a confrontation between Joe Medwick and Tigers third baseman Marv Owen. With the Cards leading 9–0 in the sixth inning, Medwick slid roughly into third base on a triple and bumped Owen hard. It appeared to the disgruntled Detroit fans that Medwick had slid in with unnecessary vigor. The two men jumped up and squared off before they were separated. When Medwick took the field after the inning, the very unhappy Detroit fans began to pelt him with tons of garbage and pop bottles. Judge Landis tried to calm the inflamed crowd by ordering Medwick out of the game. Fortunately, the expulsion had no effect on the outcome of the one-sided game.

In 1935 the Cardinals roster was unchanged except in center field where rookie Terry Moore replaced Ernie Orsatti. Years later Moore, a gifted outfielder, remembered that spring training vividly: "I think I had one of the toughest managers on earth. Frisch didn't like rookies, and every time I made a mistake he'd always yell, 'Who was your manager? I wish he'd taught you better than that!' Frisch was tough on you."

When Frisch was managing the Cardinals in spring training that year, rookie catcher Sam Narron asked Frisch how best to occupy himself. Frisch suggested that Narron pick out an established player and do everything he did. A few days later Frisch was leaning against the batting cage watching his players hit. He noticed that Narron, who should have been busy practicing, was leaning against the other corner of the batting cage. "Hey," he yelled to Narron, "Sam, what the hell are you doing? I thought I told you to pick out a player and do what he did." Narron replied, "I did pick out a player, Mr. Frisch." Frank asked, "And who did you pick?" The guileless rookie answered, "I picked you, Mr. Frisch." The quick-witted Frankie responded, "Well, I like to run so you can start out by running yourself around the field until I tell you to stop."

The Cards started the season reasonably well, residing in second place by Memorial Day, four games behind the smoothly functioning Giants. The Cardinals remained seven games out of the lead by the All-Star break. By Labor Day the Cardinals had overtaken the Giants. The same players who had spearheaded the 1934 pennant win—the Deans, Medwick, Collins, Martin, Durocher—appeared on the way to repeating their earlier triumph. But the Cubs, in fourth place in July, came on with a rush. After Labor Day they began a 21-game winning streak that carried them past the Giants and the Cards. They clinched the pennant on September 27 with their twentieth straight win, as Cubs righthander Bill Lee beat Dizzy Dean.

Several of Frisch's players had fine seasons as his team finished with a 96–58 record, four games behind the blazing Cubs. The Dean brothers practically duplicated their previous season's performance, with Dizzy winning 28 games and Paul winning 19. Medwick and Collins had good seasons. Frisch hit .294 but played in only 103 games, an indication that the 36-year-old player-manager's active career was nearing its end. But Frankie was surprisingly philosophical about his team's pennant loss, asking a writer, "How can you beat a team that wins 21 straight in September?"

It was during this season that Frisch's club became known as the "Gashouse Gang." Late in the season the Cardinals came into New York after playing a doubleheader in the rain at Boston. There was no time to have their uniforms dry-cleaned, and they showed up at the Polo Grounds in grimy, stained, and wrinkled uniforms. The New York writers wrote about the "Gashouse Gang from St. Louis" and the colorful nickname stuck.

Frisch was not immune from practical jokes just because he was the player-manager. One day in a Chicago hotel, Pepper Martin got himself a paper sack full of water and waited until Frisch came down the street, under Martin's third floor room window. Pepper dropped his water bomb on Frisch's head, then tore down to the lobby and picked up a newspaper and sat down. The drenched Frisch stormed into the lobby, wringing wet. He walked over to Martin and said, "Damn you, if you weren't sitting there reading, I'd swear it was you that did it!" Martin lowered his paper and inquired innocently, "Did what, Frank?"

Martin, with Dizzy Dean as his accomplice, was involved in off-field activities that tried Frisch's patience. Frisch knew from experience not to take a cigarette or a match if Martin offered one because Pepper only used the exploding kind. Martin was a past master at administering a hot foot. And Martin and Dean pulled one memorable prank when they broke up a womens luncheon in a Philadelphia hotel. They claimed they were house painters and they noisily brought in scaffolding in apparent preparation for painting the walls. And yet, for all their pranks that nearly drove Frisch crazy, both men insisted that they loved the manager, who they referred to as "the Dutchman." Actually, Frisch had a wonderful sense of humor. He needed it, not only to put up with his rambunctious players, but also because he often was accused of trying to get himself ejected from games in New York to give him more time for a treasured pastime—tending to his plants at home in New Rochelle.

The Cardinals got off to a good start in 1936, leading the second-place Giants by a game and a half by the end of May. The Cubs had a three game lead over the Cardinals at the All-Star break, while the Giants were in fifth place, 11 games off the pace. Frisch provided a good example of a player-manager's prerogative. The Cardinals took on the Indians in an exhibition game during the break. Frisch's eyes almost popped out when he took one look at the lightning-fast, but wild, pre-game pitches of 18-year-old righthander Bob Feller. Frisch walked over to rookie second baseman Stu Martin and, shamelessly using his authority, said, "Stu I think I'll rest my aches and pains, so I'm putting you in there today. Besides, I'm too old to risk getting killed by this wild kid."

Medwick provided most of the excitement for the Cardinals in the second half of the season, as he set two National League records. On July 21 he obtained his tenth consecutive hit, and on September 25 he clubbed his still-standing record sixty-fourth double of the year. He also took part in a free-swinging brawl in the dugout with a teammate, pitcher Ed Heusser, who criticized a poor fielding play by the slugging leftfielder. Frisch made the two men shake hands and soon all was forgiven. But the Giants came back to win the pennant after Bill Terry's club had been written off in July.

Frisch's tenure as a player-manager ended in 1937, as he played in only 17 games, all but five as a pinch hitter. He recalled the occasion when he decided to end his playing career. In a game in May he was the base runner at second base, with Terry Moore the runner at first base. Frisch struggled mightily to score on a base hit to center field. He held up, thinking the ball might be caught. As Frisch described it: "I was running with all I had, and it wasn't much, that late in my career. I finally slid for the plate, made it safely, and before I was through with my slide I felt a foot against my bottom. It was Moore sliding in behind me. He had made up ninety feet on the Old Flash in the race for the plate. I knew then that it was time to quit."

The Cardinals finished in fourth place in 1937. Frisch remained as the Cards' bench manager in 1938, leaving after the Cardinals finished in sixth place. Frankie had a long career in baseball after he left St. Louis. He announced Boston Braves games over radio in 1939 before managing the Pirates from 1940 through 1946. He returned to the booth, announcing Giants games from 1947 through 1949, and entertaining his listeners by intoning "Oh, those bases on 'bawls'" in his New York accent. His last managing job came with the Cubs, from mid-season of 1949 through the middle of the 1951 season.

Frisch played in 2311 games, hitting .316 and stealing 419 bases during his 19-year playing career. He was a great contact hitter, striking out more than 18 times in only two seasons. An exceptional fielder, he set a number of batting and fielding marks in the 50 World Series games in which he appeared. Frisch had a managerial record of 1138–1078 (.514) over 16 years, and he played in 483 games of those he managed. Frisch, inducted into the Hall of Fame in 1947, died in Wilmington, Delaware, on March 12, 1973, after an automobile accident.

JIMMY DYKES

James Joseph Dykes was born in Philadelphia on November 10, 1896, the son of an engineer at Bryn Mawr College. Dykes began playing baseball on neighborhood sandlots under the coaching of his father, who managed local teams. The chunky 5 foot, 9 inch, 185- pounder was signed as an infielder by the Philadelphia Athletics in 1917. He played for the A's in 59 games in 1918 before being called for Army service. In 1919 he was discharged, and he returned to the A's. Connie Mack sent him to the Gettysburg, Pennsylvania, club in the Blue Ridge League, and Dykes returned to the A's to finish the 1919 season. He became the Athletics' regular second baseman in 1920.

Dykes' exceptionally strong throwing arm dictated his switch to third base in 1922, and that was his predominant position throughout his career, although he played elsewhere in the infield when needed. Dykes' hitting came more slowly. Still, during the seven-year period beginning in 1924 he hit over .300 in five seasons. Dykes was a key player on Connie Mack's great 1929–31 championship teams. He expected to remain with the Athletics indefinitely and, like Eddie Collins, had the impression that he might succeed Mack when Connie stepped down as manager. So he was completely surprised when Mack, in an economy move, sold him to the White Sox after the 1932 season.

The 1934 White Sox were in last place after losing 11 of their first 15 games. Owner Lou Comiskey (Charles Comiskey's son) decided to replace play-manager Lew Fonseca with Dykes. The Sox were in Washington when Comiskey asked Dykes to come to his hotel room. He asked Jimmy, "How would you like to manage the White Sox?" Dykes thought of his friend Fonseca and answered, "I'd rather not answer that." But Comiskey said, "If you don't take it, I'm going to give it to somebody else." With that, Jimmy agreed to take over as player-manager.

The next day Dykes arrived with his lineup in mind. He even had memorized a short speech to his new underlings. But there was a problem. Comiskey had not been able to reach Fonseca to notify him of his dismissal. Dykes said later, "Hell, I wasn't going to tell him. All I know is that on my first day as manager of the White Sox, Lew Fonseca managed the team." Dykes gained added respect from his new charges for this thoughtful handling of a ticklish situation. Dykes told reporters some time later: "I welcomed the opportunity to manage, but I'd never given it a thought. Managing had never been one of my burning ambitions. But I'll never forget what Mr. Mack told me after I'd taken the job. He said, 'You're now a player with authority. Don't ever let it get the best of you. Stay a player. Think of yourself as one of the boys, and you'll never have any trouble.' I tried to follow that advice."

"The Little Round Man," as some of the writers referred to Dykes, took over a team with a few stars, but the club needed help. The infield included first baseman Henry "Zeke" Bonura, who could hit but who had no mobility; second baseman Jackie Hayes, a competent fielder but a weak hitter; shortstop Luke Appling, a decent fielder and an excellent hitter; and the 37-year-old player-manager at third. The outfield consisted of the great Al Simmons in left, fading veteran Mule Haas in center, and journeyman Evar Swanson in right. Weak-hitting Eddie Madjeski was the catcher. The only pitchers of note were righthanders George Earnshaw and Ted Lyons. Earnshaw had been a fine pitcher for Connie Mack in the A's glory years, and Lyons was a skilled knuckleballer whose performance had slipped after several good years in the 1920s.

Dykes, who played his usual steady game, was unable to improve the club, which finished in last place. Things picked up in 1935 with a fifth place finish, attributable to improved pitching, especially by Ted Lyons (15–8). Dykes was popular with his players, who found him an easy manager to play for. Jimmy followed Mack's advice, telling an interviewer years later: "I was friendly with all of my players. I didn't have many rules, but one thing I insisted upon was that my players never argue with me on the bench. If there was something they didn't like, they could come into the office later, and we could thrash it out there…. I also insisted that there be no discussion of salaries."

The White Sox, unable to equal the crosstown Cubs in personnel or fan support, matched the Cubs with a third place finish in 1936. Dykes' club benefited from a tremendous year by Appling, who led the league with a .388 average, and righthander Vern Kennedy, who had a career-best 21–9 season. Bonura had 138 RBI, and slap-hitting leftfielder Ray Radcliff had 207 hits and a .335 average. In his last year as a regular player, Dykes hit .267 in 127 games.

Dykes told of another problem he encountered as a player-manager. When he was playing third base he always told his hurlers never to throw a pitch until they looked around at him because he might be making a change. One day he waved to the bullpen for a new pitcher just before righthander Clint Brown threw to the plate. When Dykes looked around, he saw the ball rolling down the third base line. The batter had bunted in his direction. He picked up the ball and asked Brown, "You forget something?" Brown answered, "I guess so." Dykes remembered thinking to himself, "At that I was lucky—a line drive would have carried my head with it into left field."

It was the same story in 1937—a third place finish, decent hitting and pitching, but no chance to compete with the power-packed Yankees who again won the pennant in a landslide. Dykes played in only 30 games, hitting .306. The Sox did little to improve the team and slipped to sixth place in 1938 as Dykes duplicated his previous season, hitting .303 in 26 games.

Through it all, Jimmy remained a doughty, aggressive, non-stop talking manager who exasperated umpires. But he retained their respect and that of his players. He removed his name from the playing roster after the 1939 season and continued as the club's bench manager until the 1946 season when Ted Lyons replaced him 30 games into the season. Looking back on his also-ran managerial years with the White Sox, Dykes summed it up succinctly, "Winning without good players is like trying to steal first base."

Jimmy was still in demand when managerial positions became available. He managed the Athletics from 1951 through 1953, with little success, before managing the Baltimore Orioles in 1954. The Orioles, formerly the St. Louis Browns, were in their first year in Baltimore. Subsequently, he managed the Reds for part of the 1958 season, then took over the Tigers from 1959 through August 1960 when, in a bizarre deal, he traded jobs with Indians manager Joe Gordon. Dykes' managing career ended after the 1961 season. He had a batting average of .280 over his 22-year playing career. During his 21 years as a manager, during which he never had superior teams, his teams had a 1406–1541 (.477) record. Dykes, who played in 382 of the games he managed, died at age 79 in his native Philadelphia.

18

Cronin and Durocher

Joe Cronin and Leo Durocher were two other prominent infielders who also were player-managers during the pre–World War II period. Cronin was the longer-lasting player-manager because he had the good fortune to be appointed player-manager when he was only 26.

JOE CRONIN

Joseph Edward Cronin was born in San Francisco on October 12, 1906. His father, an Irish immigrant who drove a team of horses, was left with virtually nothing when the San Francisco earthquake leveled the family house and destroyed its contents. Joe, always hard-working and responsible, worked at odd jobs when he wasn't playing sandlot ball. Although baseball was his passion, he was a good all-around athlete, playing basketball and soccer, and winning the junior tennis championship of San Francisco when he was 14. The clean-cut, pink-cheeked youngster with the choir boy looks (and the devout Catholicism to match) and the jutting jaw played baseball in high school. He turned down a college baseball scholarship because his family desperately needed his financial help.

The righthand-hitting Cronin signed with the Pirates as an infielder when he was 18 and began his professional career with Johnstown in the Mid-Atlantic age. The skinny youngster played in 38 games for Pittsburgh in 1926. In 1927, after some minor league seasoning, he rejoined the pennant-bound Pirates but played very little. Pittsburgh sold him to the Kansas City Blues in 1928, and he joined the Senators in mid-season when their shortstop was injured. Cronin played in 63 games for Washington, hitting .242 but impressing with his powerful arm, poise, and baseball smarts.

Cronin became the Senators' regular shortstop in 1929, hitting .281, but his breakthrough season came in 1930. He was a major factor as the Senators moved up to second place, hitting .346 with 126 RBI and earning the MVP award. Cronin had the ability to hit to all fields and pull the ball to left field if the situation and the contours of the ball park called for it. He gained a reputation as a good clutch hitter and, later in Joe's career, Connie Mack said of him, "With a man on third and one out, I'd rather have Cronin hitting for me than anybody I've ever seen, and that includes fellows like Cobb and Al Simmons."

The Senators finished in the first division the next two years but fell well behind the pennant-winning Athletics in 1931 and Yankees in 1932, and Clark Griffith decided it was time to replace manager Walter Johnson. After the 1932 season, 26-year-old Joe Cronin became the Senators' newest "boy player-manager." It was a clever move by the wily Griffith. He was giving his future son-in-law (Cronin was engaged to Griffith's adopted daughter Mildred Robertson) a promotion while, at the same time, he was hiring a manager for a few thousand dollars more than Cronin received as a player only.

Cronin and Griffith made several trades during the off-season. They picked up catcher Luke Sewell, outfielders Fred Schulte and Goose Goslin, lefthanders Walter Stewart and Earl Whitehill, and righthander Jack Russell. Cronin's club started the season poorly but fought its way back into the race with the Yankees with powerful hitting by Heinie Manush and Cronin, and excellent pitching by starters Alvin Crowder and Whitehill and reliever Russell. The Senators gained the confidence to compete with the Yankees in their first trip to Yankee Stadium in late April after they won the first game of the series behind Lefty Stewart. With the Senators losing 1–0 with one out and a man on, Senators second baseman Buddy Myer hit a high foul fly behind the plate. Yankee catcher Bill Dickey made the catch but the umpire ruled it a foul ball, claiming it had barely grazed the screen. The furious Yankees loudly protested the foul ball decision. Given another chance, Myer hit the next pitch for a two-run homer to give the Senators a 4–3 win.

Later in the series the Senators led by three runs in the eighth inning. With Lou Gehrig the runner at second, Dixie Walker at first, and none out, Tony Lazzeri hit a long smash to deep right center. Gehrig held to tag up but Walker decided to run. The ball bounced off the wall and rightfielder Goslin recovered it quickly. Gehrig and Walker were very close as they approached third, and the crowd was so loud that the runners were unable to hear coach Art Fletcher's instructions. Cronin took the relay from Goslin and gunned the ball to catcher Luke Sewell at the plate.

Gehrig was tagged out as he slid in from the first base side of the plate, and Sewell tagged out Walker, sliding in from the third base side. The result was an incredible double play without a Yankee score and with only Lazzeri still on base.

Cronin recalled years later that those two plays made the Senators' season. He told Bob Broeg, "That's where we won it [the pennant]. When things are breaking for you, you get breaks like that. The team begins to feel it's going to keep on getting 'em and then nothing can beat 'em." And no one did beat them. The Yankees slipped in late August and the Senators won the pennant by seven games with 99 wins. All of the players obtained in pre-season deals contributed beautifully, making Cronin appear to be a genius. Manush (.336 and a league-leading 221 hits and 17 triples) and Cronin (.309, 118 RBI, and a league-leading 45 doubles) keyed a balanced hitting attack, and Crowder (24–15), Whitehill (22–8), and Russell (13 saves) led the best pitching staff in the league. The Senators faced Bill Terry's Giants in the World Series and, although favored, lost four games to one. Cronin led his club's futile effort, hitting .318. The Series is discussed in Chapter 16.

If the 1933 campaign was an unqualified success, the 1934 season was a complete disaster. Cronin's only happy recollection of the season was his managing the American League club to an All-Star game win on July 10. This was the game remembered best for Carl Hubbell's consecutive strikeouts of five future Hall of Famers, including Cronin. Otherwise, it was a year in which the Senators never contended for the pennant and finished in seventh place, largely due to a series of serious injuries. The final blow came in early September when Cronin's season ended after he fractured a bone in his arm.

Cronin's arm was still in a cast when he married Mildred Robertson just after the season ended. Joe was still on his honeymoon when he and Clark Griffith agreed to a deal with Red Sox owner Tom Yawkey. The Sox gave a staggering $250,000 and shortstop Lyn Lary for Cronin. He signed a five-year contract for $50,000 a year as the club's player-manager. Cronin replaced Bucky Harris, whose club had finished in fourth place with a .500 mark. There was a consensus in Boston that Harris was let go because he couldn't handle his players. Bucky later explained: "I would have fired the drinkers in five minutes, but you don't fire high-priced name players unless you've got adequate replacements, and you can't find those in five minutes." And besides, as Boston writer Joe Cashman told Peter Golenbock, who published it in his *Fenway*, "In Boston it mattered greatly that Cronin was an Irishman."

Cronin shook up the Sox lineup. He installed rookie Babe Dahlgren at first. Smooth-fielding second baseman Oscar Melillo was acquired from the Browns after the season began. Cronin was at short and Bill Werber was the holdover third baseman. The outfielders were hard-hitting Roy Johnson in left, slap-hitting Mel Almada in center, and journeyman Allen "Dusty" Cooke in right. Rick Ferrell was the regular catcher. The starting pitchers were the irascible but great lefthander Robert Moses "Lefty" Grove, hot-tempered righthander Wes Ferrell, and righthanders John "Dusty" Rhodes and journeyman Johnny Welch, neither of whom were as temperamental, or as talented, as Grove or Ferrell.

Cronin's first task as the Sox player-manager was to command the respect of his older players. Never a sparkling performer as a defensive shortstop, Cronin started off the season playing poorly in the field. In his third game at Fenway Park the jittery player-manager booted three ground balls, and he made another error

Joe Cronin was the 26-year-old shortstop-manager of the pennant-winning 1933 Washington Senators. He was the player-manager of the Boston Red Sox through the World War II period, ranking fourth on the player-manager list in terms of games overseen. Cronin became the Red Sox vice president before becoming American league president.

the following day. Before the next game, as Wes Ferrell took the mound in the first inning, Cronin told him, "Let's win this one, Wes." Ferrell looked at his youthful boss and quipped, "I'll do what I can, Joe. But tell me which side you're playing for today." Cronin had no choice but to laugh in response, but the criticism hurt. He began developing a complex about fielding grounders and got into the schoolboy habit of dropping down on one knee to field balls hit directly at him. It got so bad that veteran Oscar Melillo called over to his boss, "If you're going to miss 'em, Joe, miss 'em like a big leaguer."

The Red Sox played at the same .500 pace as they had under Harris and were unable to climb above fourth place. Yawkey, to whom money was no object, continued to purchase big name players over the winter. In December the Sox paid Connie Mack big bucks for two of his stars, slugging first baseman Jimmy Foxx and talented centerfielder Roger Cramer. Aging Heinie Manush was picked up from the Senators. The Red Sox began the 1936 season with a lineup of players of All-Star caliber— Foxx, Cramer, Lefty Grove, Cronin, and the brother battery of pitcher Wes Ferrell and catcher Rick Ferrell. But the club lacked pitching depth. As a result, it finished in sixth place, a full 28½ games behind the powerful Yankees, despite a great year for Foxx and decent years for Ferrell (20–15) and Grove (17–12).

Cronin, who missed half the season with a broken thumb, had continuing problems with the "Gold Sox," as some of his high-priced players were called. Wes Ferrell, who had won 25 games in 1935, gave Cronin the most trouble. His volatile temper soared out of control on August 21, 1936, when, for the second time in five days, he had a tantrum over poor fielding support and walked off the mound. Cronin fined him $1000 and suspended him, although with the dearth of pitching talent on the club the suspension was lifted after a few days. Boston fans became frustrated with the club's inability to win, especially because Tom Yawkey's optimism heightened their expectations. The frustration also increased because of the Yankees' continued success and the strong possibility that rookie Joe DiMaggio, Gehrig, Dickey, et al. would help the Yankees maintain their superiority for several more years. The situation was essentially unchanged in 1937, with the Sox finishing in fifth place. Again, the pitching was not on a par with the hitting.

The picture brightened in 1938 as Cronin's club managed a second place finish, 9½ games behind the Yankees. The Sox stayed even with the Yankees for the first six weeks until an exciting doubleheader at Yankee Stadium on Memorial Day before a record Stadium crowd. The Yankees won the first game as Red Ruffing beat Grove, who had won his last eight games. The Yanks also took the tense second game, enlivened by a fight between Cronin and firebrand Yankee outfielder Jake Powell. After that loss the Yanks moved out ahead and won the pennant without further challenge. The one promising development for the Sox was the maturation of 20-year-old second baseman Bobby Doerr.

The Ted Williams era began in 1938 when the cocky, 20-year-old youngster with the classic swing came to training camp. He was sent down for more seasoning but he returned the following Spring, confident and single-minded about his hitting as ever. Williams' obsession with his hitting, and his short temper drove Cronin crazy. Joe removed him from an exhibition game in Atlanta after he threw a ball over the grandstand to express his annoyance at a heckling fan. Cronin bawled him out, and Williams hung his head in shame. A few days later he loafed after a ball, and the furious player-manager waited for Williams after the inning, bawling him out all the way into the dugout. Later that Spring, Cronin called time to check out his outfield and saw Williams in left field taking practice swings at imaginary pitches. Cronin mimicked Williams' hitting stroke, then shouted out to him, "Hey, Bush. Never mind practicing that...." Then he went through the motions of scooping up a ground ball and bellowed, "Practice this!"

Williams had been preceded by a number of other egocentric players. These head cases included Wes Ferrell, Ben Chapman, Bill Werber, Lefty Grove, Roger Cramer, and heavy-drinking third baseman Jim "Rawhide" Tabor. Sportswriter Ed Linn, *The Irishman Who Made His Own Luck* in Sport Magazine's All-Time All Stars, wrote that after Cronin fined Wes Ferrell $1000 in 1936, Ferrell said, "I'm going to slug that so and so Irishman right on his lantern jaw." Cronin responded, "If he wants to slug me, I'll be passing through the lobby at six o'clock on my way to dinner." At six o'clock Cronin was there but Ferrell was not. Linn also described Ferrell as an advanced astrology student who felt put upon when Cronin was so unscientific as to start him when the stars forecast disaster.

Linn told of a joke going around the Boston dressing room that Cronin had to play Chapman because Cronin was afraid to let Chapman stay on the bench between innings and knock him when the player-manager was in the field. Werber had to be fined for not hustling. Lefty Grove refused to talk after losing a tough game. Linn referred to Roger Cramer as a "clubhouse lawyer," and Jim Tabor didn't take training rules too seriously. Cronin had to put up with all these idiosyncrasies.

The 1939 season was virtually a copy of the previous year. The Yankees took the lead from the start and were never seriously challenged, winning the pennant by 17 games over the second-place Red Sox. Ted Williams began his magnificent career hitting .327 and finishing among the top five hitters in every other meaningful offensive statistic. Foxx had another great year, and Cronin hit .308 and drove in 108. Lefty Grove, now a once-a-week starter, led the pitchers with a 15–4 record, but, as usual, the Sox pitching staff had to be bailed out frequently by the thundering offense.

Cronin followed the practice of calling pitches from shortstop, a practice which many of his pitchers resented. Righthander Eldon Auker was picked up from the Tigers after the 1938 season, but he lasted with Cronin's club only through the 1939 season, with a 9–10 record. When Auker was nearly 90, he gave a talk at a SABR meeting in which he discussed the year that he pitched for Cronin. Auker said: "I pitched for Cronin one year and that was enough. Joe was a good guy but he drove me crazy, always nervous and pawing the dirt down at shortstop. He'd come to the mound and say, 'Don't walk this guy but don't give him anything to hit.' And he'd signal the catcher what pitch to call without my knowing it. One day I just walked off the mound after telling him that he should do the pitching and I would play shortstop."

As a playing manager, Cronin had other disadvantages. His players respected him as a potent hitter, but they didn't feel he was worth his large salary, particularly because his fielding was poor and getting worse with the passage of time. Cronin was popular with the press because he was a congenial, cooperative man, but sometimes he hurt himself in his players' eyes when his criticisms of them appeared in the writers' stories. And Cronin was given the job of negotiating salaries with some of the lesser players, many of whom resented Cronin's hard bargaining.

And then there was the Pee Wee Reese controversy. Red Sox farm system director Billy Evans was instructed by Tom Yawkey to beef up their farm system after it became apparent to Yawkey that he could not buy a pennant by acquiring big-name players. One of Evans' first moves was to purchase the Louisville Colonels of the American Association and all of its assets for $175,000. The Colonels' main asset was their promising short-stop, 18-year-old Harold "Pee Wee" Reese. Evans felt that Reese was the Sox's shortstop of the future and that, when Reese was ready, Cronin could move to third base. According to Tony Lupien, a well-respected Harvard graduate who replaced Jimmy Foxx at first base, "What Evans hadn't anticipated was Joe Cronin's fierce fight to protect his job and Tom Yawkey's fierce loyalty in protecting Cronin…. [In 1939] Cronin was still playing, so all of a sudden Cronin cut Billy's legs off by selling Pee Wee to Brooklyn…. Joe didn't want to move to third base. And then Pee Wee was gone." Some baseball men felt the move cost the Red Sox heavily. Cronin always claimed that the sale was not a question of personalities but simply a matter of what was in the best interests of the Red Sox.

The 1940 Sox finished in a fourth place tie with Jimmy Dykes' White Sox, eight games behind the pennant-winning Tigers. Williams and Foxx hit for average and power, and Cronin complemented both sluggers with 111 RBI. But, as usual, the pitching was not good enough to make the club a legitimate contender. The 1941 club strongly resembled the 1940 version, although it finished in second place, 17 games behind the Yankees. This was the season remembered for Joe DiMaggio's 56-game hitting streak and Ted Williams' .406 average. Cronin hit .311, with 95 RBI, in his last year as a regular player.

The 1942 club had new regulars at first base and shortstop, but again the Sox finished second, nine games behind the Yankees. Cronin's regular infield included Tony Lupien at first, Bobby Doerr, Johnny Pesky at short, and Jim Tabor. Williams (wrongfully abused as a draft dodger) was in left, Dom DiMaggio in center, and Lou Finney in right. Righthanders Cecil "Tex" Hughson, Charley "Broadway" Wagner, Joe Dobson, and Dick Newsome were the starting pitchers, and veteran righthander Mace Brown was the principal reliever. Cronin hit .304 in 45 games as an occasional infielder, although he was still a tough hitter in the clutch, batting in 24 runs with his 24 hits during the season.

With the increasing intensification of the Nation's war effort and players joining the military service, the 1943 Sox finished an inconsequential seventh place. Cronin would have preferred to retire as a player but he remained on the roster and showed he could still hit. He batted .312 in 59 games, with 29 RBI on his 24 hits. His most spectacular performance came in a doubleheader against the Athletics on June 17 when he hit a three-run pinch hit home run in each game. Cronin had a strong sense of the dramatic, reflected in Ed Linn's description of Joe's 1943 pinch hitting heroics:

> Joe, who dearly loved the clutch, would wait for a key spot late in the game. Time would be called. The batter would trudge back to the dugout. There would follow perhaps 30 seconds of total inactivity on the field and a thickening of tension in the stands. Nobody doubted that Cronin would be coming up, of course, and yet a great roar would arise as, at last, he came hulking up out of the dugout, swinging half-a-dozen big bats which he strew behind him as he strode to the plate.

The Sox finished fourth and fifth in the last two years of World War II as Cronin's playing career ended in April 1945 when he broke his leg. As a bench manager he led Boston to the pennant in 1946, losing to the Cardinals on Enos Slaughter's famous dash home in the seventh game, and to a third place finish the following year. He moved into the Red Sox front office from 1947 through 1959, serving consecutively as the club's vice-president, treasurer, and general manager. He was the president of the American League from 1959 through 1973, and after that was Chairman of the American League board until his death on September 7, 1984. Cronin had a .301 career batting average and drove in 1424 runs during his 20 playing seasons. He was a player-manager in 1291 games, ranking behind only Cap Anson, Fred Clarke, and Charles Comiskey in this regard. He had an overall 1236–1055 (.540) record as a manager. Cronin was elected to the Hall of Fame in 1956.

LEO DUROCHER

Leo Ernest Durocher was born on July 27, 1905, in West Springfield, Massachusetts. His parents, railroad engineer George and Clara Durocher, were of French descent. Leo, a tough, street-smart youngster, left high school to work as a mechanic for a local electric company, playing semi-pro ball on weekends. The Yankees signed him as a shortstop when he was 19, and he impressed manager Miller Huggins as a fielder but he was a weak hitter. He was sent to the minors where he spent the 1926–7 seasons before rejoining the Yankees in the Spring of 1928.

The brash, stylishly-dressed youngster was disliked by his Yankee teammates, especially Babe Ruth, but his skill in the field continued to impress Huggins. The Yankee manager suggested that righthand-hitting Leo try to become a switch hitter so that he might be better able to beat out hits from the lefthand side. His attempt to improve his offensive skills gave rise to a joke among his teammates. Before spring training games in 1928, a Yankee player would ask a member of that day's opposing team, "Have you seen our new .400 hitter?" After receiving a "no" answer, the Yankee player would respond, "Durocher—.200 batting righthanded and .200 batting lefthanded!"

Durocher spent the 1928–9 seasons with the Yankees, making more noise with his mouth than at the plate and becoming involved repeatedly in minor brawls. The Yankees management tired of him and he moved to the Reds in 1930, remaining there until early in the 1933 campaign when he was traded to the Cardinals. He became the Cards' captain in 1934 and was a key figure in their emergence as Worlds Champions in 1934. Leo remained with St. Louis through the 1937 season, and was considered the best fielding shortstop in the National League. The Dodgers obtained Durocher after the 1937 season. He captained the Dodgers but hit only .219 in 1938 as the futile Dodgers finished in seventh place.

Larry MacPhail, the Dodgers' erratic but brilliant executive president, signed Durocher as the club's player-manager in 1939. Despite acquiring several players, the Dodgers started sluggishly in 1939. Stuck in the second division in early July, they needed a spark, and Durocher tried to provide it. In the second game of the July 4 doubleheader at the Polo

Grounds, Durocher traded insults with the Giants. In reprisal, Giants' righthander Hal Schumacher threw a fast ball close to Leo's head. Durocher shouted out something to Schumacher before hitting the next pitch to short, an easy double play ball. Leo was an easy out at first as first baseman Zeke Bonura took the inning-ending throw. As Lippy Leo crossed the bag he spiked Bonura. There was an astonishing sight as Durocher continued down the baseline. Bonura wheeled and chased Durocher, slowing only to fire the ball and then his glove at Leo's head. Zeke clamped a headlock on the smaller Dodgers' player-manager, meanwhile delivering a series of punches. Durocher returned fire with several body blows. Both teams emptied onto the field and there was some ineffectual pushing and shoving until peace was restored. But the Dodgers' field boss had tried to stir his club up, practically admitting that spiking Bonura was a deliberate attempt to accomplish that.

Later in July the Dodgers picked up outfielder Dixie Walker on waivers from Detroit. The club came on with a rush in August, at their best when Durocher was in the lineup, although he had to rest occasionally from fatigue and the strain of managing. First baseman Dolph Camilli led the offense, and righthander Luke "Hot Potato" Hamlin the pitchers, as the Dodgers polished off the Cubs to finish in third place. Durocher hit .277 in 116 games.

The Dodgers acquired shortstop Pee Wee Reese after the 1939 season, although there was a feeling in Brooklyn that Durocher was not yet ready to retire to the bench. Larry MacPhail told the writers in the Spring, "Next year Reese will definitely be in our starting lineup at short, and I predict he will be the most sensational newcomer in both leagues." Joe Williams wrote, "If Reese can send the brilliant Durocher to the bench he must be better than fair." Reese was a lot better than fair as the Dodgers won their first eight games in 1940. Further reinforcements came later in the season as youthful third baseman–outfielder Pete Reiser and Cardinals veteran leftfielder Joe Medwick joined the club.

There was a game that season when Durocher's barbed comments stirred up Cubs' righthander Claude Passeau. The big pitcher kept looking into the Dodgers dugout to spot his tormentor. After one particularly offensive remark, Passeau threw down his glove and began walking toward the Dodgers bench, shouting, "The guy who made that last crack doesn't have guts enough to come out and back it up." Player-manager Durocher looked down the bench and spotted big, strong, good-natured outfielder Joe Gallagher not paying any attention to what was going on. Leo called out, "Joe, get up there and hit." The unsuspecting Gallagher picked out a bat and walked out of the dugout towards home plate. Passeau walked up to

Gallagher and shouted, "You need a bat, you big S.O.B," and hauled off and belted the hulking Gallagher. Both players were ejected, and a laughing Durocher, pleased that he had gotten Passeau removed from the game, told a writer the next day, "I still don't think Gallagher knows what happened." Apparently, Passeau did, because the next time he faced the Dodgers, he fired a ball into the Dodgers dugout, narrowly missing Durocher.

The Dodgers played well and appeared to have a chance to overtake the Reds until they lost Reese for the season in mid–August with a fractured heel bone. Durocher replaced Reese and played reasonably well, but the overmatched Dodgers lost the pennant by 12 games to the Reds, who obtained excellent years from righthanders William "Bucky" Walters and Paul Derringer. Durocher slowed up in the field and hit .231 in 62 games.

Durocher's year-to-year contract required renewing after the season, but the mercurial MacPhail had a problem with Lippy Leo. Despite the Dodgers' fine season, MacPhail was unhappy about Durocher's failure to play regularly, instead relying so heavily on the inexperienced Reese. During one of MacPhail's frequent violent arguments with his manager, he raged, "I'm paying you to see some of that sparkling infield play I've been reading about! You don't think I'm paying you just to manage the club, do you? Hell, I could manage the club myself and do a better job than you." The argument continued until Leo shouted back, "All right, I'm fired. Get somebody else to manage your lousy club." The not-so-sober, and completely unpredictable, MacPhail calmed down suddenly and the argument was over, and Leo was re-signed for the upcoming 1941 season. With that taken care of, MacPhail filled two positions very effectively, acquiring flamethrowing righthander Kirby Higbe from the Phillies and catcher Arnold "Mickey" Owen from the Cardinals.

After a good training season in Havana, replete with some player hijinks, and then Clearwater, Florida, Durocher's club was further strengthened in May when they picked up highly skilled second baseman Billy Herman from the Cubs. Brooklyn fans had high hopes, and Durocher's club accommodated them in the first half of the season. The Dodgers and Cardinals traded first place leads in early July, and Durocher inspired his players further with a gutty move on July 2. Kirby Higbe and Cubs lefthander Verne Olsen were locked in a scoreless game in the ninth inning at Ebbets Field. In the bottom of the inning the Dodgers loaded the bases with one out and Higbe due to bat. He started for the plate, but Durocher called him back, picked up a bat, and walked to the plate. The crowd roared its disapproval, wanting to see Higbe try to win his own game. Durocher knew that the crowd would blame him if he failed, but it was characteristic of him that he took the chance. On the second pitch to him, Leo deftly rolled a bunt past the box and squeezed in Medwick from third base with the winning run. The crowd appreciated the play— but not as much as Leo's inspired players.

The Dodgers weakened later in the month but came back strong in August and September. These were the halcyon days for the long-suffering Brooklyn fans. Their team was headed for the pennant, and Brooklynites loved all their players. But their special favorites were Pee Wee Reese, Pete Reiser, Dolph Camilli, and, most of all, Dixie "The People's Cherce" Walker. Durocher's club clinched the pennant on September 25, powered by the 22-year-old Reiser, who led the league in hitting; Camilli, who led in homers; and Medwick. Higbe and fellow righthander Whitlow Wyatt led the pitchers with 22 wins apiece. The Dodgers lost the World Series to the Yankees four games to one, a Series best remembered by the Dodgers' loss of the fourth game when Hugh Casey's strikeout pitch, which appeared to have pinned down a Dodgers win, escaped Mickey Owen and opened the floodgates for the Yankees' come-from-behind win.

The 1941 season was Durocher's final campaign as a part-time player, as he hit .286 in 18 games. He did not play an inning in 1942, and his club finished two games behind the Cardinals. Even with the severe player shortage of the World War II years, Leo played in only six more games over the next three years. He managed the Dodgers through 1946 but was suspended by Commissioner Happy Chandler for the 1947 season for associating with gamblers. Just before his suspension Durocher put down a revolt by the Dodger players who were protesting the presence of black rookie Jackie Robinson. In July 1948, in a real shocker, Durocher replaced Mel Ott as manager of the hated Giants. He won a pennant and a World Championship with the Giants in seven seasons, including the 1951 flag on Bobby Thomson's historic home run. Leo also managed the Cubs from late 1966 until late 1972, and the Houston Astros from late 1972 through 1973.

Durocher's tempestuous career as a player and manager was matched by his fast track, controversial private life, which included four marriages and well-publicized involvement with gamblers and show business figures. He was controversial even nine years after his death when it was revealed that the Giants' miraculous win in 1951 may have been facilitated by opposing team signals relayed from the center field clubhouse at the Polo Grounds. Durocher-managed teams had an overall 2010–1710 (.540) record, as his clubs won three pennants and the 1954 World Series. He had a mediocre lifetime .247 batting average but was among the best defensive shortstops of his era. Durocher was elected to the Hall of Fame three years after his death at age 85 in 1991 in Palm Springs, California.

19

Boudreau, Ott, and Rose

Lou Boudreau and Mel Ott became playing managers within a week of each other, just a few days before Pearl Harbor. Both players were of Hall of Fame caliber, although Boudreau, nine years younger at 24, was yet to hit his peak as a player, and Ott's best years were behind him. Boudreau was a natural leader whose managerial appointment was more predictable than that of Ott's, a quiet, unassuming man who led by example rather than force of personality.

LOU BOUDREAU

Louis Boudreau, Jr. was born in Harvey, Illinois, on July 17, 1917, the son of a machinist and semipro baseball player of French descent. At the University of Illinois, where he had a basketball scholarship and majored in physical education, he was captain and third baseman of the baseball team, and captain of the basketball team. But his eligibility to play amateur sports was withdrawn after he signed an agreement to join the Cleveland Indians after graduation. The 5 foot 11 inch, 185-pounder played professional basketball briefly with the Hammond, Indiana, team of the National Basketball League.

In 1939 Boudreau played for Cedar Rapids and Buffalo, teaming with second baseman Ray Mack. Both Boudreau and Mack joined the Indians in early August 1939. In 1940 righthand-hitting Lou hit .295, led American League shortstops in fielding, and made the All-Star squad. He had another successful year in 1941, compensating for his lack of speed with lightning-quick reaction and an extraordinary ability to position himself.

The Indians were looking for a new manager after the 1941 season.

Boudreau applied for the job, and the 24-year-old shortstop became the Indians' new "boy wonder" player-manager. A Cleveland reporter wrote sarcastically: "Great! The Indians get a Baby Snooks for a manager and ruin the best shortstop in baseball." Less than two weeks later the Japanese bombed Pearl Harbor. In his book *Covering All the Bases*, Boudreau admitted his first mistake was trying to instill a rah-rah spirit in his team by placing sophomoric signs in the locker room. The players' sneering reactions showed Boudreau that major leaguers are professionals who react differently than collegians. The 1942 Indians included first baseman Les Fleming, Mack, Boudreau, and Ken Keltner at third. Veterans Jeff Heath and Roy "Stormy" Weatherly were in left field and center, respectively, and Oris Hockett was the rightfielder. Otto Denning and Gene DeSautels shared the catching. The experienced pitchers, with Bob Feller in the Navy, were righthanders Jim Bagby and veteran Mel Harder, and lefthanders Al Smith, Harry Eisenstat, and Alfred "Chubby" Dean. With World War II mobilization moving ahead, Boudreau was classified 4-F because of chronically bad ankles.

Boudreau's club won 13 straight games in April and May but slipped down to fourth place by the end of Memorial Day. The club finished fourth as the playing manager hit .283. Over the next three years the Indians finished third and then fifth twice in relatively meaningless seasons, with success or failure determined more by draft board roulette than any other factor. Boudreau played well during these wartime seasons. He hit .286 in 1943, then a league-leading .327 in 1944 as he led all shortstops in the league in fielding for the fifth straight year and participated in 134 double plays, a record at the time. Lou hit .307 in 1945, playing in only 97 games because of a broken ankle. But things changed in 1946 with the war over.

Boudreau started off the postwar season with a new two-year contract at an increased $45,000 a year, $25,000 for managing and $20,000 for playing. His infield included Fleming, Mack, Boudreau himself, and Keltner. The outfield starters were leftfielder George Case, centerfielder Pat Seerey, and Hank Edwards in right. Jim Hegan was the catcher, and two other promising players were outfielder Gene Woodling and third baseman Bob Lemon. Bob Feller headed a pitching staff that included righthanders Steve Gromek, Allie Reynolds, and Charles "Red" Embree.

Boudreau's early optimism faded in May with the Indians in seventh place. The only happy occasion before that came on April 30 when Feller pitched a 1–0 no-hitter in Yankee Stadium. Player-manager Boudreau made the gem possible with a great play. As Lou described it: "Nobody was thinking no-hitter in the first inning when I was fortunate enough to

Lou Boudreau was the shortstop-manager for the Cleveland Indians from 1942 to 1950, directing the club to a World Championship in 1948 while leading the American League with a .355 batting average. He had less success later as bench manager for the Red Sox, Kansas City Athletics, and the Chicago Cubs.

make a play on a hot grounder that [second baseman] Snuffy Stirnweiss hit to the right side of second base. I somehow reached the ball and, while in the process of falling, made an underhand throw to Les Fleming at first base. My momentum forced me into a somersault and I landed on my back—but Stirnweiss was out."

The Indians were well out of the race by June 21 when a group headed by Bill Veeck purchased the club. Asked about Boudreau's status, the colorful Veeck answered, "Lou is a swell fellow and a great player," but he said nothing about Lou's managerial ability. A few days later Veeck met with Lou, who was concerned about his future with the team. Veeck told him, "We know about your ball playing. You're the best.... But we have some doubts about your managerial ability.... Meanwhile, you're the manager and don't worry about anything else." Boudreau made it clear to Veeck that if he were relieved as manager he would not play under another manager. Lou had a lot to worry about as his team finished sixth, 36 games behind Joe Cronin's Red Sox. In the losing cause, Feller had a great year (26–15) and an outstanding 371 innings pitched. Pat Seerey, a home run or nothing–type hitter, had 26 homers, and Boudreau hit .293 and again led American League shortstops in fielding.

Boudreau devised the famous "Williams shift" in 1946. Some 75 percent of Ted Williams' hits were pulled into right field. Boudreau, predicting that Williams was too stubborn to hit to left, overloaded the right side of the infield and outfield, leaving the left side open. Lou stationed his first baseman and rightfielder virtually on the right field line, and placed his second baseman closer to first base and back on the grass. Boudreau positioned himself to the right of second base and had his third baseman play directly behind second. He moved his centerfielder well over towards right field and had only his leftfielder on the other side of the field, 30 feet closer to the plate than usual. One of Lou's players said, "Hell, Lou, he'll just bunt." Boudreau answered, "Fine, I hope he does." After the season Lou determined the shift was 37 percent more successful than if it had not been used.

The most important development of the winter was a trade with the Yankees for Joe "Flash" Gordon, their acrobatic second baseman, with the Tribe giving up righthander Allie Reynolds. Gordon had been the American League MVP in 1942 but had hit only .210 in 1946. But Boudreau was pleased to obtain Gordon, convinced that the 31-year-old second baseman would provide power, clutch hitting, experience, and field leadership. Veeck also decided to move the Indians out of ancient League Park, where the Indians had played part of their home games, to spacious Municipal Stadium. And Boudreau hired veteran manager Bill McKechnie as a coach.

The 1947 Indians never contended, playing .500 ball through June and finishing in fourth place, 17 games behind the pennant-winning Yankees. The most important event of the Indians' season came on July 5 when African-American Larry Doby joined the club. Feller led the league with 20 wins. Gordon hit .272, with 29 homers and 93 RBI. Under Bill Mckechnie's guidance, former infielder-outfielder Bob Lemon had become a solid (11–5) righthand reliever with his natural sinker ball delivery. Boudreau hit .307 and led the league with 45 doubles, but he was concerned about his status because his two-year contract had expired. He had reason for concern because there were strong indications that Veeck was actively seeking a change, especially in light of a report that Boudreau would be traded to the St. Louis Browns for shortstop Vern Stephens in a multi-player swap.

Veeck found himself involved in a controversy as Indians fans deluged him with some 4000 letters. Most of them urged Veeck to keep Lou in Cleveland. *The Cleveland News* ran a front page "Boudreau Ballot" for fans to vote whether or not to trade Boudreau, and the votes, tabulated each day, were largely in Boudreau's favor. The Cleveland writers also favored Boudreau's retention. Ed McAuley wrote in the *News*, "If Veeck were to trade Bob Feller, he might stab some of the fans in their judgments. If he trades Boudreau, he will stab many of the fans in their hearts." This went on for several weeks until November 27, when Veeck relented. Lou signed a two-year contract for $49,000 a year, including $25,000 for managing and a $4000 increase to $24,000 for playing.

With his immediate status clarified, Boudreau and Veeck turned their attention to the 1948 club. Hank Greenberg, retired after playing with the Pirates in 1947, became a part owner of the Indians and a close adviser to Veeck. McKechnie remained as a coach, former catcher Muddy Ruel and newly-retired Mel Harder were the new coaches, and Tris Speaker worked with outfielder Larry Doby. The infield included first baseman Eddie Robinson, Gordon, Boudreau, and Keltner. Dale Mitchell was in left, Doby started the season in right but moved to center, and Thurman Tucker was in right. Jim Hegan remained the regular catcher, and the starting pitchers included Feller, Lemon, Gromek, and, after the season's start, rookie lefthander Gene Bearden.

The Indians took over first place on Memorial Day and held the lead until July 4. On July 7, the Indians picked up legendary Negro League righthander Leroy "Satchel" Paige, he of the famed "hesitation pitch" and the indeterminate age. Veeck was accused of signing Paige as a publicity stunt, but Paige produced a 6–1 season record and a 2.48 ERA. On the next-to-last game of the season the Indians clinched a tie for the pennant as Bearden beat the Tigers for his nineteenth win. But the club lost its final game of the regular season and finished in a tie with the Red Sox, who beat the Yankees, necessitating a one-game playoff.

The crucial game was played in Boston. Boudreau surprised everyone by picking rookie Bearden to start and bypassing Feller, Lemon, and Gromek. Red Sox manager Joe McCarthy also surprised by starting righthander Denny Galehouse, who had won only eight games. The cool, nerveless Bearden won the game 8–3, with his player-manager providing heroic support. Lou homered in the first inning, and singled in the fourth inning and scored as the Indians took a 4–1 lead. In the fifth, Boudreau hit another home run to give his club a five-run cushion, and he singled in the ninth. He had gone four for four in the biggest game of his career. Veeck paid Lou the ultimate compliment: "We didn't win the pennant in 1948. We won it on November 25, 1947, the day I re-hired Lou Boudreau."

The Indians had several heroes. Bob Lemon and Gene Bearden won 20 games, and Feller won 19. Joe Gordon, who had 32 homers and 124 RBI, was the leader Boudreau had hoped for, and Ken Keltner and Dale Mitchell had career years. Player-manager Boudreau, voted the league MVP, hit .355 with 106 RBI, struck out only nine times in 560 at-bats, and led all shortstops in the league in fielding for the eighth time in the last nine years.

The Indians met the Boston Braves in the World Series. Righthander Johnny Sain beat Feller in the first game 1–0, although Feller yielded only two hits. The only run scored in the eighth after Braves' catcher Phil Masi was ruled safe at second by National League umpire Bill Stewart on a pickoff throw from Feller. Photos showed clearly that Boudreau had tagged Masi out. (Masi insisted for years that he was safe, but after Stewart died, Masi admitted that he was out.) Bob Lemon beat lefthander Warren Spahn 4–1 to tie the Series, and the Indians went up by a game the next day in Cleveland when Bearden pitched a 2–0 win. The rookie pitcher continued his sensational run, getting two of the Indians' five hits and scoring the first run. Steve Gromek beat Sain in the fourth game 2–1, as Boudreau drove in the first run and Doby homered for the winning run. The Braves took the sixth game 11–5 as Spahn beat Feller, and the Series stood at three to two. Boudreau's club clinched the Series the next day back in Boston, winning 4–3 as Lemon beat righthander Bill Voiselle. Lemon was helped by Joe Gordon's home run and the irrepressible Bearden, who came in with the bases loaded in the seventh. The lefty allowed two runs but held the lead the rest of the way. Boudreau had rewarded the fans for their support with a World Championship. Veeck tore up Lou's contract and replaced it with a new two-year pact that included a $13,000 raise. Lou became one of the highest paid major leaguers, with a $62,000 a year salary—$25,000 as a manager and $37,000 as a player.

The 1949 Indians finished third, eight games behind Casey Stengel's pennant-winning Yankees. Boudreau's club was in seventh place through the middle of June and barely beat out the Tigers for third place. Lou, who had a fair season, wrote of his relations with Veeck and Hank Greenberg:

> By mid-season, we didn't see as much of Veeck as before.... I
> know that Veeck felt I was too much of a "hunch manager,"
> that I relied on my instincts instead of managing by the book....
> I think Greenberg, with his constant second-guessing of my
> decisions, had a lot to do with formulating Veeck's opinion of
> my managerial ability, and I resented it.

With a few new regulars—first baseman Luke Easter, third baseman
Al Rosen, Ray Boone who played more games at short than Boudreau—
the 1950 club performed as well as the 1949 version, but the Yankees,
Tigers, and Red Sox simply outplayed them. The Indians stayed in third
place through August but finished fourth, six games behind the first place
Yankees. Boudreau hit .269 in half of the club's games. Veeck and Greenberg at first indicated that Boudreau would return in 1951. But the Indians released him on November 10, replacing him with Al Lopez. According
to Boudreau, Greenberg, whom he disliked, did not personally inform
him of his release.

Boudreau signed with the Red Sox in 1951 as a player under manager
Steve O'Neill. The Sox finished in third place as the slowed-down
Boudreau duplicated his 1950 season, hitting .267 in 82 games. Lou took
over as Sox manager in Spring training when O'Neill became ill. Boudreau,
not yet 35, had planned to continue playing in 1952, and he had two at-
bats in early May when he broke a bone in his hand warding off a close
pitch. He took himself off the playing roster, ending his playing career.

Boudreau managed the Red Sox for three seasons, finishing sixth in
1952 and fourth in 1953 and 1954. He took over the new Kansas City Athletics in their first two years, finishing sixth in 1955 and last in 1956. Lou
managed the A's in their first 104 games of the 1957 season, then was
replaced with the club in last place. Lou became a sports broadcaster in
Chicago in 1958 and remained there before exchanging jobs with Cubs'
manager Charlie Grimm 17 games into the 1960 season. After the Cubs
finished seventh, Boudreau returned permanently to the broadcast booth
and remained there until he retired. Over his 15 year playing career,
Boudreau hit .295 with a .973 fielding percentage. He had a 1162–1224
(.487) managing record. Boudreau was a player-manager in 1285 games,
ranking fifth on the all-time list, just six games fewer than Joe Cronin. He
was inducted into the Hall of Fame in 1970.

MEL OTT

Melvin Thomas Ott was born on March 2, 1909, in Gretna, Louisiana,
a town near New Orleans. His parents were Charles and Carrie Ott, a

hard-working couple of Dutch descent. Charles Ott, a laborer at a local cottonseed oil plant, had been a semipro pitcher and he encouraged his youngster, a gifted all-around athlete despite his short, stocky build. At 16 Mel joined the Patterson Grays, a local semipro team financed and operated by Harry Williams, a wealthy lumberman.

Williams was so impressed by the hitting and baseball savvy of his juvenile catcher that, when Williams was in Europe, he sent Mel a post-card telling the youngster to go to New York for a tryout with McGraw. At first Mel thought the card was a joke and he ignored it until Williams returned to Louisiana and insisted that he make the trip. The sturdy lit-tle teenager arrived in New York in September 1925 and so impressed McGraw that he sent Ott a contract for the 1926 season. Mel continued his powerful hitting in Spring training, and *New York Times* writer Harry Cross wrote the following:

> Sarasota, Fla., March 14, 1926—Manager McGraw has made a remarkable discovery. He has found a young ballplayer ... who is as rare a baseball possibility at ... seventeen as his experienced eyes ever rested upon.... He says that he has never seen a youth of his age and experience with such a perfect stance at the plate. As Ott is too small to measure up to McGraw's proportions for a catcher, the young find will be developed into an outfielder.

McGraw supervised Mel's development so closely that the writers began referring to him as "John McGraw's boy" or "Master Melvin." Ott had a distinctive hitting style. A lefthand hitter, he stood with his feet well apart and raised his right foot to knee height as the pitcher prepared to deliver the pitch. Mel put his foot down a split-second before the pitch was released. His swing most impressed McGraw because it was so level and well-balanced, and because the youngster kept his head perfectly still with his eyes focused on the ball. In his first two years with the Giants, Ott learned every outfielding and base running technique, including how to run properly. He would become the smallest of the great home run hit-ters, at 5 foot 9 inches, 170 pounds.

Rather than sending his prodigy to the minors, McGraw preferred to keep Mel on the bench next to him, pelting him with a continuing, some-times profane, lecture on the action before them. McGraw forbade Mel from socializing with the veterans to prevent him from adopting their undesirable habits and activities. Ott was brought along slowly, hitting .383 in 35 games in 1926, and not becoming the Giants' regular rightfielder until well into the 1928 season when he hit .322 in 124 games.

Mel's breakthrough season came in 1929 when, at 20, he hit .328 in

150 games, with a career-high 151 RBI and 42 homers. Ott was one of the great run producers and home run hitters in the National League over the next 12 years, carrying much of the offensive load in the Giants' pennant-winning seasons of 1933, 1936, and 1937 under Bill Terry. Mel also was widely considered the best defensive rightfielder in the league. He was a master judge of fly balls, had an unusually powerful and accurate throwing arm, and showed uncanny ability to play caroms off the tricky Polo Grounds right field wall.

The Giants had slipped after winning the 1937 pennant, and by 1941 they had become an old, jaded club whose fans had tired of the team's mediocre field performance. For a few years manager Bill Terry had expressed interest in moving to the front office, and some names had been mentioned as his successor, including Frankie Frisch, Gabby Hartnett, and Dick Bartell. Ott, past his peak as a player, had never been considered a possible successor. On December 2, 1941, Mel attended the annual minor league meetings in Jacksonville to talk with Terry and Giants owner Horace Stoneham about his salary for 1942. He entered the Giants' suite and was greeted by Stoneham who said, "Hi ya, manager! I have a new job for you, at more money." Mel had to be assured by Stoneham and Terry that he was indeed the Giants' new playing manager. Some baseball men questioned whether the easygoing, gentlemanly Ott was tough enough for the job. But his devoted fans and the writers were pleased, particularly reporters who felt he would be easier to deal with than Terry, now the Giants' farm system director. Five days after Ott's appointment the Japanese bombed Pearl Harbor.

Ott's first actions indicated that he, and not Terry, would be making decisions on playing personnel. Mel removed catcher Harry Danning from the trading block. Danning and Terry had not hit it off. Then outfielder Hank Leiber, also not compatible with Terry, was re-acquired from the Cubs. But the most important move was the purchase of Cardinals slugging first baseman Johnny Mize for four players plus cash.

Ott's regulars in 1942 included Mize, second baseman Mickey Witek, shortstop Billy Jurges, and third baseman Bill Werber. The outfielders were Herbert "Babe" Barna in left, rookie Willard Marshall in center, and the player-manager in right. A happier Harry Danning was the catcher. Aging Carl Hubbell and Hal Schumacher, Cliff Melton, and righthander Bob Carpenter were expected to be the starters, and righthander Ace Adams was the reliever. The writers picked the Giants to finish in fifth place.

The Giants won nine of their first 15 games as their hitting bailed out their mediocre pitching. The writers were welcomed to the clubhouse after games, a complete reversal from the Terry era, and the fans were enthused by the hitting of Ott's "Dynamite Division," comprising Ott, Mize, Marshall, Leiber, and Danning in the third through seventh batting order positions. But the club slipped down to sixth place by late May. The Giants' weaknesses were all too apparent. The offensive power was there, but the defense, speed, and, above all, pitching were not.

The Giants did not have the horses to compete with the Dodgers and the Cardinals, and they needed some spark to have any chance of finishing in the first division.

Ott, the player rather than the manager, gave them a lift in a game against the Dodgers. In the first inning Mel had started his club off with a two-run homer. But it was his base running, straight out of John McGraw's playbook, that gave the Giants a boost. In the third inning, with one out and Giants on second and third, Ott was intentionally walked to set up a double play. Johnny Mize slashed a sharp grounder to first baseman Dolph Camilli, who threw to Pee Wee Reese for a force on Ott. Instead of sliding, Mel threw his body into Reese and bowled him over, a rough but legal maneuver. Reese's relay to first base was wild, and two more key Giant runs scored, enough to win the game. The Dodgers reacted by dusting off Ott and his hitters, standard under Leo Durocher's leadership. After the game, Mel commented straight-faced, "Their pitchers were a little wild, don't you think?"

Ott showed one sign of the strain of managing and playing. He always had the habit of tapping the outfield sod with his right foot. After a few games at the Polo Grounds the small bare spot in right field grew in diameter under the pressure of his more intense foot-tapping. Ott told a writer, "Sometimes the decision as to when to pull a pitcher can be murder. My instinct tells me to take him out, but my desire to give him another chance to build up his confidence tells me to leave him in." There was another change traceable to Ott's new role. He complained to umpires more than he ever had, the climax coming when he was ejected in the first inning of a doubleheader and was finished for the rest of the day.

At the All-Star break the Giants were in fourth place, 14 games behind the league-leading Dodgers. After the break Ott decided that his club needed another shot in the arm. His solution was to start his close friend Hubbell, who had won only one game before the break. With only a trace of his old stuff, King Carl beat the tough Cardinals and repeated the feat against the Pirates in his next start. Mel revamped his lineup and the Giants rose to within half a game of third place by the end of July.

New York Sun writer Frank Graham wrote about changes in Ott:

Someone said, "Mel used to be such a mild-mannered little fellow, and now every time I see him he is arguing with the umpire
or snapping at the opposing players.... What has come over the
young man?" The answer to that question comes in two parts.
The first is that Ott [feels] that he assumed a heavy responsibility when he took over.... The second is that he felt he had to
do something drastic to shake up the Giant players.... No one
can have the faintest doubt as to who is boss.... Some must ask
themselves if this is the same quiet little guy who used to dress
over in the corner of the room and seldom had anything to say.

But Mel still had his sense of humor and could laugh at himself. Ott's
club won in the tenth inning of a game when he deftly squeezed in a runner from third with one out and the bases loaded. Complimented by a
friend on the play, Mel revealed he had intended to swing away. He tapped
the plate before the first pitch to him, which he had always done. But just
as the pitcher delivered the ball, the runner started for the plate. Mel had
inadvertently given the squeeze bunt sign by tapping the plate.

The Giants finished in third place, 20 games behind the pennant-
winning Cardinals but well above pre-season expectations. Mel missed
only one game in his seventeenth season, leading the league in home runs,
walks, and runs. Johnny Mize led the league in RBI and slugging percentage. And reliever Ace Adams broke the then-existing record by appearing in 61 games. It had been a successful first year for player-manager Ott
and his club.

The increasing impact of the war effort completely changed the game
over the next three years. In 1943 the player-depleted Giants finished in
last place, 49½ games off the pace. It was a personal disaster for Ott, who
hit a career-low .234 and missed 25 games with a stomach ailment triggered by his club's terrible performance. Despite that, he signed a three-
year player-manager contract at a small salary increase. The Giants finished
in fifth place the next two seasons as Ott bounced back, hitting .288 and
.308. Mel passed two milestones in 1945, breaking Honus Wagner's
National League record for career total bases, and hitting his 500th home
run in a night game at the Polo Grounds on August 1.

Things returned to normal in 1946 with the war over. In January the
Giants bought catcher Walker Cooper from the Cardinals for $175,000,
by far the largest sum the Giants ever paid for a player. Cooper was considered the best catcher in the game before joining the service after the
1944 season. But Ott's jubilation in acquiring Cooper did not last long.
For several months major leaguers had been approached to jump to the
Mexican League, an "outlaw" (not part of organized baseball) league operated by Mexican customs broker Jorge Pasuel and his brother Bernardo.

The Giants lost outfielders Danny Gardella, first baseman Nap Reyes, and lefthander Adrian Zabala, none of whom figured importantly in Ott's plans. But Ott was furious a month later after learning that righthanders Sal "The Barber" Maglie, Harry Feldman, pitching mainstay Ace Adams, second baseman George Hausmann, and reserve first baseman Roy Zimmerman also were jumping to Mexico.

The Giants opened the season at the Polo Grounds before 40,000, including large numbers of discharged servicemen. They saw the Giants beat the Phillies and were thrilled when Ott hit a looping fly ball into the right field grandstand, one of his least impressive home runs. It was number 511 of Mel's career and the last major league homer he would hit. The next day he dove futilely for a fly ball, injured his knee, and played infrequently and ineffectively for the rest of the season, hitting .074 in 31 games. The club played miserably and slipped into last place permanently after Labor Day. Horace Stoneham considered dismissing Ott after the season. But his close friendship with his favorite player made the decision for him. Ott would be back to manage the Giants in 1947.

Giants fans, anticipating a major trade for established pitchers, were disappointed when the team assembled for Spring training in Phoenix in 1947. The club had acquired righthanders Larry Jansen and Bill Ayers from the high minors, but otherwise the Giants were still saddled with the same pitchers who had failed them the previous season. However, Ott had assembled a group of hard hitters, including Mize, Cooper, Willard Marshall, Carroll "Whitey" Lockman, Bobby Thomson, and Sid Gordon. The Giants, picked to finish sixth, were in third place on July 4, but only because their powerful attack continually bailed out a weak pitching staff, with the exception of the very effective Larry Jansen.

The Polo Grounders finished in fourth place, 13 games behind the pennant-winning Dodgers. Ott's "windowbreakers" hit a record 221 homers (since surpassed), 39 more than the 1936 Yankees' record 182 roundtrippers. Ironically, none were hit by Ott in his last playing season. Mel began the 1948 season realizing it was his last chance if his club did not improve. After a fast start the Giants faded and found themselves in fourth place with a 37–38 record on July 16. The Giants issued a bombshell announcement that morning. Ott was stepping down (no surprise) and his replacement was Leo Durocher (major surprise). Stoneham told the writers later that Mel had recommended Durocher as his replacement. With the baseball world in an uproar, Ott left the scene to work with his old friend Carl Hubbell, then the head of the Giants' farm system.

In 1946 Frank Graham quoted Durocher as having said, "Nice guys! Do you know a nicer guy than Mel Ott? Or any of the other Giants? And where are they? The nice guys over there are in last place!" That dialogue has been distorted to create the idiom: "Nice guys finish last!" Ott has been described as being too nice to be a competent manager. A closer analysis of his managerial history would lead to the more realistic conclusion that his sweet nature was not the reason for his mediocre managerial record, but that his basic problem was that he found himself trying to win games by outslugging the opposition. Winning baseball is the product of competent pitching, dependable fielding, and adequate hitting and base running. Ott's Giants had only the hitting, and that, plus some bad luck, is why he had a disappointing managerial career.

Mel Ott had a career batting average of .304, with 511 home runs (200 more than any other National Leaguer when he retired) and 1860 RBI. When he retired he also was the National League career leader in RBI, runs, total bases, and walks. At 5 foot 9 inches and 170 pounds, Ott was the smallest of the great home run hitters. He also was rated among the top fielding rightfielders of his time. But his records hardly do him justice. In 1938 Hall of Famer and former Pirates player-manager Pie Traynor said of Ott: "When you talk about National League players, Ottie has to be the best in all of the years I've been with the Pirates. The best players are those who win the most games. I know that Mel personally has beaten the Pirates more often than any other player, and on the other teams the players I talk to express the same thought." Unfortunately, Ott was less successful as a manager, with a record of 464–530 (.467). He ranks twenty-first among player-managers, with 532 games. Ott, elected to the Hall of Fame in 1951, died at age 49 after an automobile accident. His biography in *The Ballplayers* sums him up well: "He is remembered variously as sincere, disciplined, dedicated, warm-hearted, honorable, the embodiment of sportsmanship."

PETE ROSE

Peter Edward Rose was born in Cincinnati on April 14, 1941, one of four children of bank cashier Harry and La Verne Rose. Encouraged by his athletic father, Pete played baseball and football at Western Hills High School in Cincinnati. The switch-hitting Rose signed with the Reds in 1960 and began his professional career with Geneva, New York, of the New York–Pennsylvania League. He matured physically over the next two seasons, and in 1963 the brash, crewcut, 5 foot 11 inch, 190 pounder became the Reds' regular second baseman and was named Rookie of the Year. Rose hit .273 that year while acquiring the nickname "Charley Hustle" for his habit of sprinting to first base after drawing a walk.

Rose became a bona fide star in 1965, hitting .312 with a league-leading 209 hits. The righthand-throwing Rose was not an especially gifted second baseman, and in 1967 he was shifted to the outfield where he performed adequately over the next eight seasons. Subsequently, Rose became a regular at third base and first base. Meanwhile, he was one of the most consistent, effective hitters in the game, switch-hitting and specializing in spraying hits to all fields rather than hitting for power. After 16 seasons with Cincinnati the extremely physical Rose was traded to the Phillies, where he remained for four full seasons through the 1983 season. When his hitting performance slipped, the Phillies released him and he signed with the Montreal Expos in 1984. His playing continued to deteriorate, and he was hitting .259 early in August when the Expos traded him back to Cincinnati. Pete took over as the fifth place Reds' player-manager on August 15, 1984.

Rose had 4062 hits when he rejoined the Reds, needing 129 to equal Ty Cobb's 4191 career total. In his first game before an enthusiastic crowd, the 43-year-old player-manager had two singles and twice slid into bases with his trademark headfirst slide. He played in 26 games and hit a satisfying .365, although his club remained in fifth place in the National League's Western Division.

Early in 1985 Cincinnati automobile dealer Marge Schott purchased the Reds. The club had an infield of Rose at first; scrappy, switch-hitting Ron Oester at second; smooth-fielding Dave Concepcion at short; and competent Buddy Bell at third. The outfield starters were Gary Redus in left, Eddie Milner in center, and big, power-hitting Dave Parker in right. Journeyman Dave Van Gorder was the catcher. The pitching staff was led by young lefthander Tom Browning, righthander Mario Soto, and righthanded reliever Tom Power. Under Rose's spirited leadership, and with Parker and Browning leading the way, the Reds finished in second place in the Western Division, 5½ games behind the Dodgers. The highlight of the season came in Cincinnati on September 11 when Rose singled to left center off San Diego Padres righthander Eric Show, Rose's 4192nd career hit, breaking Ty Cobb's record. Rose had tied the record against the Cubs three days earlier. Nearing the end of his playing career, Rose hit .264 in 119 games. The 1986 team, sparked by Parker and Eric Davis, duplicated its 1985 finish, losing out to the first place Houston Astros. In his last season as a player Rose hit .219 in 72 games. As a bench manager, Rose led his club to two more second place finishes in 1987–8. But his situation took a drastic turn as the 1989 season moved along.

Rose had been a compulsive gambler, à la Rogers Hornsby, for many years, as James Reston, Jr., described it in his *Collision at Home Plate*:

> At the center of Rose's greatness as a player ... was his com-
> pulsiveness. Like a child, he had trouble controlling his
> impulses.... What was he to do with his kinetic energy as he
> played baseball less and less?... How was he to sustain the thrill
> of major league competition, or the daily challenge of winning
> and losing before a huge, cheering crowd?
>   To the extent that Rose was ever questioned about his gam-
> bling before 1985, his response was always the same: with a
> smile and a twinkle, he would say he was betting no more in
> 1985 than he had bet in 1975.... He loved to gamble, sure. It
> kept him interested in sports of all kinds. By the agreement of
> virtually everyone later ... eventually including himself, Pete
> Rose's gambling had become pathological by 1985.

Extensive examination of Rose's betting activities by Commissioner
Peter Ueberroth's office had been under way well before Bart Giamatti
took over the office in 1989. In late February of that year Rose met with
Ueberroth and Commissioner-elect Giamatti. On March 20 the Commissioner's office announced that Rose was under investigation for
unnamed "serious allegations." On August 24, after weeks of legal wrangling between lawyers for Rose and for Commissioner Giamatti's office,
Giamatti banned Rose from baseball for his alleged gambling on major
league games. Giamatti's decision, containing no formal findings, was
signed by both parties, and Giamatti said that he considered Rose's accep-
tance of the ban to be a no-contest plea to the charges. Reds coach Tommy
Helms was named as Rose's interim replacement, with the team in fourth
place. The climax to the tragic episode came a week later when Giamatti
died of a heart attack.

Since Rose was banned and denied the possibility of election to the
Hall of Fame, there has been a continuing debate as to whether he should
be granted eligibility to be selected to the Hall, an honor which he otherwise deserved with his playing accomplishments. Since that time, Rose
has been a public figure. He has received large amounts of money for signing baseballs and other memorabilia. He has been permitted to appear at
a Reds' oldtimers day. And he has continued to broadcast from his restau-
rant in Boca Raton, Florida. But early in 2001 Commissioner Bud Selig
reaffirmed his intention not to change Rose's status.

Other than his gambling, Rose has had a stormy, ugly personal life.
He divorced his first wife, Karolyn, after continually philandering and
actually flaunting his affairs. However, his messy personal life did not
affect his brilliant playing performance. In addition to his .303 batting
average and record for total hits (4,256), Rose is the major league career
leader in singles (3,215), at-bats (14,053), and games played (3,562). He

is second with 746 doubles, and fourth with 2,165 runs. And Rose is the only player to have participated in at least 500 games at five different positions. *The Sporting News* named him the Player of the Decade for the 1970s.

In his six years as a manager, Rose's clubs had a 412–373 (.525) record. He had a higher winning percentage solely as a player-manager, with a 194–170 (.533) record. Pete Rose was the last player-manager in the long period that had begun with Harry Wright's field leadership of the Cincinnati Red Stockings in 1869. In all likelihood, Rose will be the last of this vanishing breed.

20

Perspective

There were two fundamental differences between player-managers and bench managers. Obviously, the playing manager had to concern himself with holding up his end as a player. This meant keeping himself in playing shape, both physically and mentally, similar to any other player. The other important difference was that playing managers tended to be much younger and less experienced at managing a team than bench managers. As a result, the player-manager usually had a more stressful, difficult job in handling problems with which older managers were more familiar.

In his *Guide to Baseball Managers from 1870 to Today*, Bill James determined that a high percentage of managers have their best seasons when they get their first chance to manage, and in their first years on the new job. James reasoned that new managers are effective because they tend to pull their teams out of ruts developed under the preceding manager. The accuracy of James' thesis was borne out by data on the first year a new player-manager took over a team. Twenty-three men were player-managers in more than 500 major league games. Team performances were studied for 16 of these 23 men. In the cases of 12 of the 16 player-managers studied, the new player-manager led his club to a higher finish than the club had attained the year before he took over. The team finish was the same in two cases and lower in the other two cases. In five of the 12 improved finishes the new player-manager's team won the pennant.

James reasoned that a new manager naturally attempts to make changes he sees as needed. And these changes tend to be beneficial in the short run. But over time the manager loses the ability to see what the club needs, to the detriment of the team's performance. A review of the performance of teams with player-managers confirms that this reasoning applies as well to teams managed by players. That review showed that improved team standings were not as great after the first year. Comparisons were made of the first half of each player-manager's tenure with the second half. Of the 16 player-managers, nine managed clubs averaging higher finishes in the first half of the playing-manager's tenure than in the second half. Five playing-managers had lower average finishes in the first half of their years as player-managers, and two experienced no change.

Teams managed by Cap Anson, Charles Comiskey, and Fred Clarke had the greatest difference in average standings from the first half to the second half of their regimes. In Anson's first 11 years his teams averaged finishes slightly higher than second place. In his last 10 years as a player-manager Anson's teams finished slightly better than fourth place. Similarly, Comiskey's clubs averaged 2.6 places higher in his first six player-manager years than in his second six years. Clarke had opposite results, finishing 2.3 places lower in his first eight years. In the modern era, Tris Speaker, Ty Cobb, Rogers Hornsby, and Bucky Harris had better average finishes in their first years than in their second, while Bill Terry and Lou Boudreau had opposite results.

It is difficult to determine how much the player-manager role affected a player's performance on the field because of the variables involved. One important variable was the experience a player had before taking on the added responsibility of managing. Another was his playing workload. A third was his temperament. For example, there was a big difference between inexperienced, 24-year-old shortstop-manager Lou Boudreau, with the bulk of his playing career ahead of him, and veteran shortstop-manager Leo Durocher, nearing the end of his playing days. There also was a big difference between young player-manager Joe Cronin, concerned over his fielding problems, and player-manager Rogers Hornsby, whose supreme confidence overcame the stress of his managerial duties. And there also was a big difference in the physical demands of playing and managing between catcher-manager Mickey Cochrane, physically and emotionally exhausted from catching every day, and catcher-manager Bill Carrigan, who was a part-time player in his four years as a player-manager.

Probably the best indicators of the impact of managing on playing are the performances and views of the playing managers and their players. Cleveland's Napoleon Lajoie happily stepped down as playing manager in August 1909 because he felt that his managing responsibilities had adversely affected his playing. Relieved of his managing role, Lajoie rebounded to hit .324. In his two previous years as the club's player manager, he had sub-par .299 and .289 seasons. George Sisler was another great player glad to step down as the St. Louis Browns' player-manager after a mediocre 1926 season, who had a fine year in 1927 as a player only. Mickey Cochrane's great second baseman Charley Gehringer felt that Cochrane was a much better manager when he was a player-manager than when he was forced to become a bench manager. Mel Ott was the Giants' regular rightfielder-manager from 1942 through 1945. He played creditably in three of the years, but in 1943 he hit a career-low .234 and missed three weeks with a stomach ailment brought on by frustrations with his last-place team.

Tris Speaker's field performance apparently was affected adversely in his first year as a player-manager in 1919 when he was in his prime. He hit .296, his only sub-.300 average in his 19 seasons as a regular player. But over the next six years as a player-manager he adjusted to his expanded responsibilities with averages of .388, .362, .378, .380, .344, and .389. Becoming a player-manager had no discernible impact on Ty Cobb's performance. He hit .389 in 1921, his first year after taking over the Tigers, and over the following five years of his player-manager years he hit .401, .340, .338, .378, and .339. Mickey Cochrane's play also was unaffected in his first two years as the Tigers' player-manager, indicated when he hit .320 and .319 in leading the Tigers to pennants in 1934 and 1935. Rogers Hornsby, in his first playing-managing year, hit .403 in 1925. Joe Cronin, Bill Terry, and Lou Boudreau also played at their usual levels as new player-managers despite the added stress they encountered.

The responsibilities of playing and managing took their physical and emotional toll. Frank Chance provides one example After playing his last season as a regular and winning a second straight pennant in 1910, Chance, looking and acting much older than 32, commented, "This business is making a crab out of me." After Mickey Cochrane's first two successful years, he suffered a nervous breakdown in his third year. Red Sox outfielder-manager Chick Stahl, unable to juggle both roles, had a tragic ending. Stahl managed the 1906 Sox in their last 40 games to a miserable 14–26 record, and he began the 1907 season in a severe state of depression over his team's problems and his dual responsibilities. He committed suicide one morning during spring training, gulping down several ounces of carbolic acid and leaving a note to his players reading, "Boys, I just couldn't help it.

After their careers were over, what did former player-managers think about the dual role they had played? Al Stump wrote in his *The Life and Times of the Meanest Man Who Ever Played Baseball* that, 40 years after Ty Cobb had taken over the Detroit Tigers, Cobb bemoaned, "I had signed away my independence. Up [till then] I'd been judged on what I did, alone. But no manager who ever lived could beat the blame when his men fucked up—didn't give it everything they had, boozed it up, alibied their mistakes, faked injuries."

Johnny Evers, a great second baseman and an extremely intense man, was a playing manager for one season and a bench manager after his playing career ended. Apparently he preferred the player-manager role. In the 1914 *Reach Guide* he was quoted: "There is too much fretting [in managing a team from the bench].... Watching a game from the bench is tiresome, and I don't know how some of them do it. I believe that [Pirates manager] Fred Clarke often pines for the days when he was in there himself instead of sitting on the bench and pulling for others."

Frankie Frisch agreed with Evers, although he found a down side to the player-manager role. He told a writer: "I think managing shortened my playing career, but I was a better manager when I was playing, when I could lead like a platoon sergeant in the field rather than as a general sitting back on his duff in a command post. But I won't apologize for having wanted my players to be as good as I was supposed to be. If intolerance of mediocrity is a crime, I plead guilty."

During John McGraw's days as a playing manager he occasionally left his third base post, removing himself from the game, feeling that he could do a better job of managing from the bench. In his *My Thirty Years in Baseball*, in comparing a coach's (or a player's) position on the field with that of the bench manager, McGraw wrote in 1923:

> Though I did not realize it then [during the 1890s] I am now convinced that the bench manager has a decided advantage.... I see things on the field that would escape me if I was on the coaching lines.... While coaching [or playing] at third I overlooked chances for shifting the attack....To get the best results, I find it more advantageous to ... direct the whole team from the bench.

Cubs first baseman Phil Cavarretta, a playing manager in 1951 through 1953, agreed with McGraw. In retrospect, he took a dim view of the player-manager role. After retiring from the game, he told a writer, "Looking back, I think I made a mistake [in becoming a player-manager]. I think I accepted the job too quickly. I didn't have enough experience. I should have worked in the minors first. Being a playing manager was rough; there are so many things to think about. You really can't do both jobs well."

Christy Mathewson wrote in his *Pitching in a Pinch*: "It is my opinion that it is a big advantage to a team to have the manager on the bench rather than in the game. Frank Chance ... is a great leader, but I think he would be a greater one if he could find one of his mechanical ability to play first base, and he could sit on the bench as the director general. He is occupied with the duties of his position and often little things get by him. I believe that we beat the Cubs in two games in 1909 because Chance was playing first base instead of directing the game from the bench."

Hall of Fame second baseman Charlie Gehringer could see a difference between a manager's effectiveness as a player-manager and the same individual as a bench manager. He told a writer, "[Mickey] Cochrane was a super leader when he was playing, but after he got beaned and had to manage from the bench, he didn't call them quite so well because he wasn't close enough to the scene. I think if he can handle it, a playing manager is great, especially if he's a catcher because the catcher is the quarterback. When Mickey was managing the Tigers from behind the plate I can't remember him ever fouling up anything. Seemed like he made snap judgments that always worked out well, especially in '34 and '35 when we were winning our two pennants. After he became a bench manager it seemed like he weighed everything a little more, and you can't do that in baseball...."

Joe Cronin managed Ted Williams for six years, four of the years when Cronin was a player-manager and for two years after World War II when Cronin was a bench manager. Williams compared Cronin in the two capacities in Anthony J. Connor's *Voices from Cooperstown* as follows:

> Cronin had the greatest obstacle to beat in the fact that he was playing shortstop, trying to be manager, and planning day by day and long range. I mean that's pretty near impossible. I know Lou Boudreau was able to do it over in Cleveland. He managed superbly, worked his pitching staff, played great shortstop, and had great years. But remember, nobody in baseball had better coaches surrounding him than Lou Boudreau. Cronin didn't have that group around him.... Now when he [Cronin] quit playing he was the greatest manager I ever played for.

Cronin, a successful playing manager for 15 years, also spoke for many player-managers when he told Connor:

> Looking back, I wish I'd been a player first and a manager later, but not both at once. I think player-managing is the toughest job in the world. You just can't win. There's a lot more to the job than just playing and running the ball game. You've got to plan, and handle the men—and every personality is different. You've got to cooperate with the [front] office and cooperate

with the press. And it's all in a goldfish bowl. From the very first I had doubts about it and almost asked to step down after that first year. But I didn't. And looking back, I regret it.

Player-managers' contracts broke down salaries into two figures, one amount for managing and the other for playing. This created a problem when Roger Bresnahan was fired by the Cardinals before he had fulfilled his multi-year player-manager contract. Eventually a settlement was reached, but this illustrated the difficulty involved in terminating a dual service contract. If the player-manager stepped down or was fired as a manager, there was a question as to how well he would accept the orders of another manager. When the Cleveland Indians' Bill Veeck considered replacing player-manager Lou Boudreau in 1946, Boudreau made it clear that he would have to be traded if he was relieved as manager; he would not play for the Indians under another manager. Released by the Indians after the 1950 season, he joined the Red Sox as a player in 1951. Boudreau played harmoniously for his old friend Steve O'Neill before replacing O'Neill in 1952.

First baseman–manager Fred Tenney, released by the Boston Bean-eaters in 1907 after managing the club for three years, played for the Giants for two years before returning to Boston as the club's player-manager. John McGraw was lavish in his praise of Tenney's willingness to join the Giants as a player and contribute to the Giants' success. Napoleon Lajoie welcomed his return to the player ranks in 1909 after serving as Cleveland's player-manager for almost five years. Lajoie did not even have a problem playing under first baseman–manager George Stovall who, while a player under Lajoie, had hit the Frenchman over the head in a fit of anger. Third baseman Jimmy Collins, after serving as player-manager of the Red Sox for six years, was relieved as manager in 1906 but remained unhappily as a player with the club until the following year when he joined the Athletics.

Appendix Table 4 lists pennant winners led by player-managers. Cap Anson's Chicago clubs dominated the1880–1887 period, winning five pennants. In the "modern" era since 1901, Frank Chance's Cubs won four flags and twice finished second against the spirited competition provided by three time pennant-winning player-manager Fred Clarke's Pirates, and part-time player and manager John McGraw's Giants. The other playing managers who won two pennants were Bill Carrigan, Bucky Harris, and Mickey Cochrane. First basemen–managers won 13 of the 34 pennants won by player-managers; catcher-managers ranked second with five flags. Only two pitcher-managers, Al Spalding and Clark Griffith, won pennants, both of them in the earlier days of the game.

A number of pennant-winning player-managers also had fine seasons as their teams excelled. Al Spalding had a magnificent year in 1876, winning 47 of the 66 games won by his flag-winning Chicago club. His protégé, Cap Anson, played brilliantly as his teams won five pennants in the 1880s. Anson led the National League in RBI in each of the five seasons and was especially effective in 1886 when he had 147 RBI, 52 more than his closest competitor. The durable Anson missed only four games during those seasons.

Clark Griffith, the pitcher-manager of the 1901 Chicago White Sox, led the new American League's pitchers with a 24–7 (.774) season as his club won the league's first pennant. Outfielder-manager Fred Clarke hit .351 while directing the 1903 Pirates to their first pennant. Tris Speaker hit .388 and ranked high in many offensive categories as his Indians won the World Championship in 1920. The Cardinals won the 1926 World Championship, sparked by Rogers Hornsby, who hit .317 with 93 RBI.

Player-managers Bill Terry and Joe Cronin played well as their clubs won pennants in 1933. First baseman–manager Terry hit .322 and led his Giants to a World Series triumph over Cronin's Washington Senators. Shortstop-manager Cronin had an excellent year, hitting .309 and leading the league in doubles, and league shortstops in fielding. Cardinals second baseman–manager Frankie Frisch hit .305 while leading his 1934 "Gashouse Gang" to a World Championship victory over catcher-manager Mickey Cochrane's Tigers. Cochrane came back the next year with a .319 average as his club won the World Series against the Cubs. Cleveland shortstop-manager Lou Boudreau was the last player-manager to lead his team to a pennant and World Championship. Boudreau hit .355 and almost singlehandededly won the 1948 playoff game against the Red Sox to win the pennant. His club went on to win the World Championship.

Baseball has seen many important changes over the years. There have been a number of changes in the rules of the game and in the ball parks. Every type of equipment has been modified and improved. The dead ball era was replaced by the live ball era after World War I. The designated hitter has changed American League offensive strategy. Pitching strategy has changed with the decline of the complete game pitcher and the advent of the long reliever and the ninth inning pitching specialist. And the colorful player-manager era has ended.

Appendix

Table 1
Games Played by Non-Pitching Player-Managers

Rank	Player-Manager	Games Played While Managing	Position
1	Cap Anson	2155	1B
2	Fred Clarke	1848	OF
3	Charles Comiskey	1312	1B
4	Joe Cronin	1291	SS
5	Lou Boudreau	1285	SS
6	Patsy Donovan	1022	OF
7	Patsy Tebeau	1011	1B, 3B
8	John M. Ward	854	SS, 2B, P
9	Ty Cobb	765	OF
10	Tris Speaker	741	OF
11	Bob Ferguson	714	2B, 3B
12	Fielder Jones	714	OF
13	Frank Chance	678	1B
14	John Morrill	677	1B
15	Jimmy Collins	663	3B
16	Napoleon Lajoie	639	2B
17	Bill Terry	614	1B
18	George Stovall	585	1B
19	Bucky Harris	556	2B
20	Fred Tenney	544	1B
21	Mel Ott	532	OF
22	Rogers Hornsby	508	2B
23	Jim O'Rourke	505	OF
24	Frankie Frisch	483	2B
25	George Sisler	451	1B
26	Dave Bancroft	445	SS
27	Jimmy Dykes	382	3B

Rank	Player-Manager	Games Played While Managing	Position
28	Miller Huggins	376	2B
29	Jake Stahl	373	1B
30	Buck Herzog	372	SS
31	Red Dooin	354	C
32	Charlie Grimm	331	1B
33	Roger Bresnahan	324	C
34	Mickey Cochrane	315	C
35	King Kelly	299	C, OF
36	Bill Joyce	287	3B
37	Jimmy Wilson	269	C
38	Eddie Collins	251	2B
39	Buck Ewing	247	C, 1B
40	John McGraw	245	3B
41	George Davis	241	3B, SS
42	Joe Tinker	236	SS
43	Bill Carrigan	231	C
44	Pete Rose	194	1B
45	Leo Durocher	178	SS
46	Harry Wright	177	OF
47	Gabby Hartnett	170	C

Source: Compiled from *Total Baseball, Fourth Edition*, 1999, based upon career games played by player-managers while regulars or semi-regulars.

Table 2
Records of Pitcher-Managers as Regular Starters

Pitcher-Manager	Games	Won	Lost
Clark Griffith	146	69	38
John M. Ward	117	35	21
Albert Spalding	61	47	12
Kid Nichols	36	21	13

Source: Compiled from *Total Baseball, Fourth Edition*, 1999, based upon career games pitched by pitcher-managers.

Table 3
Percentage of Active Players Who Were Player-Managers

Decade	Percentage
1870–1879	68
1880–1889	41
1890–1899	51
1900–1909	57

Decade	Percentage
1910–1919	44
1920–1929	24
1930–1939	32
1940–1949	19
1950–1959	7
1960–1969	Less than one
1970–1979	2
1980–1989	1 (Pete Rose retired as a player after 1986)
1990–present	none

Source: *The Bill James Guide to Baseball Managers from 1870 to Today*, 1997

Table 4
Pennant Winners Managed by Players, 1876 to Present

Year	League	Team	Player-Manager	Position
1876	NL	Chicago	Albert Spalding	P
1879	NL	Providence	George Wright	SS
1880	NL	Chicago	Cap Anson	1B
1881	NL	Chicago	Cap Anson	1B
1882	NL	Chicago	Cap Anson	1B
1883	NL	Boston	John Morrill	1B
1885	NL	Chicago	Cap Anson	1B
1886	NL	Chicago	Cap Anson	1B
1901	NL	Pittsburgh	Fred Clarke	LF
1901	AL	Chicago	Clark Griffith	P
1902	NL	Pittsburgh	Fred Clarke	LF
1903	NL	Pittsburgh	Fred Clarke	LF
1903	AL	Boston	Jimmy Collins	3B
1906	NL	Chicago	Frank Chance	1B
1906	AL	Chicago	Fielder Jones	CF
1907	NL	Chicago	Frank Chance	1B
1908	NL	Chicago	Frank Chance	1B
1909	NL	Pittsburgh	Fred Clarke	LF
1910	NL	Chicago	Frank Chance	1B
1912	AL	Boston	Jake Stahl	1B
1915	AL	Boston	Bill Carrigan	C
1916	AL	Boston	Bill Carrigan	C
1920	AL	Cleveland	Tris Speaker	CF
1924	AL	Washington	Bucky Harris	2B
1925	AL	Washington	Bucky Harris	2B
1926	NL	St. Louis	Rogers Hornsby	2B
1932	NL	Chicago	Charlie Grimm	1B
1933	NL	New York	Bill Terry	1B
1933	AL	Washington	Joe Cronin	SS
1934	NL	St. Louis	Frankie Frisch	2B

Appendix

Year	League	Team	Player-Manager	Position
1934	AL	Detroit	Mickey Cochrane	C
1935	AL	Detroit	Mickey Cochrane	C
1938	NL	Chicago	Gabby Hartnett	C
1948	AL	Cleveland	Lou Boudreau	SS

Source: *USA Today Baseball Weekly*, August 19–25, 1992

Bibliography

Following are the sources of information used in the writing of this work:

Newspapers

The Detroit News
The New York Clipper
The Sporting News
The New York Sun

USA Today Baseball Weekly
The New York World-Telegram
The New York Daily Mirror

Books

Alexander, Charles C. *John McGraw* (New York: Viking, 1988)

Bartell, Dick. *Rowdy Richard* (Berkeley, CA: North Atlantic Books, 1987)

Bjarkman, Peter C., ed. *Encyclopedia of Major League Baseball Team Histories: National League* (Westport, CT: Meckler, 1991)

Boudreau, Lou. *Covering All the Bases* (Champaign, IL: Sagamore, 1993)

Broeg, Bob. *Super Stars of Baseball* (St. Louis: The Sporting News, 1971)

Cobb, Ty. *My Life in Baseball* (New York: Doubleday, 1961)

Cochrane, Mickey. *Baseball: The Fan's Game* (Cleveland: SABR, 1992)

Connor, Anthony J. *Voices from Cooperstown* (New York: Macmillan,1982)

Creamer, Robert. *Babe* (New York: Simon and Schuster, 1974)

Goldstein, Warren. *Playing for Keeps* (Ithaca, NY: Cornell University Press, 1989)

Golenbock, Peter. *Fenway* (New York: G.P. Putnam, 1992)

_____. *Wrigleyville* (New York: St. Martin's Press, 1996)

Graham, Frank. *The Brooklyn Dodgers* (New York: G.P. Putnam, 1948)

_____. *McGraw of the Giants* (New York: G.P. Putnam, 1944)

Honig, Donald. *The Man in the Dugout* (Chicago: Follett, 1977)

Hynd, Noel. *The Giants of the Polo Grounds* (New York: Doubleday, 1988)

Ivor-Campbell, Frederick. *Baseball's First Stars* (Cleveland: SABR, 1996)

James, Bill. *The Bill James Baseball Guide to Baseball Managers from 1870 to Today* (New York: Scribner, 1997)

_____. *The Bill James Historical Baseball Abstract* (New York: Villard, 1986)

Langford, Walter M. *Legends of Baseball* (South Bend, IN: Diamond Communications, 1987)

Mathewson, Christy. *Pitching in a Pinch* (New York: G.P. Putnam, 1912)

McGraw, John J. *My Thirty Years in Baseball* (New York: Boni & Liveright, 1923)

Murray, Tom, ed. *Sport Magazine's All-Stars* (New York: Atheneum, 1977)

Porter, Daniel L., ed. *Biographical Dictionary of American Sports* (Westport, CT: Greenwood, 1987)

Reston, James Jr. *Collision at Home Plate — The Lives of Pete Rose and Bart Giamatti* (Lincoln: University of Nebraska, 1991)

Ritter, Lawrence S. *The Glory of Their Times* (Macmillan, 1966)

Seymour, Harold. *Baseball: The Early Years* (New York: Oxford University Press, 1960)

_____. *Baseball: The Golden Age* (New York: Oxford University Press, 1971)

Shatzkin, Mike, ed. *The Ballplayers* (New York: William Morrow, 1990)

Spalding, Albert G. *America's National Game* (Lincoln: University of Nebraska Press, 1992)

Stein, Fred *Mel Ott: The Little Giant of Baseball* (Jefferson, NC: McFarland, 1999)

_____. *Under Coogan's Bluff* (Glenshaw, PA: Chapter and Cask, 1978)

Stockton, J. Roy. *The Gashouse Gang* (New York: A.S. Barnes, 1945)

Stump, Al. *The Life and Times of the Meanest Man Who Ever Played Baseball* (Chapel Hill, NC: Algonquin, 1994)

Thomas, Henry. *Walter Johnson: Baseball's Big Train* (Lincoln, NE: Bison Books, 1995)

Thorn, John, and Pete Palmer, eds. *Total Baseball,* First Edition (New York: Total Sports, Warner, 1989)

_____. *Total Baseball,* Sixth Edition (New York: Total Sports, Warner, 1999)

Williams, Peter. *When the Giants Were Giants* (Chapel Hill, NC: Algonquin, 1994)

Index